LABOR RELATIONS AND PUBLIC POLICY SERIES

NO. 21 343-7
23

UNIONS' RIGHTS TO COMPANY INFORMATION

by

JAMES T. O'REILLY

*Member of the Bar
of Virginia and Ohio*

with the assistance of

GALE P. SIMON

*Research Assistant
Industrial Research Unit*

INDUSTRIAL RESEARCH UNIT
The Wharton School, Vance Hall/CS
University of Pennsylvania
Philadelphia, Pennsylvania 19104
U.S.A.

© 1980 by the Trustees of the University of Pennsylvania
MANUFACTURED IN THE UNITED STATES OF AMERICA
Library of Congress Catalog Number 80-53300
ISBN: 0-89546-023-8
ISSN: 0075-7470

Foreword

In 1968, the Industrial Research Unit inaugurated its Labor Relations and Public Policy Series as a means of examining issues and stimulating discussions in the complex and controversial areas of collective bargaining and the regulation of labor-management disputes. This study, *Unions' Rights to Company Information*, is the twenty-first monograph published in the series. Eleven of these monographs, as well as a major portion of this one, deal with various aspects of the National Labor Relations Board's procedures and policies. The other nine explain significant and controversial issues such as welfare and strikes; opening the skilled construction trades to blacks; the Davis-Bacon Act; the labor-management situation in urban school systems; old age, handicapped, and Vietnam-era antidiscrimination legislation; the impact of the Occupational Safety and Health Act; and the effects of the AT&T-EEO consent decree.

In recent years, a surge of conflicting laws and regulations have emanated from Congress, federal agencies, and the courts concerning the right of individuals and organizations to obtain what heretofore had been considered private information, and the right of individuals and organizations to maintain the privacy of such information. The result has been a conflict of rights, a plethora of regulations, and an increasing invasion of the privilege both to withhold and to provide information. The National Labor Relations Board requires employers to give "relevant" information to unions to help the latter bargain. Are medical records "relevant"? The NLRB, seconded by the Occupational Safety and Health Administration, claims that they are, but many medical practitioners are outraged by such prospective dissemination of personal records. Similarly, the NLRB and the Equal Employment Opportunity Commission want testing records and results, affirmative action plans, and other information handed over to unions without any practical safeguards. Should this be permitted? Where do the Freedom of Information Act and various laws concerning privacy fit into the picture? What should be government policy in this regard?

What about the future? What about the impact of the United Automobile, Aerospace, and Agricultural Implement Workers' winning a seat on the Chrysler Board of Directors for its president? Will there henceforth be any limit to unions' rights to company information? The experience in Germany, where codetermination has had its longest experience, indicates that there are few limits, if any, to information sharing and that, when union officials, in contrast to company employees, become board members, privileged company information given to union officials is not maintained in confidence, despite legislation requiring secrecy. For example, when the supervisory board of AEG-Telefunken, the giant electrical firm, decided to reduce operations in order to curtail deficits, union members of the board broadcast the information publicly before the company could make an official announcement. Many other examples could be given of union use and misuse of board roles for union gains since the 1976 amendments to the German codetermination law added outside union members to German company boards.

To answer the host of questions involved in unions' rights to company information, the Wharton Industrial Research Unit commissioned James T. O'Reilly, Esq., to make this study. A graduate of the University of Virginia Law School, a member of the Virginia and Ohio bars, Mr. O'Reilly is a distinguished corporate attorney, a prolific author, and an authority on the Freedom of Information Act, privacy laws, and their application both in practice and to other legislation. His books include the two-volume *Federal Income Disclosure: Procedures, Forms and the Law* and *Food and Drug Administration*, both published by McGraw-Hill/Shepards, and he has contributed numerous articles to business and professional journals.

Mr. O'Reilly received material assistance from Ms. Gale P. Simon, a third-year student in the University of Pennsylvania Law School, who wrote the drafts of the chapters dealing with the Taft-Hartley Act and the NLRB. Professor Clyde W. Summers, Jefferson B. Fordham Professor of Law, University of Pennsylvania Law School, and a labor law advisor to the Industrial Research Unit, and Patrick M. Stanton, Esq., of the Ohio Bar, read this section of the manuscript and made valuable suggestions. Earlier work by Timothy J. Boyce, Esq., was helpful in the sections dealing with Title VII of the Civil Rights Act of 1964, as amended.

The manuscript was edited by the Industrial Research Unit's Chief Editor, Mr. Robert E. Bolick, Jr., and the footnotes were edited and checked by Eric Raun, Esq. The manuscript was typed by Ms. Janet Vest, Ms. Kathryn Hunter, and Ms. Nancy E.

Chiang. Mrs. Margaret E. Doyle handled the administrative matters.

Interviews for the text were graciously provided by Robert Saloschin and Katherine Braeman, Department of Justice; Soffia Petters and Robert Shapiro, Department of Labor; David Vaughn, Federal Mediation and Conciliation Service; Constance duPre, Equal Employment Opportunity Commission; Stanley Weinbrecht, NLRB; and Elizabeth Medaglia, Federal Labor Relations Authority. Excellent research material was very kindly provided by Douglas S. McDowell, counsel for the Equal Employment Advisory Council, and by the staff of Mr. Philip M. Knox, Jr., of Sears, Roebuck for the Business Roundtable. The assistance of Bureau of National Affairs, Inc., experts Lila Crane and Charlotte Kuenan was very helpful on private sector sources of labor information. Robert Gellman of the House Government Operations Committee was very helpful on the issue of medical records privacy. And the membership of the Chemical Manufacturers Association group on chemical identity disclosure and medical records, led by Mr. Roger Batchelor of Diamond Shamrock Corporation, provided much of the basic introduction into those two important subjects. Last, but far from least, the author is grateful to his wife and family for support while he spent extracurricular hours writing this book.

Research for this book was financed by the generous grants from the J. Howard Pew Freedom Trust in support of the Labor Relations and Public Policy Series, by grants from the Gulf, Rollin M. Gerstacker and A. O. Smith foundations, by Mobil Oil Corporation, and from the membership contributions of the ninety-five corporations that constitute the Industrial Research Unit's Research Advisory Group. Editing was financed by grants from the John M. Olin Foundation and publication by the Pew Trust grants.

As in all works published by the Wharton Industrial Research Unit, the senior author is solely responsible for the research and for all opinions expressed, which should not be attributed to any organization with which he is affiliated, to the grantors, or to the University of Pennsylvania.

HERBERT R. NORTHRUP, *Director*
Industrial Research Unit
The Wharton School

Philadelphia
September 1980

TABLE OF CONTENTS

PART FIVE

FRONTIERS OF DISCLOSURE: THE NLRB AS A
SOURCE OF SAFETY AND EQUALITY DATA

PART SIX

CONCLUDING REMARKS

PART ONE

Introduction to Disclosure

Direct - info. flows from employer to the bargainer rep.

Indirect - info. flows thru the FoIA + Privacy Act.

CHAPTER I

The Nature of Disclosure

The subject of information exchange is a controversial one in every case in which information withheld is power denied. For a military operation, information withheld may be crucial to a successful attack on an enemy position. For an adversarial legal assault on an opponent's position, confidential information of the opponent may be crucial to success. The opponent who wins the information may win the substantive battles that accompany the possession and exploitation of that information.

A reader who is new to the field of information law and practice should bring an ample supply of skepticism to the study of its application to labor relations. Adversary positions in labor relations often involve the games of denying information or sharing pieces of data that might be minimally sufficient to convince an opposing party of the information holder's strong position. Because indirect sources of information are becoming as important as direct employer-to-union delivery of documents, the reader must understand the nontraditional routes of information access, such as the federal Freedom of Information Act,[1] the Privacy Act,[2] and state disclosure statutes on medical,[3] personnel,[4] and exposure records. These statutes impinge on the games in which information can be a tool for adversarial success. The forced dissemination of information to an adversary occurs in both direct and indirect manners.

Disclosure under the National Labor Relations Act and pursuant to orders from the National Labor Relations Board (NLRB) constitutes a direct delivery (or direct refusal) of information, flowing from the employer to the collective bargaining repre-

---

[1] 5 U.S.C. § 552 (1976); *see* chapters XI-XV *infra*.

[2] 5 U.S.C. § 552a (1976); *see* chapter VIII *infra*.

[3] *See, e.g.*, Bullard-Plawecki Employee Right to Know Act, MICH. COMP. LAWS § 423.501-.512 (West Supp. 1979).

[4] *See, e.g.*, CALIF. LAB. CODE § 1198.5 (West Supp. 1980).

3

sentative.[5] The avenues of indirect access include the federal
Freedom of Information Act and Privacy Act. These permit
private persons to gain information from federal files. When a
union or an employer files a report or is investigated by a government official, the Freedom of Information Act and Privacy
Act govern dissemination from the federal file of those reports
or investigative files.[6] Another indirect means of access is the
employee's right of access under state law or federal regulation
to certain employer files. An individual's access to medical records, personnel files, and the like is covered by some state requirements. Another means of the union's access to information,
which is on the horizon rather than in actual practice, is the
codetermination system in which union representatives actively
participate in corporate management.[7]

A large amount of information that can be useful to either side
in collective bargaining is already available and public. For
unions, the employer's annual report and Securities & Exchange
Commission reports (such as the Form 10-K)[8] are helpful to
understanding the employer's economic posture. If the employer's
financial statements are a maze of qualifications and exceptions
noted by the auditing firm that reviewed the balance sheets, then
the union will need to be aware of that information. State corporate reports and product line reports filed with state or federal
agencies also give information that is readily available to researchers. The general health of the industry is determinable
from periodic Census Bureau statistical reports and from the
Bureau of Labor Statistics documents published by the Department of Labor.

Contract information is routinely available to unions and to
managers from the Bureau of National Affairs publication *Collective Bargaining Negotiations and Contracts*. The employer
and union parties to a contract generally permit public release
of basic information about a contract, including wage informa-

---

[5] *See* chapters II-V *infra*.

[6] *See* chapter XIII *infra*.

[7] *See* Foreword *supra*.

[8] The 10-K is a more detailed annual report; other forms are filed on
other activities of the corporation, such as acquisitions or mergers, that may
be of great interest to labor unions.

tion, term of the contract, workers covered, locations, etc.[9] The
results of union elections are routinely distributed by the NLRB's
election statistics office. That organization publishes the monthly
Election Reports, which the NLRB is required to publish.
Listings are by union, company name, number of employees
eligible, outcome of the vote, and Standard Industrial Code (SIC)
applicable to the unit in which the voting took place.

Misconduct by unions is the subject of a third routine publication. The Labor Department's annual report under the Labor-
Management Reporting and Disclosure Act lists the names of
individuals convicted of violations, their union affiliations, the
charges, dates of conviction, and penalties imposed.

By the use of the published services and generally available
library sources, a union knows the employer's financial position,
the general health of its market, its record with union elections,
the existing and new contracts governing its workers, and the
sites at which particular union successes or failures have occurred. The employer has access to the same information and
can plan to respond to a union campaign with information on
subjects such as criminal conduct by union officials, losses suf-
fered by the union in related firms' elections, and weaknesses in
other contracts for other facilities.

At that point, the public sources may be exhausted, and the
amount of information that the union can gather through direct
observation may be exhausted. The statutes and the contractual
obligations governing normally undisclosed information become
essential to successful bargaining—if they can be understood and
managed. For the employer, defending some of the same data
against disclosure may likewise be essential to successful bargaining positions on important issues.

So, with appropriate caution, skepticism, and the necessary
attention to detail, the reader is welcome to begin the use of
information law and practice to assist in the collective bargaining
process.

---

[9] This voluntary service depends, however, upon acquiescence of the contracting parties. Some contracts are provided through the Labor Department's
contract files, and others come to the Bureau of National Affairs (a private
publisher) directly from the parties. Interview with Lila Crane, Bureau of
National Affairs (March 11, 1980).

PART TWO

Disclosure Pursuant to the Taft-Hartley Act

CHAPTER II

The Duty to Disclose in the Collective
Bargaining Process

The axiom that "Knowledge is power" captures the spirit with which information sharing is imbued in the context of collective bargaining. The American legal system recognizes the truth of that axiom as it applies to the bargaining responsibilities of firms subject to the National Labor Relations (Taft-Hartley) Act, as amended. Employers and employee organizations are required to exchange all information relevant and useful in the collective bargaining process.

The duty to share information has been developed and expanded over the five decades since the enactment of the National Labor Relations Act. Today, although other government agencies and other information-sharing systems exist, the greatest quantity of information sharing occurs in the context of bargaining between employers and employee representatives.

ORIGIN OF THE DUTY

A stated purpose of the National Labor Relations Act, as amended, is the protection of worker rights "by encouraging practices fundamental to the friendly adjustment of industrial disputes" that relate to "wages, hours, or other working conditions" and by "restoring equality of bargaining power between employers and employees." [1] The Act guarantees to employees the right to "bargain collectively through representatives of their own choosing." [2] Once employees choose a collective bargaining agent, that agent becomes the exclusive spokesman for those employees on matters relating to "rates of pay, wages, hours of employment and other terms and conditions of em-

---

[1] 29 U.S.C. § 151 (1976).

[2] 29 U.S.C. § 157 (1976).

ployment." [3] The Act also imposes upon employers and properly
designated employee bargaining agents the duty to "bargain
collectively." [4] Section 8(d) of the Act defines this duty to
bargain as

> . . . the performance of the mutual obligation of the employer and
> the representative of the employees to meet at reasonable times and
> confer in good faith with respect to wages, hours and other terms
> and conditions of employment, or the negotiation of an agreement,
> or any question arising thereunder, and the execution of a written
> contract incorporating any agreement reached if requested by either
> party, but such obligation does not compel either party to agree
> to a proposal or require the making of a concession. . . .[5]

There is no express requirement in the Act that either party
provide specific information as part of the duty to bargain.
Within a year after the passage of the Act, however, the new
National Labor Relations Board had recognized that "communication of facts peculiarly within the knowledge of either party
is of the essence in the bargaining process." [6]

Disclosure almost invariably involves the dissemination by the
employer of relevant information that has been requested by a
union representing the employer's workers. The information is
generally used by the union to gain knowledge that it deems
necessary to reach informed decisions and thereby to perform
efficiently its responsibilities as the employees' exclusive spokesman.[7] The National Labor Relations Board also recognizes that
the union has a similar duty to supply data upon request by the
employer.[8] Disclosure also encourages the parties to focus upon

---

[3] 29 U.S.C. § 159a (1976).

[4] 29 U.S.C. §§ 158(a) (5), (b) (3) (1976).

[5] 29 U.S.C. § 158(d) (1976).

[6] S. & L. Allen Co., 1 N.L.R.B. 714, 728 (1936), *enforced*, 2 L.R.R.M. 780
(3d Cir. 1938).

[7] Oregon Coast Operators Association, 113 N.L.R.B. 1334, 1338 (1955),
enforced per curiam, 246 F.2d 280 (9th Cir. 1957); Bartosic and Hartley, *The
Employer's Duty to Supply Information to the Union—A Study of the Inter-
play of Administrative and Judicial Rationalization*, 58 CORNELL L. REV. 23
(1972).

[8] Local 13, Detroit Newspaper Printing & Graphic Communications Union,
233 N.L.R.B. 994 (1977), *enforced*, 598 F.2d 267 (D.C. Cir. 1979) (where
expired contract required company first to consider applicants recommended
by the union and also required use of competent substitutes in lieu of overtime, union was required to give employer data requested on number of
substitutes available for union referral and an explanation of how referrals
are handled).

the real positions of both the employees and the employer. This furthers the statutory goal of resolving labor disagreements through mutually agreed settlements.[9]

REQUESTS FOR INFORMATION

As a general principle, the employer is under no duty to provide information until the union makes a *specific* request for *relevant* information.[10] This request may be either written or oral,[11] as long as it places the employer on notice as to the information requested.[12]

A *specific* request is needed. If the request is vague, ambiguous, or confusing, then failure to disclose is not a refusal to disclose as defined in section 8(a)(5) of the Act.[13] The employer, however, bears the burden to demonstrate good faith doubts. An ambiguity will serve as grounds for failure to disclose only if the employer notifies the union shortly after the demand has been made that the request was unclear or that clarification is sought.[14]

Absolute precision is not required; it is unrealistic to expect the bargaining representative to be aware of all the potentially relevant information that the employer may possess.[15] The

---

[9] Curtiss-Wright Corp., Wright Aeronautical Div. v. NLRB, 347 F.2d 61, 69 (3d Cir. 1965).

[10] A. H. Belo Corp. v. NLRB, 411 F.2d 959 (5th Cir. 1969), *cert. denied,* 396 U.S. 1007 (1970); International Tel. & Tel. Corp. v. NLRB, 382 F.2d 366, 371 (3d Cir. 1967), *cert. denied,* 389 U.S. 1039 (1968); United States Smelting, Ref. & Mining Co., 179 N.L.R.B. 1018 (1969). *But see* Ozark Trailers, Inc., 161 N.L.R.B. 561 (1966) (must notify union of desire to close plant prior to date of actual closure); Standard Handkerchief, Inc., 151 N.L.R.B. 15 (1965) (must inform union during negotiations of plans to transfer plant to new location); Vac Art, Inc., 124 N.L.R.B. 989 (1959) (must inform union during contract negotiations of decision to close plant).

[11] International Tel. & Tel. Corp. v. NLRB, 382 F.2d 366, 371 (3d Cir. 1967), *cert. denied,* 389 U.S. 1039 (1968).

[12] Crane Co., 244 N.L.R.B. No. 15 (Aug. 10, 1979).

[13] M. F. A. Milling Co., 170 N.L.R.B. 1079 (1968), *enforced per curiam,* 463 F.2d 953 (D.C. Cir. 1972); Snively Groves, Inc., 109 N.L.R.B. 1394 (1954).

[14] Hughes Tool Co., 100 N.L.R.B. 208, 210 (1952).

[15] Ellsworth Sheet Metal, Inc., 232 N.L.R.B. 109 (1977); Fifty Div., Hayes-Abion Corp., 190 N.L.R.B. 109 (1977).

union's right to information is limited, however, by the terms of its request.[16]

When the request for information is sufficiently specific, the union need not repeat its request.[17] If the employer seeks in good faith a clarification of the request, however, the union's failure to respond relieves the employer of the duty to provide the information sought.[18]

THE REQUIREMENT OF RELEVANCE

The union's right to information does not entitle it to conduct a "fishing expedition" into the employer's records.[19] Instead, the union has a right that extends to information that is *probably or potentially relevant* to the performance of its function as exclusive bargaining representative of the employees.

Information that relates to the wages, hours, and other terms and conditions of employment is presumptively relevant.[20] Failure to disclose that information is not a violation per se of the employer's duty to bargain.[21] Instead, the Board must look to the circumstances of the particular case to determine whether the employer's refusal was in good faith.[22] Absent some strong showing of good faith reasons by the employer in support of its refusal to disclose, however, a refusal to disclose will be held in violation of the Act, and disclosure will be ordered.[23]

A union seeking information must set forth the particular reasons for its request when it seeks information that is not

[16] Westinghouse Elec. Supply Co. v. NLRB, 196 F.2d 1012 (3d Cir. 1952) (where union requested data supporting employer's claim that its wages were equal to or higher than its competitors, employer did not have to produce wage survey which did not support its claim).

[17] DePalma Printing Co., 204 N.L.R.B. 31 (1973); Aero-Motive Mfg. Co., 195 N.L.R.B. 790, 792 (1972), *enforced*, 475 F.2d 27 (6th Cir. 1973).

[18] NLRB v. Pacific Grinding Wheel Co., 572 F.2d 1343 (9th Cir. 1978).

[19] Albany Garage, Inc., 126 N.L.R.B. 417, 432 (1960).

[20] Whitin Mach. Works, 108 N.L.R.B. 1537, *enforced*, 217 F.2d 593 (4th Cir. 1954), *cert. denied*, 349 U.S. 905 (1955); *see* chapter III *infra*.

[21] NLRB v. Truitt Mfg. Co., 351 U.S. 149, 153 (1956).

[22] *Id.*

[23] *See, e.g.*, Westinghouse Elec. Corp., 239 N.L.R.B. No. 19 (Oct. 31, 1978) (where employer sought to avoid disclosure of presumptively relevant statistical data on race and sex of unit employees by claiming disclosure would place an undue burden on it, employer must substantiate its claim).

normally related to its role as the employees' exclusive bargaining agent.[24] Disclosure will be required only if this showing demonstrates that the information sought is both relevant and necessary to bargaining over the represented employees' terms and conditions of employment.[25] The requirement for relevance is satisfied as long as one of the purposes—but not the sole purpose—for which the union seeks the data is germane to its collective bargaining responsibilities.[26] If, however, the information is sought solely for purposes that are unrelated to the union's bargaining duties, no disclosure is necessary.[27]

THE TIMING OF REQUESTS

The duty to furnish requested information is not limited to requests made during the negotiation of the collective bargaining agreement.[28] The union, as exclusive representative of the employees, has a responsibility for the policing and administering of existing contracts as well as the negotiation of new ones. Accordingly, information needed in connection with its ongoing

[24] San Diego Newspaper Guild, Local 95 v. NLRB, 548 F.2d 863, 867 (9th Cir. 1977); *see* chapter IV *infra*.

[25] Texaco, Inc., 170 N.L.R.B. 142, 146 (1968), *enforced*, 407 F.2d 754 (7th Cir. 1969) (absent a showing of relevance and necessity, disclosure of sensitive financial and technical data used in manpower reduction program not required; data related only to a basic managerial decision); White Furniture Co., 161 N.L.R.B. 444 (1966), *aff'd sub nom.* United Furniture Workers v. NLRB, 388 F.2d 880 (4th Cir. 1967). For an example of a well-presented demand resulting in disclosure of sensitive information, *see* North Am. Soccer League, 245 N.L.R.B. No. 168 (Sept. 28, 1979) (where the players' union obtained, inter alia, copies of the league commissioner's contract and the league's television contracts, league regulations on transfer of franchises, and plans for expansion and movement of franchises).

[26] Utica Observer-Dispatch, Inc. v. NLRB, 229 F.2d 575, 577 (2d Cir. 1956) (names and wages of employees must be disclosed even if information sought in part to assist the union in collecting dues).

[27] Sign & Pictorial Union, Local 1175 v. NLRB, 419 F.2d 726 (D.C. Cir. 1969) (where strikers were threatening and assaulting replacements, disclosure of payroll information unnecessary; record established that the union sought the information to intimidate the replacements, not to represent the unit employees). *See also* J. I. Case Co. v. NLRB, 253 F.2d 149, 153 (7th Cir. 1958); Annot. *Duty of Furnishing Information to Employee Representatives Under National Labor Relations Act*, 2 A.L.R.3d 880 (1965).

[28] J. I. Case Co. v. NLRB, 253 F.2d 149, 153 (7th Cir. 1958) (information on piecework rates requested during the term of contract must be disclosed).

functions must be furnished during the term of the existing agreement.[29]

THE FORM IN WHICH DATA ARE FURNISHED

An employer is not required to provide information in the precise form requested by the union.[30] If, however, the employer has or should have the information requested, the employer must present the information to the union in some reasonably clear and understandable format.[31]

If the employer objects to the form or extent of the information requested, the employer must advise the union of its objections.[32] The union must be afforded some opportunity to discuss the matter and to attempt to reach some acceptable compromise.[33] The resolution of disputes over the form or extent of the information to be produced should, ideally, be resolved by the parties' bargaining in good faith.[34] If the employer both raises good faith objections to the union demands and offers alternatives that would satisfy the union's needs, no violation will be found, even if the union refuses to accept the information in the form offered.[35]

---

[29] NLRB v. Acme Indus. Co., 385 U.S. 432, 436 (1967). *But see* Laidlaw Corp., 171 N.L.R.B. 1366 (1968), *enforced*, 414 F.2d 99 (7th Cir. 1969), *cert. denied*, 397 U.S. 920 (1970) (where information relating to a wage reopener was properly refused because the time for negotiating the reopener had expired).

[30] American Cyanamid Co., 129 N.L.R.B. 683, 684 (1960) (no duty to provide exact copies of job evaluation and job description records as requested; documents requested included information on unique manufacturing techniques and processes).

[31] Westinghouse Elec. Corp., 239 N.L.R.B. No. 19 (Oct. 31, 1978); Food Employer Council, Inc., 197 N.L.R.B. 651 (1972); Texaco, Inc., 170 N.L.R.B. 142, 149 (1968), *enforced*, 407 F.2d 754 (7th Cir. 1969).

[32] J. I. Case v. NLRB, 253 F.2d 149 (7th Cir. 1958).

[33] *Id.*

[34] Food Employer Council, Inc., 197 N.L.R.B. 651 (1972).

[35] Detroit Edison Co. v. NLRB, 440 U.S. 301 (1979) (where employer told employees that test scores would be confidential, employer's offer to disclose scores without names for employees who do not give written consent for disclosure of names is sufficient); Emeryville Research Center v. NLRB, 441 F.2d 880 (9th Cir. 1971) (where employer promised confidentiality to other employers participating in wage survey, disclosure of summary data linked to the companies not required; union, by refusing to explain how it intended to use the data, made it impossible for the employer to offer the

Financial data raise special problems because they are often highly confidential.[36] Special considerations govern the form of disclosure of financial data. The employer is entitled to regulate access to sensitive financial data if the limitations are necessary to avoid disclosure of such information to competitors or other third parties.[37] For example, an employer could require that a union's request for an audit be met by having a certified or licensed public accountant perform the audit at the union's expense, with all books and records being examined on company property and with all sales and purchase information remaining in the offices of the employer.[38]

The duty to disclose existing information does not require the employer to undertake a study, or survey, to gather information that is not already in his possession.[39] When the union requests information that is available only to the employer but is not available in the requested form, however, the employer must make a reasonably diligent effort to obtain the information, including investigating the available alternatives for obtaining this information.[40] If, after so investigating, the employer is unable to gather the information, it must be able to explain the reasons why it is not available.[41]

---

information on an alternative basis). *But see* General Elec. Co. v. NLRB, 466 F.2d 1177 (6th Cir. 1972) (wage surveys with rates identified by participating companies must be disclosed).

[36] *See* chapter V *infra.*

[37] Fruit & Vegetable Packers & Warehousemen Local 760 v. NLRB, 316 F.2d 389 (D.C. Cir. 1963).

[38] *Id.*

[39] Taylor Forge & Pipe Works v. NLRB, 234 F.2d 227 (7th Cir.), *cert. denied*, 352 U.S. 942 (1956).

[40] Borden, Inc., 235 N.L.R.B. 982 (1978), *enforced in part*, 600 F.2d 313 (1st Cir. 1979); General Elec. Co., 150 N.L.R.B. 192, 259 (1964), *vacated on other grounds*, 382 U.S. 366 (1966), *enforced*, 418 F.2d 736 (2d Cir. 1969), *cert. denied*, 397 U.S. 965 (1970) (coverage cost per employee in local negotiations of insurance and pension programs run on a nationwide basis).

[41] General Motors Corp., 243 N.L.R.B. No. 19 (June 29, 1979) (where the employer contended that compilation of the data requested would require 18,000 to 20,000 man-hours, the Board ordered the parties to bargain over the cost of such effects. The Board noted that, in *Food Employer*, 197 N.L.R.B. at 651, it had said that, if no agreement on payment of the costs was reached, the union should be given "access to records for which it can reasonably compile such information"); Food Employer Council, Inc., 197 N.L.R.B. 651 (1972).

If the new data are available and compilation of the data requires substantial effort, the employer must either present the information to the union on some mutually agreeable basis or offer the union access to the available raw data.

THE COSTS OF FURNISHING DATA

The information requested is usually of a type, such as wage records, that has been normally maintained by the employer. The expense in supplying the information is generally minimal. At times, however, the cost of compiling and delivering the information is so substantial that the employer is unwilling to bear the costs. In that case, the employer must notify the union of its objection to the burdensome nature of the request. Thereafter, the employer must bargain with the union over the issue.[42] This will give the union the opportunity to limit its demands. In the course of that bargaining, the parties can discuss the limitation of the scope of the demands or payment by the union of some or all of the costs of gathering and duplicating the information.[43] If the parties cannot agree, then the employer may simply make the files available to the union so that the union can compile the information itself.[44]

DELAY IN SUPPLYING REQUESTED INFORMATION

Data that are not provided promptly grow stale and oftentimes lose their relevance. Accordingly, an unreasonable delay in producing requested information violates the employer's duty to

---

[42] General Motors Corp., 243 N.L.R.B. No. 19 (June 29, 1979); Food Employer Council, Inc., 197 N.L.R.B. 651 (1972).

[43] General Motors Corp., 243 N.L.R.B. No. 19 (June 29, 1979); Food Employer Council, Inc., 197 N.L.R.B. 651 (1972). The employer cannot, however, insist that the union pay the costs of information deleted at the employer's insistence, such as information relating to non-bargaining unit employees, unless the employer can provide an adequate explanation for demanding the deletions. United Aircraft Corp., 192 N.L.R.B. 382 (1971), *modified sub nom.* IAM v. United Aircraft Corp., 534 F.2d 422 (2d Cir. 1975); Fruit & Vegetable Packers & Warehousemen Local 760 v. NLRB, 316 F.2d 389, 391 (D.C. Cir. 1963) (admonishing the parties not to use the allocation of costs as a "tool" for harassment).

[44] Globe-Union, Inc., 233 N.L.R.B. 1458 (1977).

disclose.[45] The length of time that constitutes an "unreasonable" delay varies with the particular facts and circumstances of each case. In a case in which the union submitted a broad request for wage data, a six-week delay due to the complexity of gathering and transmitting the information to the union was not considered evidence of a violation.[46] Similarly, in another case, the union made a "copious" request for information prior to the start of bargaining, and the employer's supplying the information piecemeal over a one-month period did not violate the Act, even though the last piece of information was not made available to the union until two weeks before bargaining began.[47]

Other circumstances that have excused a brief delay include the organization of the firm's payroll by employee wage rate rather than by job classification, the unavailability of the firm's bookkeeper, and the mailing of the information to a negotiator based in another city for transmittal by him to the union.[48] Finally, if the delay is caused by the union representative's failure to make an adequate and timely request for the data, the employer's failure to disclose is not a violation.[49]

As a general rule, the Board and the courts have found that delays of two months or more violate the Act. A delay of as little as three weeks has been found unlawful in the presence of other circumstances suggesting that the delay had been in bad faith.[50]

---

[45] Reed & Prince Mfg. Co., 96 N.L.R.B. 850, 858, *enforced,* 205 F.2d 131 (1st Cir. 1951).

[46] Preterm, Inc., 240 N.L.R.B. No. 81 (Feb. 9, 1979).

[47] United Engines, Inc., 222 N.L.R.B. 50 (1976).

[48] Partee Flooring Mill, 107 N.L.R.B. 1177 (1954) (fifteen-day delay).

[49] Alkahn Silk Label Co., 193 N.L.R.B. 167 (1971).

[50] Hollywood Film Co., 213 N.L.R.B. 584 (1974) (other supporting circumstances present included illegibility of materials furnished, failure to explain data, and provision of only part of data requested); Colonial Press, Inc., 204 N.L.R.B. 852 (1973) (delay of two months in furnishing names, classification, and rates of pay of employees constitutes a violation in the absence of any explanation for the delay); May Aluminum, Inc., 160 N.L.R.B. 575 (1966), *enforced,* 398 F.2d 47 (5th Cir. 1968) (two-month delay in furnishing list of employees, prestrike job classifications, rates of pay, and dates of hire, requested at the end of a strike); Diercke Forests, Inc., 148 N.L.R.B. 923 (1964) (two-month delay in informing union that permanent job classifications did not exist); Kit Mfg. Co., 142 N.L.R.B. 957 (1963), *modified on other grounds,* 335 F.2d 166 (9th Cir. 1964) (two-month delay in furnishing names and addresses of unit employees, dates of hire, job classifications, and wages).

THE EXCELSIOR LIST ISSUE

One of the controversial conflicts between mandatory access to employer data and the rights of individual employees to privacy has centered on the NLRB's *Excelsior* rule. In *Excelsior Underwear, Inc.*,[51] the Board established a new rule requiring the disclosure to the Board of lists of names and addresses of unit employees within seven days after the Regional Director of the NLRB has approved a consent-election agreement (or within the same period after the Director has ordered an election).[52] The Regional Director takes this eligibility list and disseminates it to the election parties. If the employer fails to deliver the list, the Board can either set aside the election in response to proper objections from the losing side,[53] or it can subpoena the information, delay the election, and try to force disclosure of the lists through the courts.[54]

The Board's order in *Excelsior* was eventually found to have been an illegal adoption of a rule, without compliance with the Administrative Procedure Act.[55] Notwithstanding that rejection of the rule as a rule, the Supreme Court went on to approve the substance of the rule in its endorsement of judicially enforced subpoenas to obtain the same information from reluctant employers. By subpoena, if not by rule, the Board's officials receive the list and can then disclose it to the union.[56]

Insufficient attention has been given to the arguments for employees' privacy rights affected by each forced disclosure of a name and address list. Because unions are free to pay personal visits to the individuals named in the Board-supplied or employer-supplied list,[57] there is at least some invasion of privacy for the affected workers.[58] If a person other than a union

---

[31] 156 N.L.R.B. 1236 (1966).

[52] *Id.* 1239-40.

[53] *Id.*

[54] NLRB v. Wyman-Gordon Co., 394 U.S. 759 (1969); NLRB v. Rohlen, 385 F.2d 52 (7th Cir. 1967); NLRB v. Hanes Hosiery Div., 384 F.2d 188 (4th Cir. 1967).

[55] NLRB v. Wyman-Gordon Co., 394 U.S. 759 (1969).

[56] *Id.*; *see* NLRB v. Hanes Hosiery Div., 384 F.2d 188 (4th Cir. 1967).

[57] Excelsior Underwear, Inc., 156 N.L.R.B. 1236 (1966).

[58] Getman v. NLRB, 450 F.2d 670 (D.C. Cir.), *application for stay denied,* 404 U.S. 1204 (1971).

seeks access to the Board's file containing the names and addresses, the Board can be expected to fight any disclosure, into the courts if necessary, to preserve secrecy.[59] If the Board wished to preserve individual privacy at a cost of some marginal paperwork, it could establish a single umbrella "system of records" under the Privacy Act into which the employees' names and addresses could be filed.[60] By doing so, the Board would place the information effectively off limits to anyone other than persons having access as a "routine use," such as a union whose access is compatible with the purpose which collection of the list had served.[61] The Board has chosen, however, to stay out of the Privacy Act field as much as possible and avoids creating "systems of records" despite their third-party access limitations.[62]

The labor law promulgated in *Excelsior* developed in an era of exceptionally adversary relations between employers and employee representatives, during which the Board and the courts lost sight of the privacy rights of individuals. The privacy considerations to which all federal agencies (and millions of individual workers) have become attuned in the 1980s were brushed aside as an employer ploy when they were used as arguments in *Excelsior* [63] and *Wyman-Gordon*.[64] Perhaps a future case, one dealing with a union infiltrated by organized crime elements and a workplace electorate susceptible to coercive conduct, would bring to a head the privacy issues left unanalyzed in *Excelsior*. If the attitude of the courts toward disclosure to

---

[59] This is what the Board did in the Freedom of Information Act case in which two labor law professors sought disclosure to them of Excelsior lists for their use in a survey of opinions and attitudes regarding elections. *Id.*

[60] The Privacy Act of 1974 permits an agency to treat any group of records from which information can be retrieved by individual identities as a "system of records." *See* chapter IX *infra.*

[61] *See* Local 2047, Am. Fed'n of Gov't Employees v. Defense Gen. Supply Center, 423 F. Supp. 481 (E.D. Va. 1976), *aff'd*, 573 F.2d 184 (4th Cir. 1978).

[62] Interview with Stan Weinbrecht, Associate General Counsel, NLRB, in Washington, D.C. (Jan. 14, 1980).

[63] Excelsior Underwear, Inc., 156 N.L.R.B. 1236 (1966).

[64] NLRB v. Wyman-Gordon Co., 394 U.S. 759 (1969).

third parties is sensitive and cautious, as it has been,[65] perhaps future courts will be led to reexamine the wisdom and practical impact of mandatory disclosure of personal privacy information. Like the reexamination of environmental effects after environmental policy legislation became law, the time may come when the courts will reexamine the efficacy of *Excelsior* lists in the context and spirit of federal privacy legislation.

---

[65] *See, e.g.,* Local 2047, Am. Fed'n of Gov't Employees v. Defense Gen. Supply Center, 423 F. Supp. 481 (E.D. Va. 1976), *aff'd,* 573 F.2d 184 (4th Cir. 1978); Getman v. NLRB, 450 F.2d 670 (D.C. Cir.), *application for stay denied,* 404 U.S. 1204 (1971).

CHAPTER III

Presumptively Relevant Data

To obtain disclosure of employer information, the union usually must demonstrate that the requested information is relevant and necessary to the performance of its functions as bargaining representative. If, however, the requested information pertains *directly* to one of the mandatory subjects of collective bargaining—"wages, hours and other terms and conditions of employment" as specified in section 8(d)—then both the National Labor Relations Board and the courts will presume that the information is relevant.

The rule of "presumptively relevant" information was explained by the Second Circuit in *NLRB v. Yawman & Erbe Mfg. Co.*[1]

> The rule governing disclosure of data is not unlike that prevailing in discovery procedures under modern codes. There the information must be disclosed unless it appears plainly irrelevant. Any less lenient rule in labor disputes would greatly hamper the bargaining process, for it is virtually impossible to tell in advance whether the requested data will be relevant except in those infrequent instances in which the inquiry is patently outside the bargaining issue.[2]

PURPOSE OF THE PRESUMPTION

The focal points of most labor negotiations are wages and hours; these form the "heart and core of the employer-employee relationship."[3] It follows that most requests for information relate to these subjects as they affect the employees in the unit represented by the union. The disclosure of information directly

---

[1] 187 F.2d 947 (2d Cir. 1951).

[2] *Id.* at 949. Rule 26 of the Federal Rules of Civil Procedure requires disclosure of any nonprivileged information bearing on the subject matter of the case.

[3] International Woodworkers v. NLRB, 263 F.2d 483, 485 (D.C. Cir. 1959).

bearing on compensation and work time stimulates more productive and better-informed collective bargaining.

By establishing a presumption that certain information will be pertinent and thus must be shared between employer and employee bargaining representatives, the Board and the courts conserve time and energy that would otherwise have to be expended in a determination of relevance for information almost always of crucial significance for intelligent negotiations. The existence of a presumption that certain information will be relevant and ordinarily must be disclosed also provides the parties with a degree of certainty about the information that should be furnished upon request. This eliminates many disputes about the employer's duty to honor such requests routinely.[4]

ORIGIN OF THE PRESUMPTION

The National Labor Relations Board first gave a clear statement of the presumption of relevance in *Whitin Machine Works*.[5] There, the union requested the wage rate of all employees. The company responded by providing a list of employee names, job classifications, and dates hired. In a separate document, the employer listed hourly wage rates for that plant.

The Board ruled that the employer was required to provide the union with a list that linked names to wage rates. The Board rejected the employer's claim that the union had failed to show a specific need for the information. Instead, such a need would be presumed. Chairman Farmer concurred with the majority opinion, commenting:

> This broad rule is necessary to avoid the disruptive effect of the endless bickering and jockeying which has heretofore been characteristic of union demands and employer reaction to requests by unions for wage-related information. . . . I conceive the proper rule to be that wage and related information pertaining to employees in the bargaining unit should, upon request, be made available to the bargaining agent without regard to its immediate relationship to the negotiations or administration of the collective bargaining agreement.[6]

---

[4] NLRB v. Yawman & Erbe Mfg. Co., 187 F.2d 947, 949 (2d Cir. 1951).

[5] 108 N.L.R.B. 1537, *enforced*, 217 F.2d 593 (4th Cir. 1954), *cert. denied*, 349 U.S. 905 (1955).

[6] Whitin Mach. Works, 108 N.L.R.B. 1537, 1541, *enforced*, 217 F.2d 593 (4th Cir. 1954), *cert. denied*, 349 U.S. 905 (1955).

The Fourth Circuit enforced the Board's order and cited with approval the Second Circuit's opinion in *Yawman & Erbe,* quoted above.[7] The doctrine of presumptive relevance was further solidified in the following year by the First Circuit's decision in *Boston Herald-Traveler Corp. v. NLRB.*[8] There, the court ruled that linked wage data dealing with employees' job classifications, dates of employment, salaries, and commissions were presumptively relevant data and must be disclosed. Although the court relied primarily on *Whitin,* the Fourth Circuit expressed the view that the rule had been implied in cases preceding *Whitin.*[9]

REBUTTAL OF THE PRESUMPTION

The adverse party, normally the employer, is able to rebut the presumption of relevance. Once the employer has rebutted the presumption—a rare event—the burden shifts to the union to demonstrate relevance.[10] At that point, the union must then demonstrate the precise relevance of the desired data by reference to the particular circumstances of the case.[11] For example, if the employer pays a year-end bonus equal to a certain percentage of its profits, the union may not obtain profitability data merely by asserting that profits are wages.[12]

WAGE DATA

One means that the Board and the courts have used to expand the presumption of relevance is the expansion of the definition of wage-related data. The traditional set of information that had been assumed pertinent included the wage history of em-

---

[7] NLRB v. Whitin Mach. Works, 217 F.2d 593, 594 (4th Cir. 1954).

[8] 223 F.2d 58 (1st Cir. 1955).

[9] *Id.* at 62-64.

[10] Bendix Corp., 242 N.L.R.B. No. 8 (May 8, 1979) ; White Furniture Co., 161 N.L.R.B. 444 (1966), *aff'd sub nom.* United Furniture Workers v. NLRB, 388 F.2d 880 (4th Cir. 1967).

[11] Bendix Corp., 242 N.L.R.B. No. 8 (May 8, 1979) ; White Furniture Co., 161 N.L.R.B. 444 (1966), *aff'd sub nom.* United Furniture Workers v. NLRB, 388 F.2d 880 (4th Cir. 1967).

[12] United Furniture Workers v. NLRB, 388 F.2d 880, 882-83 (4th Cir. 1967) ; *accord,* NLRB v. Leland-Gifford Co., 200 F.2d 620 (1st Cir. 1952).

ployees,[13] number of hours worked at straight and overtime rates,[14] wage rates,[15] and employee benefits.[16]

The First Circuit enlarged this group of wage-related items in *Sylvania Electric Products Inc. v. NLRB.*[17] There, the employer proposed to improve the insurance and welfare benefits that were provided solely at the employer's cost. The union requested a breakdown of this coverage and its costs, so that the union might determine whether workers would prefer expanded benefits instead of an equivalent increase in wages. The employer refused, relying on an earlier First Circuit decision that, involving the same firm, had held that employer payments to a noncontributory insurance plan were neither "wages" nor "terms and conditions of employment."[18] The First Circuit in this case, however, enforced the Board's disclosure order, holding that refusal to disclose may be a violation of the duty to bargain when the union demands information to determine if it should seek improved welfare benefits or an equivalent increase in wages. Even though the information was collateral, it was deemed necessary to an informed, intelligent decision on the part of the union.

In *Sylvania,*[19] the information became presumptively relevant when it was tied to a specific union decision. The Fourth Circuit used this notion of "derivative" or "bootstrap" presumptive relevance in *Cone Mills Corp. v. NLRB*[20] to require that an

[13] Utica Observer-Dispatch, Inc. v. NLRB, 229 F.2d 575 (2d Cir. 1956) (employer must link employee names with individual wages); Aluminum Ore Co. v. NLRB, 131 F.2d 485 (7th Cir. 1942) (employer who refused to reveal wage rates for preceding three years acted unlawfully).

[14] NLRB v. F. W. Woolworth Co., 352 U.S. 938 (1956) (employer must divulge hours information).

[15] Hekman Furniture Co., 101 N.L.R.B. 631 (1952), *enforced per curiam,* 207 F.2d 561 (6th Cir. 1953) (rate ranges must be disclosed).

[16] John Swift & Co., 124 N.L.R.B. 394 (1959), *enforced in part,* 277 F.2d 641 (7th Cir. 1960) (respective premium payments by employer and employees for insurance plan must be disclosed).

[17] 358 F.2d 591 (1st Cir.), *cert. denied,* 385 U.S. 852 (1966).

[18] Sylvania Elec. Prods., Inc. v. NLRB, 291 F.2d 128 (1st Cir.), *cert. denied,* 368 U.S. 926 (1961).

[19] Sylvania Elec. Prods., Inc. v. NLRB, 358 F.2d 591, 592-93 (1st Cir.), *cert. denied,* 385 U.S. 852 (1966).

[20] 413 F.2d 445 (4th Cir. 1969).

employer disclose the cost of a noncontributory pension plan that it had proposed during negotiations. The union desired to use the cost information to develop a feasible counterproposal. That desire to make a counterproposal meant that cost data were the equivalent of wages for purposes of that negotiation, and thus they were presumptively relevant.[21]

WAGE SURVEYS

Presumptively relevant information includes not only actual wages paid but also information dealing with the manner in which wages are set. In *General Electric Co. v. NLRB*,[22] the employer asserted during bargaining that its wage rates were competitive in the local market. The union demanded access to the wage surveys. The Board ordered disclosure, and on appeal, the order was upheld. The company was required to reveal wage surveys that were done in linked or correlated form, i.e., with each piece of information identified by the name of the company that supplied the data.[23] The court held that the union's need to verify the accuracy of the study outweighed the employer's pledge of confidentiality to other companies that had participated in the survey.[24]

The *General Electric* line of cases has established that correlated wage surveys are presumptively relevant if they are used at all in developing the wage structure.[25] It is not material that, at the time of the request, no negotiations or grievance proceedings are underway.[26]

---

[21] *Id.*

[22] 466 F.2d 1177 (6th Cir. 1972).

[23] *Id.* at 1183-84.

[24] *Id.* at 1185.

[25] General Elec. Co., 163 N.L.R.B. 198 (1967).

[26] General Elec. Co. v. NLRB, 466 F.2d 1177 (6th Cir. 1972). General Electric has been singularly unsuccessful in its attempts to prevent disclosure of its wage surveys. *See* General Elec. Co. v. NLRB, 414 F.2d 918 (4th Cir. 1969), *cert. denied*, 396 U.S. 1005 (1970); General Elec. Co. v. NLRB, 443 F.2d 602 (5th Cir. 1968). As a result of these decisions, companies have employed outside consulting firms to perform such wage studies. Since the companies do not actually possess the survey but only the results thereof, they arguably cannot be required under the Act to provide the union with such surveys.

TIME STUDIES

Time study data used to determine wages are also presumptively relevant. In *J. I. Case Co. v. NLRB*,[27] piece rates were computed by the employer based upon a time study that it had conducted. When the company converted the job from a one-machine to a two-machine operation and did not increase the wage rate for that job, the union sought data relating to that particular job, including portions of the time study bearing on the changes in the job. The court held that the information was relevant to the determination of wages, and the employer's refusal to supply this information was held to be a violation of the Act.[28]

An employer is not obligated to furnish studies that are not used to determine wage rates or otherwise affect the terms and conditions of employment. In *General Aniline & Film Corp.*,[29] the union sought the disclosure of reports used exclusively for cost purposes and for development of a more efficient system of managerial work scheduling. The Board ruled that, since such data would not aid the union in bargaining intelligently on behalf of the workers, it need not be disclosed.[30]

PERFORMANCE OF A LIVE STUDY

A union may not only receive time study data from the employer but may also, under certain circumstances, conduct its own time study on the company's premises during working hours.

In *Fafnir Bearing Co. v. NLRB*,[31] the contract in force provided that piece rates "shall be set so that the average qualified operator working under normal job conditions and applying normal incentive efforts shall be able, after a reasonable trial period, to earn 5% above the standard earning grade of his labor grade."[32] The company permitted wide use of personal discretion by the industrial engineering personnel who conducted the

---

[27] 253 F.2d 149 (7th Cir. 1958).

[28] *Id.* at 155-56.

[29] 124 N.L.R.B. 1217 (1959).

[30] *Id.* at 1219.

[31] 362 F.2d 716 (2d Cir. 1966).

[32] *Id.* at 718.

company's time studies. The contract provided that piece rates could be adjusted when there had been a "measurable change or accumulation of changes over a period of time in material, method, or processes not previously taken into account." [33]

The company proposed changes in piece rates, and the union filed grievances. The union sought to perform its own time study to determine if the company's actions were justified, but the company refused permission for the study. When the case reached the Second Circuit, the court ordered that the union be permitted to perform the time study on the employer's premises during working time. The court concluded that a live study was the only way in which the union could fully assess the employer's proposed modifications.[34]

Two conditions must be met before live in-plant time studies will be required, according to the court in *Fafnir*. First, the repetition of the study must be essential for the union to function intelligently on behalf of the employees. Second, the study must be conducted so as not to disrupt company operations.[35]

An employer may impose conditions on the manner in which a union-initiated study is conducted inside the plant if it can demonstrate that an absence of restrictions will unnecessarily burden or interfere with production or discipline.[36] A refusal to permit an unconditional study, however, will be held to be unlawful if the employer cannot demonstrate that restrictions are necessary to ensure uninterrupted plant operations.[37]

The union's right to conduct such a live study in the plant is derived from the Act, and limitations on the statutory right

---

[33] *Id.*

[34] *Id.* at 720.

[35] Fafnir Bearing Co. v. NLRB, 362 F.2d 716 (2d Cir. 1966); *accord*, Waycross Sportswear, Inc. v. NLRB, 403 F.2d 832 (5th Cir. 1968).

[36] Wilson Athletic Goods Mfg. Co., 169 N.L.R.B. 621 (1968); *see* Winn-Dixie Stores, Inc., 224 N.L.R.B. 1418, 1443 (1976), *modified on other grounds*, 567 F.2d 1343 (5th Cir. 1978) ("compliance with the good faith bargaining prescribed by the Act required Respondent (employer) to cooperate with the Union by making plant facilities available to the Union for the conduct by the latter of its own time studies, *unless the Union's request was improper for some other reason or imposed an unreasonable burden on Respondent*") (emphasis added) (quoting Wilson Athletic Goods Mfg. Co., 169 N.L.R.B. 621 (1968)).

[37] Winn-Dixie Stores, Inc., 224 N.L.R.B. 1418, 1443 (1976), *modified on other grounds*, 567 F.2d 1343 (5th Cir. 1978).

will be viewed narrowly by the courts.[38] For example, if the
employer's time study would be unintelligible without explanation, the employer could not require the union to request and
review the employer's study before granting authorization for
the union to conduct its own study.[39] Similarly, the employer
cannot deny the union the right to conduct a live study by
offering to allow the union to view videotapes of the operation.[40]
Furthermore, the company cannot require that the union hire
an independent engineer to conduct the study.[41]

WAGE METHODS AND MERIT AND BONUS PROGRAMS

An employer's method of computing wages must be revealed
upon request to the union. In *Taylor Forge & Pipe Works v.
NLRB*,[42] disclosure was ordered where the employer had assigned
points to each of eleven factors for every job, with the sum of
the points used to determine the wage rate paid for each job.

Because wage rates are affected by merit increases, incentive
rates, and bonuses, information relating to these issues is presumptively relevant to the union's statutory bargaining duties.
As stated by the Sixth Circuit in *NLRB v. J. H. Allison & Co.*: [43]
"The labeling of a wage increase as a gratuity does not obviate
the fact that a gratuitous increase on the basis of merit does,
in actuality, effectuate changes in rates of pay and wages which
are by the Act made the subject of collective bargaining." [44]

Under this principle, an employer would violate section 8(a)(5)
of the Act by refusing to furnish the result of an employee's
merit review [45] or by refusing to disclose the factors used in

---

[38] General Elec. Co., 173 N.L.R.B. 164 (1968), *enforced*, 414 F.2d 918 (4th
Cir. 1969), *cert. denied*, 396 U.S. 1005 (1970).

[39] Wilson Athletic Goods Mfg. Co., 169 N.L.R.B. 621 (1968).

[40] General Elec. Co., 186 N.L.R.B. 14 (1970).

[41] Winn-Dixie Stores, Inc., 224 N.L.R.B. 1418 (1976), *modified on other
grounds*, 567 F.2d 1343 (5th Cir. 1978).

[42] 234 F.2d 227 (7th Cir.), *cert. denied*, 352 U.S. 942 (1956).

[43] 165 F.2d 766 (6th Cir.), *cert. denied*, 335 U.S. 814 (1948).

[44] *Id.* at 768.

[45] Otis Elevator, 170 N.L.R.B. 395 (1968) (results of merit review).

computation of merit-wage increases.[46] It would also be a violation to refuse to provide a list of workers receiving merit raises, along with the size of their increases.[47]

When the selling prices of goods are an essential element in the calculation of worker bonus payments, the prices are presumptively relevant and must be disclosed.[48] Similarly, information that is used to compute employees' benefits under profit-sharing plans is deemed to be presumptively relevant.[49]

NON-BARGAINING UNIT WAGES

Information concerning workers outside the bargaining unit is not presumed pertinent. This general rule has exceptions. If non-bargaining unit employees perform the same work as unit members, the Board has ruled that information relating to wages of the excluded workers is presumptively relevant. In a series of four cases that concerned the duty of newspaper owners to disclose the amounts paid to non-bargaining unit columnists and correspondents, the Board regarded the information on those payments as pertinent to the union's responsibility to bargain over wages.[50] It held:

> The Union's immediate and continuing need for information about [nonunit workers'] earnings and methods of payment, when examined in light of the [nonunit workers'] work and the Union's duties is apparent. . . . The pay received by [nonunit workers] . . . for performing bargaining unit work and the method of pay have a direct bearing on the pay of the employees represented by the union.[51]

---

[46] International Tel. & Tel. Corp. v. NLRB, 382 F.2d 366 (3d Cir. 1967), *cert. denied*, 389 U.S. 1039 (1968) (employer must furnish factors used in recommending individuals for merit increases).

[47] Boston Herald-Traveler Corp. v. NLRB, 223 F.2d 58 (1st Cir. 1955) (employer must reveal the names of employees receiving increases and the size of the increase granted).

[48] NLRB v. Frontier Homes Corp., 371 F.2d 974 (8th Cir. 1967).

[49] NLRB v. Toffenetti Restaurant Co., 311 F.2d 219 (2d Cir.), *cert. denied*, 372 U.S. 977 (1962).

[50] Brown Newspaper Publishing Co., 238 N.L.R.B. No. 187 (Sept. 29, 1978); Press Democrat Publishing Co., 237 N.L.R.B. 1335 (1978); Amphlett Printing Co., 237 N.L.R.B. 955 (1978); Times-Herald, Inc., 237 N.L.R.B. 922 (1978).

[51] Northwest Publications, Inc., 211 N.L.R.B. 464, 466 (1974) (quoted in Times-Herald, Inc., 237 N.L.R.B. 922 (1978)).

Therefore, if the requested data about nonunit workers concern wages that are paid for work also performed by unit members, the information may be considered pertinent, and the employer may be ordered to disclose it. The Board gives little weight to the fact that such information may be requested for organizing rather than bargaining purposes.

INSURANCE, PENSION, AND HEALTH BENEFITS

Insurance, pension, and health and welfare benefits are encompassed within the concept of "wages," and as such, information concerning these benefits must be furnished upon request.[52] Employers must disclose the types of insurance coverage provided for employees, the portions of the premiums paid by the company and the workers, copies of insurance and health plans (along with their annual reports), and the costs per employee and employee-dependent for each new insurance benefit or each improvement in an existing benefit.[53] If the information is not disaggregated for individual employees, the employer must try to break it down so that it is.[54]

JOB CLASSIFICATIONS AND JOB DESCRIPTIONS

Job classifications usually have a direct bearing on wages. Correlated classifications of bargaining unit employees must be revealed on request.[55] Moreover, if written job descriptions are available, the employer must also furnish them upon request.[56]

---

[52] Stowe-Woodward, Inc., 123 N.L.R.B. 287 (1959) ; Skyland Hosiery Mills, Inc., 108 N.L.R.B. 1600 (1954).

[53] NLRB v. General Elec. Co., 418 F.2d 736 (2d Cir. 1969), *cert. denied*, 397 U.S. 965 (1970); Borden, Inc., 235 N.L.R.B. 982 (1978), *enforced in part*, 600 F.2d 313 (1st Cir. 1979) ; B. GOTTLEIB & C. WERNER, STATUTORY OBLIGATION OF AN EMPLOYER TO FURNISH INFORMATION TO A UNION, 15 (1971).

[54] Borden, Inc., 235 N.L.R.B. 982 (1978), *enforced in part*, 600 F.2d 313 (1st Cir. 1979).

[55] Lock Joint Pipe Co., 141 N.L.R.B. 943 (1963); Aluminum Ore Co., 39 N.L.R.B. 1286, *enforced*, 131 F.2d 485 (7th Cir. 1942).

[56] Sawbrook Steel Castings Co., 173 N.L.R.B. 381 (1968) ; American Sugar Refining Co., 130 N.L.R.B. 634 (1961).

EMPLOYEE NAMES AND ADDRESSES

The National Labor Relations Board has long held that the names and addresses of unit employees must be provided to the union if the union claims the need for such information to communicate effectively with unit employees.[57]

In the *Georgetown Associates, Inc.*, decision,[58] the Board expressly ruled that name and address information on unit employees is presumptively relevant. The union had made numerous requests for a list of names and addresses of employees who were hired to replace strikers. The company provided the names but refused to provide the addresses. Overruling its Administrative Law Judge, the Board found that the employer's refusal to provide addresses violated section 8(a)(5): ". . . it is well settled that the names and addresses of unit employees, like wage data, are presumptively relevant to the Union's role as bargaining agent either during contract negotiations or during the term of an agreement. Hence no showing of particularized need was necessary." [59]

The courts have not yet commented on the *Georgetown* holding. In the past, courts have required a union to demonstrate the relevance of names and addresses by showing the impracticability of reaching unit employees through alternate means of communication.[60] Factors such as the size of the unit, the rate of turnover, and the existence of a contractual union security clause are important in establishing the relevance of the name and address information.

Name and address information is sometimes essential. In *Prudential Insurance Company of America v. NLRB*,[61] the union represented 16,795 agents in thirty-four states, with a rate of

---

[57] *See, e.g.*, Magma Copper Co., San Manuel Div., 208 N.L.R.B. 329 (1974); Shell Oil Co., 190 N.L.R.B. 101 (1971), *enforcement denied*, 457 F.2d 615 (9th Cir. 1972); Prudential Ins. Co. of America, 173 N.L.R.B. 792 (1968), *enforced*, 412 F.2d 77 (2d Cir.), *cert. denied*, 396 U.S. 928 (1969); Standard Oil of Calif., 166 N.L.R.B. 343 (1967), *enforced*, 399 F.2d 639 (9th Cir. 1968).

[58] 235 N.L.R.B. 485 (1978); *cf.* DePalma Printing Co., 204 N.L.R.B. 31 (1973).

[59] Georgetown Assocs., Inc., 235 N.L.R.B. 485 (1978).

[60] NLRB v. Pearl Bookbinding Co., 517 F.2d 1108, 1113 (1st Cir. 1975); Magma Copper Co., San Manuel Div., 208 N.L.R.B. 329 (1974).

[61] Prudential Ins. Co. of America v. NLRB, 412 F.2d 77 (2d Cir.), *cert. denied*, 396 U.S. 928 (1969).

turnover of 25 percent per year. Alternative means of communication were inadequate.[62] The Board ruled (and the Second Circuit agreed) that the name and address information was essential.[63] The appellate court gave strong support to the disclosure arguments raised by the union:

> The kind of information requested by the Union in this case [names and addresses of bargaining unit employees] has an even more fundamental relevance than that considered presumptively relevant . . . [D]ata without which a union cannot even communicate with employees whom it represents is, by its very nature, fundamental to the entire expanse of a union's relationship with the employees. . . . Because this information is therefore so basically related to the proper performance of the union's statutory duties, we believe any special showing of specific relevance would be superfluous.[64]

Just one year later, however, the same court required the union to make a special showing of pertinence of the home addresses of unit workers.[65]

The strike situation is a special problem for disclosures of name and address information. *Georgetown Associates* is a case of special importance on that issue. In the past, employers have had some success in refusing to provide name and address information for those employees who were working during a strike. In *W. L. McKnight, d/b/a Webster Outdoor Advertising, Inc.*,[66] the Board upheld the employer's refusal to give name and wage data for permanent replacements because the replacements had been harassed and threatened for working during a strike.

---

[62] *Id.* at 79-80, 81-83.

[63] *Id.* at 84.

[64] *Id.*

[65] United Aircraft Corp. v. NLRB, 434 F.2d 1198 (2d Cir. 1970), *cert. denied*, 401 U.S. 933 (1971) (after noting that handbills, distribution racks, bulletin boards, shop union stewards, and employer forwarding of union correspondence were ineffective means of communication, and that only a small percentage of workers in the bargaining unit were union members, court held disclosure of the names and addresses of bargaining unit employees was necessary because the union could not rely on its members to represent adequately the views of the other employees for whom it was bargaining); *accord*, Standard Oil Co. of Calif., 166 N.L.R.B. 343 (1967), *enforced*, 399 F.2d 639 (9th Cir. 1968).

[66] 170 N.L.R.B. 1395 (1968), *affirmed sub nom.* Sign & Pictorial Union, Local 1175 v. NLRB, 419 F.2d 726 (D.C. Cir. 1969).

Similarly, in *Nordstrom, Inc.*,[67] the NLRB upheld the employer's refusal to disclose the names and addresses of unit employees who remained at work during a strike. The employer had refused because the sole reason for the union's request was to discipline union members for crossing the picket line.[68]

The presumption in favor of disclosure is, therefore, rebuttable. Even after *Georgetown Associates,* the employer is probably legally as well as practically correct in refusing to disclose names and addresses of employees who are working during violent strike situations. Demonstration of an improper motive by the union and of the threatening nature of the strike situation should be sufficient.

LAYOFF INFORMATION

Information bearing on layoffs within the unit is presumptively relevant. As explained by the Board:

> The matter of the layoff or termination of bargaining unit personnel is a mandatory subject of bargaining. This means that [the employer] . . . was required to notify the Union in advance of its intentions and give it an opportunity to bargain over the matter, promptly to supply information in this regard, and also to bargain over the effects of the terminations upon the employees.[69]

In layoff situations, the presumptive relevance principle applies if layoffs are presently occurring, have occurred, or are about to occur and if the information requested relates to the decision to terminate unit jobs, to the method by which the employees will be laid off, or to the effects of the reductions and policies of rehiring upon the workers.[70] Then the information, e.g., the schedule of an announced layoff program, is considered presumptively relevant.

---

67 229 N.L.R.B. 601 (1977); *see* Shell Oil Co. v. NLRB, 457 F.2d 615 (9th Cir. 1972). *But see* Westinghouse Learning Corp., 211 N.L.R.B. 19 (1974) (presumption not rebutted as union has legitimate interest as their statutorily designated bargaining representative in contacting replacements).

68 Nordstrom, Inc., 229 N.L.R.B. 601 (1977).

69 The Shaw College, 232 N.L.R.B. 191, 204 (1977).

70 Florida Steel Corp., 235 N.L.R.B. 941 (1978), *enforced in part,* 601 F.2d 125 (4th Cir. 1979).

TRAINING DATA

Information on the training of unit employees was held presumptively relevant in the case of *A. S. Abell Co.*[71] Abell, publisher of the *Baltimore Sun*, offered certain members of the bargaining unit an opportunity to learn how to perform nonunit work. The union sought information about the cross-training program. The employer refused to comply with the labor organization's request. The Board held that training data were included in the category "wage and related information pertaining to unit employees" and thus were presumed pertinent.[72]

EQUAL EMPLOYMENT DATA

The principle of presumptively relevant data has been applied in several recent cases involving equal employment opportunity reporting data. These cases are discussed at length in chapter XVII of this text, and since the leading case, *Westinghouse Electric Corp.*,[73] is presently on appeal to the District of Columbia Circuit as this text goes to press, any conclusions on the subject are tentative ones.

In *Westinghouse*, the NLRB majority, over a strident dissent by member Murphy, examined the statutory right of the union to correct discriminatory practices, and it held that information bearing upon the existence of discrimination within the bargaining unit is presumptively relevant.[74] Citing the *Tanner Motor Livery Ltd.*[75] case, the Board found that the presumption of relevance can arise from the union's duty of fair representation. Discrimination, the Board held, is a term or condition of employment that makes the delivery of data for use in bargaining necessary.

Because hiring discrimination can "inherently affect" terms and conditions of employment[76] and because the union has a

---

[71] 230 N.L.R.B. 1112 (1977).

[72] *Id.* at 1113.

[73] 239 N.L.R.B. No. 19 (Oct. 31, 1978), *appeal docketed*, No. 78-2067 (D.C. Cir. Nov. 1, 1978).

[74] 239 N.L.R.B. No. 19 (Oct. 31, 1978).

[75] Tanner Motor Livery, Ltd., 148 N.L.R.B. 1402, 1404 (1964), *enforcement denied on other grounds*, 419 F.2d 216 (9th Cir. 1969) (cited in East Dayton Tool & Die Co., 239 N.L.R.B. No. 20 (Oct. 31, 1978)).

[76] *Id.*

duty to make a good faith effort to correct discrimination, the statistical information as it applied to unit personnel was held to be presumptively relevant.[77] The company was not required to provide statistical data on nonunit employees because the union failed to demonstrate the pertinence of data bearing on those employees.[78]

Motives for the union's request were important in *East Dayton Tool & Die Co.*,[79] which was a companion case to *Westinghouse*. A detailed set of data on hiring applicants and new hires was requested,[80] and the data were held to be presumptively relevant.[81] The employer made a strong showing that the union was seeking the data to help it refute a charge of union actions in support of discrimination. The Board found, however, that one of the union's motives was related to its functioning as bargaining representative; therefore, the existence of other defensive motives was irrelevant in the view of the Board.[82]

PLANT SAFETY CONDITIONS

An administrative law judge's opinion in *Borden Chemical*[83] held that plant chemicals' identities and compositions were presumptively relevant. The information had been withheld for protection of a trade secret.[84] The ruling was that the union would be incapable of policing the portion of the contract related to worker safety unless detailed chemical information was available.[85] The case is currently on appeal to the Board.[86]

---

[77] Westinghouse Elec. Corp., 239 N.L.R.B. No. 19 (Oct. 31, 1978).

[78] *Id.*

[79] 239 N.L.R.B. No. 20 (Oct. 31, 1978).

[80] *Id.*

[81] *Id.*

[82] *Id.*

[83] No. 32-CA-551 (N.L.R.B., filed Apr. 25, 1979).

[84] *Id.*

[85] *Id.*

[86] *Id.*

OTHER DATA AFFECTING MANDATORY SUBJECTS

Other data used to effectuate a change in "wages, hours and other terms and conditions of employment" also are presumptively relevant. In *Texaco, Inc. v. NLRB*,[87] the employer undertook an economy and efficiency study that resulted in the elimination of certain job categories. The union requested all the study data that the firm had used in reaching its decision to reduce the number of employees. The employer refused.

The Board and the Seventh Circuit viewed the study as part of a cost-reduction program that had led to elimination of job classifications. The court held the data to be presumptively relevant and ordered it disclosed.[88]

[87] 407 F.2d 754 (7th Cir. 1969).

[88] *Id.* at 755-58; *accord*, Kendall Co., 196 N.L.R.B. 588 (1972).

CHAPTER IV

The Demonstration of Relevance

As shown in chapter III, presumptively relevant documents must be provided to the union by the employer for policy reasons of certainty and judicial economy. If, however, the union requests information that is *not* presumptively relevant, then the union must demonstrate that the information is "relevant and necessary" to its responsibilities as the collective bargaining representative of the workers.

The National Labor Relations Board makes the initial determination of relevance. The Board's decision has been accorded great deference by the courts.[1] The courts can view the determination of relevance either as a finding of fact, which cannot be overturned if supported by substantial evidence, or as a finding on an issue of both law and fact, which is within the presumed expertise of the Board.

This chapter details the types of commonly requested information that have been involved in past NLRB and judicial decisions and the manner in which relevance has been shown for them.

SUBCONTRACTING INFORMATION

The issue of an employer's subcontracting unit work is a complex one. Depending on the circumstances of a particular case, subcontracting may be a mandatory subject of bargaining. If the employer simply continues an established pattern of subcontracting work for economic reasons and no notable harm to unit employees results from the subcontracting, then the employer need not bargain over the particular subcontracting decision.[2]

---

[1] San Diego Newspaper Guild, Local 95 v. NLRB, 548 F.2d 863, 867 (9th Cir. 1977).

[2] Allied Chem. Corp., 151 N.L.R.B. 718 (1965), *enforced sub nom.* District 50, UMW v. NLRB, 358 F.2d 234 (4th Cir. 1966); Westinghouse Elec. Corp., 150 N.L.R.B. 1574 (1965).

The obligation to transfer information, however, arises in two separate instances. If the subcontracting significantly affects the unit employees or if it increases in relation to prior patterns, then the employer must give notice of the subcontracting decision. The employer then must bargain about the decision and the effects of that decision.[3] In such circumstances, the employer must also provide all requested information relevant to the issues involved in the bargaining.[4]

In *United Auto Workers v. NLRB*,[5] the employer assembled new automobiles. Cars were parked in two successive steps; the first step used bargaining unit employees, while the second step was performed by nonunit employees. Six unit members who were parking attendants were displaced when the steps were combined and placed under the control of the nonunit employees. Although all of the six were placed in other jobs, the number of positions in the bargaining unit was diminished. The union requested both the opportunity to bargain and certain information relative to the elimination of the unit work. The employer refused.

After Board proceedings were completed, the Court of Appeals for the District of Columbia Circuit reversed the Board and held that, because the decision of the employer had an adverse impact on the unit, bargaining was required.[6] The appellate court also ruled that the admitted adverse impact on the bargaining unit made the information requested regarding the new parking procedure presumptively relevant information.[7]

Determinative Sources of Relevance

If the adverse impact of the subcontracting decision upon the unit employees is not obvious, then the union must show that the subcontracting information is relevant. One way in which the union could demonstrate relevance is to show that subcontracting resulted in a loss of straight time or overtime hours.

---

[3] Fibreboard Paper Prods. Corp. v. NLRB, 379 U.S. 203 (1959); Western Mass. Elec. Co. v. NLRB, 573 F.2d 101 (1st Cir. 1978); UAW v. NLRB, 381 F.2d 265 (D.C. Cir.), *cert. denied*, 389 U.S. 857 (1967).

[4] *See* the cases cited in note 3 *supra.*

[5] *See* the cases cited in note 3 *supra.*

[6] *See* the cases cited in note 3 *supra.*

[7] *See* the cases cited in note 3 *supra.*

The union could also show that subcontracting has resulted or will result in layoffs of union employees.[8] A union could make the same demonstration by showing that the requested data are necessary for the administration or policing of the collective bargaining agreement. If the agreement has a specific provision limiting subcontracting, information requested in connection with a specific grievance filed on subcontracting will be deemed relevant.[9]

A contract clause that limits subcontracting may make requested information relevant. In *Fawcett Printing Corp.*, the contract provided:

> ". . . The Fawcett-Haynes Printing Corporation . . . agrees that it will not subcontract work, (a) while there is any unemployment of any kind among the employees doing work in the plant, or (b) where any reduction in the work force is contemplated among the employees doing such work in the plant or (c) within thirty (30) days after there has been any such unemployment." [10]

Citing decreased consumer demand, the company began to lay off some unit employees and reduced the length of the workweek for others. The union did not believe the employer's explanation for the layoffs. Instead, the union suspected that the decline in unit work may have resulted from subcontracting in violation of the contract provision rather than from a decline in customer demand.

The union filed a grievance over this decline in work. The union cited its right to administer the subcontracting clause, and it asked for the identity of the company's customers, copies of contracts and correspondence involving the customers, and information regarding the relationship between the company and suspected subcontractors. The employer refused the requested information.

The NLRB found that the company's refusal violated the Act.[11] The Board premised its decision on its conclusion that the information requested by the union was clearly relevant to the

---

[8] District 50, UMW v. NLRB, 358 F.2d 234 (4th Cir. 1966).

[9] American Oil Co., 164 N.L.R.B. 29 (1967).

[10] 201 N.L.R.B. 964, 966 (1973).

[11] *Id.* at 964.

administration of the contract provision limiting subcontracting.[12]

Information on subcontracting may also be reached by the use of other contract clauses. In *Davol, Inc.*,[13] the agreement did not limit the company's right to subcontract the unit work. The agreement did, however, grant limited recall rights to employees who were laid off, and it also provided for severance pay for employees who were affected by a plant closure. The employer notified the union that one of the company's two plants might be closed at a future date. The company also announced that production work from both this plant and another installation were being subcontracted.

After these announcements, the union noted a decrease in the size of the unit, and it became concerned that, if layoffs continued, the employees on layoff might exhaust their time-limited contractual recall rights. The union also suspected that the subcontracting was just one element in a plan to shut down the plant after the workers on layoff had exhausted their recall rights and thereby had lost their rights to severance pay to which employees were otherwise entitled. The union requested that the employer supply information on the nature and amount of the subcontracting, and the employer refused to disclose it.

Both the Board[14] and the First Circuit[15] found that the employer's refusal violated the Act because the information requested was relevant and necessary in policing the contractual rights relating to recall and severance pay. Both the Board and the appellate court deemed it immaterial that the contract had not expressly proscribed or limited the subcontracting.[16]

Information Available in Subcontracting Situations

Where relevance to the subcontracting issue has been established, the Board and the courts have ordered disclosure of a great variety of requested information. This information has

---

12 *Id.* at 970-73; *accord,* Davol, Inc., 237 N.L.R.B. 431 (1978), *enforced,* 597 F.2d 782 (1st Cir. 1979). *But see* Western Mass. Elec. Co. v. NLRB, 573 F.2d 101, 104 (1st Cir. 1978).

13 237 N.L.R.B. 431 (1978), *enforced,* 597 F.2d 782 (1st Cir. 1979).

14 *Id.*

15 *Id.*

16 *Id.*

included lists of subcontracts in effect,[17] details of the financial arrangements between the employer and the subcontractor,[18] and copies of the subcontracts.[19] In addition, disclosure of the business and corporate relationship of the employer and the subcontractor has been required if the union has raised a significant question about whether the particular subcontractor was actually the alter ego of the employer.[20]

EVASION OF THE COLLECTIVE BARGAINING AGREEMENT

A union's belief, based in fact, that an employer is attempting to circumvent completely the contractual obligation of the collective bargaining agreement warrants disclosure of employer information. In *Associated General Contractors of California*,[21] a trade association of employers in the building construction trade negotiated "master agreements" for its unionized members. The number of association members who were not signatories to the master agreement, however, was increasing substantially. The union began to suspect that some of the members who had been bound by the agreements were attempting to evade the agreement by altering their names, styles, and corporate structures. Their nonunion successor firms were not bound by the agreements. Seeking to verify this pattern, the union requested, and was denied, information relating to the members of the Associated General Contractors who were not covered by the negotiated agreements. The National Labor Relations Board ordered the association to furnish the union with a full membership roster. It held that the data were relevant not only to the policing of current agreements but also to the pending negotiations for a new contract.[22]

---

17 Amcar Div., ACF Indus., Inc., 234 N.L.R.B. 1063 (1978).

18 Davol, Inc., 237 N.L.R.B. 431 (1978), *enforced*, 597 F.2d 782 (1st Cir. 1979); Western Mass. Elec. Co., 228 N.L.R.B. 607 (1977), *enforced*, 573 F.2d 101 (1st Cir. 1978); B. F. Goodrich Gen. Prods. Co., 221 N.L.R.B. 288 (1975).

19 Equitable Gas Co., 245 N.L.R.B. No. 38 (Sept. 24, 1979); Wallace Metal Prods., 244 N.L.R.B. No. 10 (Aug. 9, 1979); Trustees of Boston Univ., 210 N.L.R.B. 330 (1974).

20 Doubarn Sheet Metal, 243 N.L.R.B. No. 104 (July 31, 1979); Fawcett Printing Corp., 201 N.L.R.B. 964 (1973).

21 242 N.L.R.B. No. 124 (June 8, 1979).

22 *Id.*

INFORMATION REGARDING WORKERS OUTSIDE THE UNIT

The right of the union to information is not limited per se to data that immediately relate to the bargaining unit employees.[23] If, however, the union seeks information about employees outside the bargaining unit, the union must demonstrate that the information is both relevant and necessary to a particular subject for bargaining.[24]

Sometimes the issue is one of erosion of the bargaining unit. Union requests for information on workers outside of the bargaining unit usually result from a suspicion that the employer is deliberately eroding the bargaining unit. The union has a legitimate concern about such erosion, and information bearing on the diminution of the unit is generally held to be relevant.

In *NLRB v. Rockwell-Standard Corp.*,[25] the union feared that the movement of certain automotive divisions of the employer into a new office building might cause a loss of unit work. The union requested the names, classifications, job descriptions, and rates of pay for all nonconfidential employees at the new location. The employer refused, contending that the information on workers outside of the bargaining unit could not be relevant to performance of the union's statutory duties. The Sixth Circuit summarily rejected the employer's argument and enforced the Board's order for disclosure.[26] The appellate court held that the desired data were relevant to the determination of whether unit work was improperly being transferred.[27] The decision favored disclosure even though the union demand was arguably made for organizing, not for bargaining, purposes.

In *San Diego Newspaper Guild, Local 95 v. NLRB,* the union failed to demonstrate how data concerning non-bargaining unit workers were pertinent to the erosion of the unit.[28] The employer

---

[23] Hollywood Brands, Inc., 142 N.L.R.B. 304 (1963), *enforced per curiam*, 324 F.2d 956 (5th Cir. 1963), *rehearing denied*, 326 F.2d 400 (5th Cir.), *cert. denied*, 377 U.S. 923 (1964).

[24] A. S. Abell Co., 230 N.L.R.B. 1112 (1977).

[25] 410 F.2d 953 (6th Cir. 1969).

[26] *Id.*

[27] *Id.* at 958; *accord*, Temple-Eastex, Inc., 228 N.L.R.B. 203 (1977), *enforcement denied on other grounds*, 579 F.2d 932 (5th Cir. 1978).

[28] 548 F.2d 863, 867 (9th Cir. 1977).

had instituted a program in anticipation of a strike, which was a training course for nonunit employees. Although the employees in the training program ordinarily did not do production work, the program trained them to be ready for production work if and when the production employees struck. The union was concerned about the impact of the program on the effectiveness of a strike. The union requested details of the program, and the employer refused. Both the National Labor Relations Board [29] and the Ninth Circuit [30] upheld the company's refusal, because the union could not show that the plan in any way eroded the bargaining unit.

Information on Misclassification of Employees

A classification scheme set forth in a collective bargaining agreement can be important to a relevance determination. The job classification system can, as a corollary to the "unit erosion" argument, be used as a justification for relevance of information on nonunit employees. A well-founded suspicion of misclassification may show relevance.

The misclassification issue arose in *Curtiss-Wright Corp., Wright Aeronautical Division v. NLRB*.[31] The union observed that the number of bargaining unit employees was declining while the number of nonunit employees was increasing. The union suspected that employees who were performing bargaining unit work were being misclassified as administrative employees. The union sought to verify its belief by requesting disclosure of summaries of job classifications and/or titles of all administrative employees. It also sought the functions of all confidential and administrative employees and the rates of pay for each job classification. The employer eventually provided some but not all of the data. In an enforcement proceeding, the conduct of the employer in withholding was held to be unlawful because the union had successfully demonstrated that the information was relevant to its responsibility to administer the provisions of the collective bargaining agreement as it dealt with job categories.[32]

---

[29] Union-Tribune Publishing Co., 220 N.L.R.B. 1226 (1975).

[30] San Diego Newspaper Guild, Local 95 v. NLRB, 548 F.2d 863, 867 (9th Cir. 1977).

[31] 347 F.2d 61 (3d Cir. 1965).

[32] *Id.* at 69; *accord*, NLRB v. Goodyear Aero. Corp., 388 F.2d 673 (6th Cir. 1968).

Indications of faulty job classifications were alleged but not demonstrated in *NLRB v. Western Electric Co.*[33] The employer had declared a number of workers, both unit and nonunit, to be "surplus." A number of unit employees were laid off, and several nonunit employees with high seniority were transferred into the unit. Because the transferees ranked above unit employees on the seniority roster, they were unlikely to lose their jobs if the layoffs continued.

The union then demanded job qualification information for both the transferees and nonunit employees with high seniority who had not yet been transferred. The union's claim was that other employees may have been misclassified. When the employer refused, the Board ordered disclosure of the information.[34] The Eighth Circuit issued a decision that treated the two groups in separate ways. The appellate court enforced the Board's order requiring disclosure of information regarding those employees who had transferred into the unit. The court refused, however, to enforce the order of the Board requiring disclosure related to "potential transferees." The court noted that the number of *both* unit and nonunit employees was shrinking. This was a contrast to the *Curtiss-Wright* situation discussed above. Because both groups were declining, the union could not rely upon the decline in numbers as a basis for asserting misclassification of the potential transferees. Because the union had no other proof that the information on nonunit employees was relevant, the court ruled that the union had failed to carry the burden of proving relevance.[35]

Wording of the Agreement

The relevance of information relating to workers outside the bargaining unit may be established by referring to a specific provision of the collective bargaining agreement. In *Torrington Company v. NLRB,*[36] the agreement contained a transfer clause.

---

[33] 559 F.2d 1131 (8th Cir. 1977).

[34] 225 N.L.R.B. 1374 (1976).

[35] NLRB v. Western Elec. Co., 559 F.2d 1131, 1133-34 (8th Cir. 1977).

[36] 545 F.2d 840 (2d Cir. 1976).

Under the clause, if operations were moved to any plant within a seventy-five-mile radius, the employees would be transferred to the new plant with no loss of seniority. The union learned that the company was reassigning work among plants, and it then demanded information on the number of employees and products manufactured in other installations and information on any transfer of production to other installations from the original plant at which the bargaining unit was located. The Board and the Second Circuit ordered disclosure because the information was deemed relevant to the policing of the work-transfer clause in the contract.[37]

Seniority of Nonunit Employees

A request for seniority information will generally be granted if it is sought in regard to a mandatory subject of bargaining that involves seniority rights, such as promotion, demotion, lay-off, and recall.[38] A union's interest in preserving a seniority system that affects promotions, demotions, etc., will not, however, justify disclosure of seniority data for all employees, even if it is possible that non-bargaining unit employees will be transferred into the unit with their accrued seniority intact.

In *International Telephone & Telegraph Corp. v. NLRB*,[39] the Third Circuit rejected the Board's decision with respect to blanket disclosure of seniority data on potential transferees into the bargaining unit. The appellate court ruled that the employer need only provide the union with seniority information on individual non-bargaining unit employees whose transfer into the unit was imminent. These data would satisfy the union's need for data and the employer's duty to disclose.[40] The Third Circuit reasoned that disclosure of seniority data for all nonmember employees who were eligible for transfer into the unit would not aid the union in the performance of its statutory duties in any

---

[37] *Id.*

[38] Kayser-Roth Hosiery Co., Inc. v. NLRB, 447 F.2d 396 (6th Cir. 1971).

[39] 382 F.2d 366 (3d Cir. 1967), *cert. denied*, 389 U.S. 1039 (1968).

[40] *Id.* at 371-72.

manner not accomplished by the disclosure of the same information for those about to be transferred.[41]

RETIREE INFORMATION

The Supreme Court held in *Allied Chemical & Alkali Workers, Local 1 v. Pittsburgh Plate Glass Co.*[42] that retired workers are not *employees* as that term is defined in the Act. Disclosure of data concerning retirees is governed by the rules regarding provision of non-bargaining unit employee information. Relevance of the information must be demonstrated. If a union wishes to obtain information from the employer about benefits received by retirees under the pension and insurance plans currently in force, the union must show that such data will enable it to bargain more intelligently for active employees.[43]

EQUAL EMPLOYMENT OPPORTUNITY DATA

The very controversial subject of employer-prepared, government-required equal employment opportunity reports is dealt with extensively in chapter XVII. Under present Board interpretations, currently on review at the District of Columbia Circuit, information is presumptively relevant if it is statistical data that reveal possible discrimination on the part of the employer.[44] The pertinence of all other equal employment data, beyond the Work Force Analyses documents, must be demonstrated by the union.

In *Westinghouse Electric Corp.*,[45] the Board found much of this data to be relevant because the union had demonstrated that statistical information on nonunit employees and the statistical information in the Work Force Analyses would assist the union in determining the success (or lack of success) of the company's equal opportunity programs. The Board held that the substance of the charges was relevant because the complaints would show the level of employee discontent with the employer's equal em-

---

[41] *Id.*

[42] 404 U.S. 157 (1971).

[43] Union Carbide Corp., 197 N.L.R.B. 717 (1972).

[44] Westinghouse Elec. Corp., 239 N.L.R.B. No. 19 (Oct. 31, 1978), *appeal docketed*, No. 78-2067 (D.C. Cir. Nov. 1, 1978).

[45] *Id.*

ployment practices, as well as necessary information in the responses by the company to the workers' discontent. Therefore, the employer was ordered to disclose Work Force Analysis statistical documents, lists or copies of complaints and charges filed by unit employees, and statistical information on nonunit employees.[46]

An example of information not presumptively relevant is the set of charges and complaints filed against the employer by unit employees asserting to some governmental authority the presence of discriminatory conduct by the employer. In the case above, the union also requested a list of all charges and complaints filed by both unit and nonunit employees, statistical information on nonunit employees, and copies of the Affirmative Action Plans prepared by the employer in developing the required governmental reports. The Board ruled that these items were not presumptively relevant,[47] because the union had failed to make a sufficient showing of relevance of the names of individual workers who had filed the charges and complaints. The union had also failed to show that information on charges and complaints by nonunit employees was relevant to the bargaining obligations of the union for unit employees. Finally, the union had failed to show the relevance of the Affirmative Action Plan reports, including future goals, timetables, and projections, to its bargaining duties.[48]

East Dayton Tool and Die Co.,[49] a companion case, presented an additional issue. The union demanded that the employer explain why so few minorities and women had been employed in the bargaining unit. The employer refused to respond to the "why" question. The Board upheld the employer's refusal to respond, concluding that the union's right to information was limited to facts, not to hypotheses.[50] The matter of relevance will ultimately be decided by the appellate courts, with *East Dayton* and several other cases placed in suspense pending an adjudication of the union's request for review of the *Westinghouse* decision.

---

[46] *Id.*

[47] *Id.*

[48] *Id.*

[49] 239 N.L.R.B. No. 20 (Oct. 31, 1978).

[50] *Id.*

INFORMATION ON PROBATIONARY EMPLOYEES

Information relating to employees placed on probation has been held pertinent if the union has demonstrated that it needs such data to enable it to present modifications to the existing contract in future bargaining sessions.[51] This showing of relevance can be based on such contract provisions as a limitation on the length of probations or a provision listing the reasons for discharge of probationary employees.[52]

OTHER INFORMATION

Witness statements that may be used in arbitration proceedings need not be produced by the employer upon the union's demand.[53] The Board has concluded that the union's claimed need for the statements is outweighed by the possibility that scheduled witnesses would refuse to cooperate because of a fear of harassment or other retaliation.[54]

Many other types of information may be the subject of a disclosure order if the union demonstrates that circumstances make the desired material pertinent.[55] For example, in *NLRB v. Custom Excavating, Inc.*,[56] a union representative observed that an employee in the bargaining unit was at work on a particular day but that no work hours had been recorded on the employer's time sheets for that work. Upon investigating the matter, he discovered that other employees were required to submit two time cards per week, one completed and the other blank. Because of these irregularities in the company's payroll system, the union filed a grievance charging the employer with failure to pay the negotiated wages and fringe benefits.

The union in *Custom Excavating* requested a list of customers for whom work was done by the bargaining unit employees. The

---

[51] Oliver Corp., 162 N.L.R.B. 813 (1967).

[52] *Id.*

[53] Anheuser-Busch, Inc., 237 N.L.R.B. No. 146 (Aug. 25, 1978).

[54] *Id.; cf.,* NLRB v. Robbins Tire & Rubber Co., 437 U.S. 214 (1978).

[55] NLRB v. Custom Excavating, Inc., 575 F.2d 102 (7th Cir. 1978); NLRB v. Celotex Corp., 364 F.2d 552 (5th Cir. 1966) ; Pine Indus. Relations Comm., Inc., 118 N.L.R.B. 1055 (1957), *modified sub nom.* International Woodworkers v. NLRB, 263 F.2d 483 (D.C. Cir. 1959).

[56] 575 F.2d 102 (7th Cir. 1978).

list was to be used by the union in support of its grievance. The union planned to consult with the firm's customers to determine whether the employer was falsifying payroll records for work done for the customers. The Seventh Circuit enforced a Board disclosure order because, under the circumstances, the reasons stated by the union demonstrated that the information was relevant to the union's collective bargaining responsibilities.[57]

One type of information not generally reached by disclosure orders concerns industrial facilities' closings, a currently heated labor relations issue in which the exchange of advance information is extremely controversial. As an example of social versus economic goals in legislation, current efforts to force formal advance notification would trade cushioned work force impacts for diminished opportunities of exiting firms to sell facilities as viable operations.[58] As a general rule, plant closings cannot be enjoined on theories of promissory estoppel if the employer had merely informed employees that continued operation depended on profitability.[59] Even if the union as charging party succeeds in making an NLRB case under section 8(a)(5) for failure to bargain, the total departure of the firm from its line of activity leaves the union remediless.[60] The existence of alternate facilities, transfer rights, and arbitration clauses complicate closing decisions when management seeks to plan the labor relations consequences of only a partial departure from the field,[61] and litigation testimony in closing cases can reveal sensitive corporate and plant-specific profitability data.[62] Generally, to date, no advance notification of closing has been required in the absence of a statutory or contractual duty of notification.

---

[57] *Id.* at 106.

[58] State and federal legislation is discussed in Freedman, *Plant Closed—No Jobs*, ACROSS THE BOARD/THE CONFERENCE BOARD MAGAZINE, Aug. 1980, at 12. Because of the legislated additional costs of transferral from operating to post-closing remedies such as supplemental unemployment and taxing payments, a facility's sale price is diminished, and the "capital is held hostage."

[59] United Steelworkers, Local 1330 v. U.S. Steel Corp., 103 L.R.R.M. 2925 (N.D. Ohio 1980).

[60] Brockway Motor Trucks v. NLRB, 582 F.2d 720 (3d Cir. 1978).

[61] *See, e.g.,* Retail Store Employees Union, Local 400 v. Great Atlantic & Pacific Tea Co., Inc., 480 F. Supp. 88 (D. Md. 1979).

[62] At the trial of the injunction action, U.S. Steel's two highest corporate officers disclosed plant-specific profitability figures, customarily held as confidential business information.

CHAPTER V

Financial Disclosures and the Employer's Duty to Substantiate

Information regarding a firm's sales and profits is commonly regarded as highly sensitive, confidential data.[1] Although such financial information is of great advantage to the collective bargaining representative in determining how vigorously to press its economic demands, employers commonly desire to safeguard its confidential status.[2] In the landmark Supreme Court decision in *NLRB v. Truitt Manufacturing Co.*,[3] the Supreme Court ruled that the employer's duty to bargain in good faith requires that financial information be made available upon request if the information would substantiate claims concerning the employer's ability to pay increased wages and benefits. No prior showing of relevance is necessary. Once the employer has made a claim of inability during negotiations, that claim establishes the pertinence of the corroborating data.

THE TRUITT DECISION

In *Truitt*, the union demanded a ten cents per hour wage increase. The employer countered by claiming that a raise of more than two and one-half cents per hour would force it out of business. To determine the truth of that claim, the union sought permission to have a certified public accountant review the books. The employer refused. The union then requested any data in

---

[1] White Furniture Co., 161 N.L.R.B. 444 (1966), *affirmed sub nom.* United Furniture Workers v. NLRB, 388 F.2d 880 (4th Cir. 1967).

[2] *Id.*; Pine Indus. Relations Comm., Inc., 118 N.L.R.B. 1055 (1957), *modified sub nom.* International Woodworkers v. NLRB, 263 F.2d 483 (D.C. Cir. 1959).

[3] 351 U.S. 149 (1956).

the employer's possession that supported the inability-to-pay claim. Again, the employer refused.[4]

Ordering the employer to disclose the information to the union, the National Labor Relations Board ruled that the refusal to substantiate the claim of dire financial straits violated section 8(a)(5). The Supreme Court granted enforcement of the Board's order, holding:

> Good faith bargaining necessarily requires that claims made by either bargainer be honest claims. This is true about an asserted inability to pay an increase in wages. If such an argument is important enough to present in the give and take of bargaining, it is important enough to require some proof of its accuracy.[5]

The Supreme Court asserted that the employer's failure to come forward with substantiating data in support of the claimed inability to pay was not a per se violation of the Act.[6] Rather, the Court concluded, each case must be decided in light of its own peculiar facts and circumstances.[7] Subsequent decisions, however, have suggested that the employer's failure to furnish relevant requested financial data, in a *Truitt* situation, may be treated as a per se violation of the Act.[8]

DUTY TO SUBSTANTIATE STATEMENTS MADE IN NEGOTIATIONS

Much of the litigation on disclosure of financial information has centered on whether statements in a bargaining context have amounted to a claim of inability to pay.

Ambiguous statements lead to disagreements. If the employer states that it *will* not pay the wages demanded by the union, it will not be required to provide substantiation data.[9] In many cases, the issue becomes whether the employer is saying that it can-

---

[4] Truitt Mfg. Co., 110 N.L.R.B. 856, 856-57 (1954), *enforcement denied,* 224 F.2d 869 (4th Cir. 1955), *enforced,* 351 U.S. 149 (1956).

[5] NLRB v. Truitt Mfg. Co., 351 U.S. 149, 152-53 (1956).

[6] *Id.* at 153-54.

[7] *Id.*

[8] United Fire Proof Warehouse Co. v. NLRB, 356 F.2d 494 (7th Cir. 1966); Milbin Printing, Inc., 218 N.L.R.B. 223 (1975), *rev'd sub nom.* New York Printing Pressmen, Local 51 v. NLRB, 538 F.2d 496 (2d Cir. 1976).

[9] Huston, *Furnishing Information As An Element of the Employer's Good Faith Bargaining,* 38 U. DET. L. J. 471, 486 (1958).

not pay or is saying that it will not pay. Typically, an employer that for financial reasons does not want to grant one requested increase but does not wish to open its books to the union will either give no reasons for its position or give some reason other than the inability to pay.[10] On occasion, this "other reason" may be construed as a disguised claim of inability to pay.

An employer acts at its peril when it explains its position on a wage demand without stating that it is *not* claiming inability to pay. An employer's assertion that it would pay "what is right" was regarded as a claim of inability to pay when the employer had complained during negotiations about high wage costs.[11] The statement that "the employees came to the wrong well . . . the well is dry," even though made in the course of hard, good-faith bargaining, resulted in an order for disclosure of substantiation data.[12]

In one case, the Second Circuit, disagreeing with the Board, has held that an employer's statement that it "couldn't reach the union's numbers" because of a desire to keep a balance between wage costs and capital expenditures was not a statement of policy but expressed instead an inability to pay.[13]

LOSS OF COMPETITIVE POSITION

The duty to substantiate a bargaining claim arises not only when an employer refuses to grant union demands because of a present inability to pay but also when the refusal is based on a claim that increased wages and benefits would put the employer at a competitive disadvantage that would eventually result in losses.[14]

Disclosure orders can be based upon something less than an express statement that the employer would go out of business if the demands of the union are met. Stating that the company cannot pay higher fringe benefits and "remain competitive" is

---

[10] *Id.*

[11] NLRB v. Celotex Corp., 364 F.2d 552 (5th Cir. 1966).

[12] NLRB v. Unoco Apparel Co., 508 F.2d 1368 (5th Cir. 1975).

[13] New York Printing Pressmen, Local 51 v. NLRB, 538 F.2d 496 (2d Cir. 1976).

[14] NLRB v. Western Wirebound Box Co., 356 F.2d 88 (9th Cir. 1966); Cincinnati Cordage & Paper Co., 141 N.L.R.B. 72 (1963).

enough to force disclosure of substantiating information.[15] Disclosure has been ordered when the employer complained that costs were higher for wages and benefits than competitors paid and that this would result in the loss of competitively bid contracts.[16] Similarly, demanding substantial reductions in present wages and benefits because of the adverse effects of increased competition will require disclosure of employer records that reflect the effects of that increased competition.[17]

The duty to substantiate is not limited to the employer's position on economic issues. Claims that restrictions upon the employer's power to schedule production operations and assign jobs to individual workers must be relaxed to make the employer competitive can result in required disclosure of "gross profit" figures for the employer that has asserted its losses of competitive position.[18]

An allegation that the employer's wage rates are equal to or higher than those its competitors pay also warrants substantiation when the claim is made in opposition to union demands.[19] The employer must substantiate by furnishing information that reveals the average wage rates paid by both the company and its competitors.[20] Similarly, if the employer declares that it is company policy to pay similar wage rates at all of its plants, it must demonstrate the truth of this statement by disclosing wage data for its various installations.[21]

[15] Stanley Bldg. Specialties Co., 166 N.L.R.B. 984 (1967), *enforced sub nom.* Steelworkers, Local 5571 v. NLRB, 401 F.2d 434 (D.C. Cir. 1968), *cert. denied*, 395 U.S. 946 (1969).

[16] International Tel. & Tel. Corp., 159 N.L.R.B. 1757 (1966), *enforced*, 382 F.2d 366 (3d Cir. 1967), *cert. denied*, 389 U.S. 1039 (1968); Bud's Cabinet & Fixture Co., 154 N.L.R.B. 1168 (1966).

[17] NLRB v. Bagel Bakers Council of Greater New York, 434 F.2d 884, 887-88 (2d Cir. 1970); *accord*, NLRB v. Palomar Corp., 465 F.2d 731 (5th Cir. 1972).

[18] NLRB v. Celotex Corp., 364 F.2d 552 (5th Cir. 1966); *accord*, NLRB v. Bagel Bakers Council of Greater New York, 434 F.2d 884, 887-88 (2d Cir. 1970).

[19] General Elec. Co. v. NLRB, 466 F.2d 1177 (6th Cir. 1972) (disclosure of area wage surveys); note, however, that simply stating that wages are or will remain competitive with those paid in the area is *not* a claim of inability to pay. *See* Charles E. Honaker, 147 N.L.R.B. 1184 (1964).

[20] Dallas Gen. Drivers, Local No. 745 v. NLRB, 355 F.2d 842 (D.C. Cir. 1966).

[21] Hollywood Brands, Inc., 142 N.L.R.B. 304, *enforced per curiam*, 324 F.2d 956 (5th Cir. 1963), *rehearing denied*, 326 F.2d 400 (5th Cir.), *cert. denied*, 377 U.S. 923 (1964).

ECONOMIC CLAIMS DURING THE CONTRACT TERM

An employer claim during the term of the contract that certain actions were motivated by economic considerations also must be substantiated upon request. In *Puerto Rico Telephone Co. v. NLRB,*[22] the company had been subcontracting a major portion of its business because of a massive modernization and expansion program that was then being undertaken. The union filed a grievance when the company began to lay off employees.

The employer asserted that the work force reduction was due to an economic reorganization of the company. The union sought data dealing with the volume of business, earnings, and wage savings from the layoffs, so that it could determine for itself the motive behind the layoffs. The Board ordered disclosure, and the First Circuit agreed. The appellate court ruled that the *Truitt* disclosure principles apply not only to claims of financial inability raised at bargaining sessions but also to claims made during the life of the contract in support of an employer's position in a grievance proceeding.

Similarly, if an employer cites economic reasons as the justification for a decision to subcontract work from the unit or to transfer unit work from one plant to another, it must disclose the financial information necessary to validate that claim.[23]

EXTENT OF SUBSTANTIATION NEEDED

Another area of difficulty involves the question of how much information an employer must furnish to satisfy the duty to substantiate. *Truitt* itself required only that the company's position be supported by "substantial proof." [24]

There is disagreement among the courts of appeals on the measure of evidence that must be disclosed under *Truitt*. At one extreme, the Third Circuit in *International Telephone & Telegraph Corp. v. NLRB* [25] ordered "full disclosure" of all data on

---

[22] 359 F.2d 983 (1st Cir. 1966).

[23] A. O. Smith Corp., 223 N.L.R.B. 838 (1976) (subcontracting); American Needle & Novelty Co., 206 N.L.R.B. 534 (1973) (transfer of unit work to another plant).

[24] NLRB v. Truitt Mfg. Co., 351 U.S. 149 (1956).

[25] 382 F.2d 366 (3d Cir. 1967); *accord,* NLRB v. Jacobs Mfg. Co., 196 F.2d 680 (2d Cir. 1952).

which the company's claim was based. But the Ninth Circuit was more lenient in *Metlox Manufacturing Co. v. NLRB* [26] and required only the disclosure of a "reasonable amount of explanation and elaboration" of the findings of an audit of the company's books instead of the results of the audit itself.[27] After examination of these two positions, the First Circuit ruled in *NLRB v. Teleprompter Corp.*[28] that substantiation requires the disclosure of as much information as the union "reasonably needs to make a meaningful assessment" of the employer's claim.[29]

MULTIPLE LOCATIONS

If the claimed inability is asserted for one of a multilocation firm's operations, the union is entitled to data solely for that one location rather than company-wide operations.[30] An employer asserting an inability to pay in negotiations that involve a corporate subsidiary, however, cannot meet the burden of substantiation with corporate-wide financial data.[31] Instead, financial information on the profitability of the subsidiary in question must be provided.[32]

PENSION PLAN INFORMATION

The Employee Retirement Income Security Act of 1974 (ERISA)[33] imposes three means of delivery of information by plan administrators (including employers and some unions) to plan beneficiaries (usually employees). Information can be a type that must be distributed (e.g., the annual report of a

---

[26] 378 F.2d 728 (9th Cir.), *cert. denied,* 389 U.S. 1037 (1967).

[27] *Id.* at 730 (requiring disclosure of management salaries because of union's claim that problem could be a deliberate bleeding of assets).

[28] 570 F.2d 4 (1st Cir. 1977).

[29] *Id.* at 11 n.3.

[30] United Fire Proof Warehouse Co. v. NLRB, 356 F.2d 494 (7th Cir. 1966); Roman Catholic Diocese of Brooklyn, 236 N.L.R.B. 1 (1978); Memorial Consultants, Inc., 153 N.L.R.B. 1 (1965).

[31] NLRB v. Teleprompter Corp., 570 F.2d 4 (1st Cir. 1977).

[32] *Id.* at 10.

[33] Pub. L. 93-406, 88 Stat. 829 (codified in scattered sections of 5, 18, 26, 29, 31, 42 U.S.C.).

qualified plan)[34] or a type that can be viewed in detail at the employer's office by any affected person.[35] In addition, an affected person could, upon proper request, receive even more detailed information about the plan.[36]

Shortly after the passage of ERISA, a pension plan expert noted that the Act established "an entirely new atmosphere and framework for employee benefit plans" and that ERISA "will embrace practically every aspect of plan negotiations, establishments and administration" that collective bargaining parties must consider.[37] That prediction was quite correct.

The ERISA process for assuring employee participation in plan approvals by government agencies is the process of plan "qualification." That process requires that the employer transmit a great deal of information to the employee beneficiaries of the plan.[38] An employee benefit plan, including a retirement plan, must be in written form and must contain the elements required by ERISA. The employees covered by the plan must be notified of its adoption by the employer.[39] Because ERISA's structure includes an overlay of both the Internal Revenue Service's and the Labor Department's jurisdictions, the transfer of plan information from employers to employees is governed by regulatory requirements administered by both IRS and Labor Department officials.[40]

An administrator of a qualified retirement plan subject to ERISA is required to make information about the plan available. For unionized employees participating in the plan, the collective bargaining agreement under which the plan was es-

---

[34] 29 U.S.C. § 1024(b)(1) (1976).

[35] 29 U.S.C. § 1024(b)(2) (1976).

[36] 29 U.S.C. §§ 1024(b)(4), 1025(a) (1976).

[37] Tilove, *ERISA—Its Effect on Collective Bargaining*, in PROCEEDINGS OF NEW YORK UNIVERSITY TWENTY-NINTH ANNUAL CONFERENCE ON LABOR 187, 198 (R. Adelman ed. 1976).

[38] 29 C.F.R. § 2520.104b-1 (1979). *See generally,* M. CANAN, QUALIFIED RETIREMENT PLANS §§ 6.2, 11.2 (West's Handbook Series 1977).

[39] M. CANAN, *supra* note 38, at § 7.2; *see* 29 C.F.R. §§ 2520.101-1 to 104b-30 (1979).

[40] This cumbersome structure is beyond the scope of this text. *See* Employee Retirement Income Security Act of 1974, § 103, 29 U.S.C. § 1023 (1976); M. CANAN, *supra* note 38.

tablished will become part of the public record.[41] The trust
agreement, contracts, and other legal documents relating to the
formation of the plan will also be made available to any participant or beneficiary of the plan.[42] In that way, persons who
are not union members themselves but who may be beneficiaries,
such as spouses or children, will in some cases have rights of
access to the employer-employee collective bargaining agreement.

Financial information about the employer is also available
under ERISA. A summary of the financial information about
assets, such as the value of the plan's stock in the employer's
firm, must be made available to all participants. The detailed
annual report can be obtained by any participant or beneficiary
from the plan administrator by making a written request and
paying the cost of copying the report.[43] In some cases, the statutory requirement for a showing of assets and changes in assets
can reveal a decline in the value of the employer's business that
might not have been publicly known for private firms.[44] As a
measure of the employer's actual financial condition, the information available under ERISA may be of great value to unions
and other interested parties.

UNION MEMBERS' RIGHTS TO INFORMATION

In addition to their rights under ERISA for union-sponsored
plans, union members have specific statutory rights under the
Landrum-Griffin Act to information about the affairs of their
unions. In that situation, the union has an affirmative duty to
disclose. This subject is covered fully in an earlier volume of
this series, *The Landrum-Griffin Act*.[45]

---

[41] 29 C.F.R. § 2520.104b-1(b) (3) (1979).

[42] *Id.*

[43] 29 C.F.R. § 2520.104b-30 (1979).

[44] *See* forms of notice in the Labor Department regulations, 29 C.F.R.
§ 2520.104b-10(c) (3) (1979).

[45] J. BELLACE & A. BERKOWITZ, THE LANDRUM-GRIFFIN ACT (Labor & Public
Policy Series No. 19, 1979).

CHAPTER VI

Effects of the Collective Bargaining Agreement on the Duty to Disclose

The provisions of the collective bargaining agreement may be a source of relevant requested information because data that have a bearing on possible contract infractions are pertinent to the union's duty to police the current contract.[1] The agreement may affect the employer's obligation to provide information in other ways. This chapter examines the effect upon the employer's duty to disclose caused by the adoption of certain common clauses in the collective bargaining agreement.

In *NLRB v. Acme Industrial Co.*, the collective bargaining agreement provided in part that:

> "in the event the equipment of the plant . . . is hereafter moved to another location of the Company, employees working in the plant . . . who are subject to reduction in classification or layoff as a result thereof may transfer to the new location with full rights and seniority, unless there is then in existence at the new location a collective bargaining agreement covering . . . employees at such location."[2]

The agreement also contained a grievance procedure terminating in compulsory arbitration.

Upon learning that machinery was being removed from the plant, the union in *Acme* filed grievances and sought data bearing on the equipment transfer. The union sought to determine if the equipment was being sold, moved, or scrapped. The employer refused to provide the information and suggested that the union should seek the information by taking a grievance on the question to arbitration.

The National Labor Relations Board held that the information had to be disclosed at the outset of the processing of the

---

[1] *See* chapter III *supra*.

[2] 385 U.S. 432 (1967).

grievance,[3] but the Seventh Circuit denied enforcement. The court held that the presence of the arbitration clause in the contract modified the union's statutory right to the information.[4] Then, the Supreme Court reversed and ordered enforcement of the Board's disclosure order.[5]

In *Acme,* the Supreme Court held that the existence of an arbitration clause does not obligate the union to take requests for information to arbitration. The Court concluded that, since the NLRB does not make a binding construction of the contract when it determines the relevance of requested information, the issuance of a disclosure order does not usurp the function of the arbitrator to resolve contract-interpretation disputes.[6]

The Court noted that, if the union were required to press each information request and pursue each into arbitration, the procedure would be very costly for the union. The cost would be imposed while the union was unaware of the real merits of the underlying claim. The Court reasoned that, with more information, the union would be able to sift out nonmeritorious claims and to concentrate its efforts and finances on the strongest grievances.[7] Thus, disclosure before arbitration would promote, rather than hinder, the national policy favoring arbitration in resolving industrial disputes.

THE USE OF ARBITRATION TO OBTAIN INFORMATION

Even if the contract itself specifies that certain information must be disclosed and provides that arbitration shall be the final phase of a grievance procedure, disputes concerning the supplying of information may be a question of contract inter-

---

[3] Acme Indus. Co., 150 N.L.R.B. 1463, *enforcement denied,* 351 F.2d 258 (7th Cir. 1965), *enforced,* 385 U.S. 432 (1967).

[4] Acme Indus. Co. v. NLRB, 351 F.2d 258 (7th Cir. 1965), *enforced,* 385 U.S. 432 (1967).

[5] NLRB v. Acme Indus. Co., 385 U.S. 432 (1967).

[6] *Id.* at 437; *accord,* NLRB v. Davol, Inc., 597 F.2d 782 (1st Cir. 1979); P.R. Mallory & Co. v. NLRB, 411 F.2d 948, 954 (7th Cir. 1969).

[7] NLRB v. Acme Indus. Co., 385 U.S. 432, 438 (1967); *accord,* NLRB v. Twin City Lines, Inc., 425 F.2d 164 (8th Cir. 1970); Hekman Furniture Co., 101 N.L.R.B. 631, 632 (1952), *enforced per curiam,* 207 F.2d 561 (6th Cir. 1953). In *Hekman,* the Board stated that the employer cannot substitute the "grievance procedure of the contract for its obligation to furnish the union with information it needs to perform its statutory functions." *Id.* at 632 (quoting Leland-Gifford Co., 95 N.L.R.B. 1322 (1951)).

pretation to be decided by an arbitrator rather than by the
Board or the courts. In *United Aircraft Corp.*,[8] the contract
stated that, at the second step of the grievance procedure, "The
Company will produce such pertinent existing production, payroll,
attendance records and other disciplinary notices pertaining to
the employee as may be necessary to the settlement of a grievance at this step of the grievance procedure." Both the Board
and the Second Circuit agreed that questions about the timing
and extent of disclosure were issues of contractual interpretation to be resolved by the arbitrator.[9]

A Fifth Circuit case that antedated *Acme Industrial* provides
another circumstance in which disclosure issues must be determined by an arbitrator. In *Sinclair Refining Co.*,[10] the contract
provided that suspensions and discharge were subject to the
grievance and arbitration machinery but that layoffs and demotions due to lack of work were not. In pursuing a grievance
of two employees who had alleged that their demotions were in
violation of the contract, the union sought information relating
to the allocation of work. The employer refused, claiming that
the decision to demote was not subject to grievance or arbitration because it was caused by a lack of work. The employer argued that, until the arbitrator determined otherwise, the information regarding the demotions was not relevant to the union's
duties as bargaining agent. When the union pressed its demand, the employer suggested that the issue be resolved through
the grievance and arbitration procedures.

The Board in *Sinclair* held against the employer and ordered
disclosure.[11] The Fifth Circuit, however, denied enforcement of
the Board's order.[12] The court held that the duty to disclose the
information in question hinged upon whether or not the underlying grievance was itself arbitrable, and the union had no right
to the information if the grievance was not arbitrable. The
Fifth Circuit opinion also noted that the Board had, in effect,

---

[8] 204 N.L.R.B. 879 (1973), *aff'd sub nom.* Lodges 700, 743, 1746, Int'l
Assoc. of Machinists & Aerospace Workers v. NLRB, 525 F.2d 237 (2d Cir.
1975).

[9] *Id.* at 880.

[10] 132 N.L.R.B. 1660 (1961), *rev'd*, 306 F.2d 569 (5th Cir. 1962).

[11] *Id.*

[12] Sinclair Refining Co. v. NLRB, 306 F.2d 569 (5th Cir. 1962).

decided a substantive question of arbitrability, while that issue instead should have been left to the arbitrator. The current viability of the *Sinclair* approach is unclear. The Supreme Court in *Acme Industrial* was not faced with this argument and did not comment on it. The *Sinclair* decision seems to be inconsistent with a line of cases holding that information must be disclosed if it is helpful in intelligently disposing of grievances.[13] Accordingly, reliance on that decision will unquestionably pose some risks for the employer before the Board today.

DISCLOSURE CLAUSES

The union may expand its right to information by obtaining a contractual disclosure provision. Such a provision may also be used to establish a contractual right to information that the Board might not order to be disclosed. For example, a union can bargain for individual access to certain personnel files—as the United Auto Workers has done, building upon a Michigan state statute heavily supported by the UAW [14]—or the union can bargain for its own access to all employee records.

These disclosure clauses permit union access to personnel data without showing relevance; the union may either use its contractual right to obtain certain data or can ask individual workers to divulge certain facts that are found in their personnel files.[15]

"ZIPPER CLAUSES"

Frequently, the employer and the union agree that their contract constitutes the entire agreement between the parties and further that the employer and union are relieved of any obligation during the contract term to discuss subjects that are covered by the agreement. These are known as "zipper clauses."

---

[13] *Compare* Timken Roller Bearing Co. v. NLRB, 325 F.2d 746 (6th Cir. 1963), *cert. denied*, 376 U.S. 971 (1964), *with* Curtiss-Wright Corp., Wright Aeronautical Div. v. NLRB, 347 F.2d 61 (3d Cir. 1965). The latter court held that use of grievance and arbitration machinery will be required only when such information requests are expressly subject to that machinery.

[14] *See* chapters VIII, IX, and X *infra.*

[15] For the issue of employees' personal privacy and the limitations that the federal Privacy Act places upon public sector unions' contractual access to certain systems of public employees' files, see chapters VIII, IX, and X *infra.*

Such exclusivity clauses do not relieve the employer of all disclosure obligations. In *Leland-Gifford Co.*,[16] one of the clauses of the contract read: "This agreement contains the entire agreement between the parties and no matters shall be considered which are covered by the written provisions stated herein." Although the employer was not obligated to disclose information related to bargaining, the employer was required to furnish data needed by the union to police the existing contract.[17]

MANAGEMENT RIGHTS PROVISIONS

The argument that various other contract provisions release the employer from the obligation to furnish requested information to the union have met with little success. In *Texaco, Inc. v. NLRB*,[18] the contract had a clause specifying that an employee or the union could complain to management of unreasonably hazardous conditions, and it also contained a clause stating that the employer could institute job changes only after consulting with the union. The employer maintained that these provisions precluded the union from receiving data regarding safety conditions and regarding the elimination of various job classifications. Noting that the information that the union requested was necessary for it to determine whether contract violations were occurring, the Seventh Circuit enforced the Board's order requiring disclosure of information requested on the disputed issues.[19]

If the union clearly and unmistakably waives its right to bargain over an item during the term of the agreement, the union may lose its right to demand information regarding that topic. In *Hughes Tool Co.*,[20] the union agreed to a management rights clause in which it waived its right to bargain during

---

[16] 95 N.L.R.B. 1306 (1951), *enforced in part*, 200 F.2d 620 (1st Cir. 1952).

[17] *Id.* at 1310; *accord*, General Elec. Co. v. NLRB, 414 F.2d 918 (4th Cir. 1969), *cert. denied*, 396 U.S. 1005 (1970); J. I. Case Co. v. NLRB, 253 F.2d 149 (7th Cir. 1958); California Portland Cement Co., 103 N.L.R.B. 1375 (1953); Hekman Furniture Co., 101 N.L.R.B. 631 (1952), *enforced per curiam*, 207 F.2d 561 (6th Cir. 1953).

[18] 407 F.2d 754 (7th Cir. 1969).

[19] *Id.* at 758.

[20] 100 N.L.R.B. 208 (1952).

the contract term on the issue of subcontracting. Thereafter, the union sought information on the subcontracting of unit work. The employer refused, citing the management rights clause. The Board upheld the employer's refusal. It reasoned that the union granted to the employer sole discretion to subcontract work, and this made the requested data irrelevant. The remaining bargaining duties of the union were not affected, and the refusal to disclose the information covered by the management rights clause was not a violation of the Act.[21]

A management rights clause, however, only functions as a contractual waiver if it indicates that the union has contractually surrendered its right to protest certain managerial actions. In *Worcester Polytechnic Institute,* the contract provided that:

> "The Union . . . recognizes the right of the college to operate and manage the college including but not limited to the rights . . . to promote, demote, suspend, discipline or discharge employees for just cause, to lay off employees for lack of work or other legitimate reasons. . . ."[22]

The agreement in *Worcester* did not contain language granting the employer the right to lay off employees at its discretion, and it did not preclude the union from using the grievance machinery to protest layoffs.

The employer laid off eleven workers in the unit and asserted that budgetary considerations caused a work force reduction. The union's request for financial reports to substantiate the employer's claim was denied. The union filed a grievance protesting the layoffs. It also filed an unfair labor practice charge concerning the refusal to provide substantiation data. The Board concluded that the contract provision quoted above did not clearly and unmistakably waive the union's right to contest the layoffs.[23] Therefore, disclosure was ordered.[24]

---

[21] *Id.* at 209; *cf.* Boston Mut. Life Ins. Co., 170 N.L.R.B. 1672 (1968) (waiver of right to contest discharge of probationary employee waives rights to information on discharges).

[22] 213 N.L.R.B. 306, 308 (1974).

[23] *Id.* at 308-9.

[24] *Id.* at 309.

CHAPTER VII

Employer Defenses against NLRB Demands

After some early successes in defending refusals to provide relevant information, employers in recent years have found the traditional defenses to be of little value before the Board.[1] In *Detroit Edison Co. v. NLRB,*[2] however, the Supreme Court gave new life to the use by employers of substantial and legitimate business justifications in defense against information demands. By its decision, the Supreme Court has undoubtedly set the stage for a whole new wave of litigation over the refusal of employers to acquiesce to union demands for information.

DETROIT EDISON

Detroit Edison involved a union's demand for information relating to the utility firm's aptitude testing of employees prior to promotion. Tests were administered with an express assurance that individual scores would remain confidential. The actual examinations and the raw scores were available only to the company's psychologist.

Six members of the bargaining unit took the exam for the position of "Instrument Man B." All six failed. The jobs then were filled by applicants from outside the plant. The union filed a grievance alleging that the company had unfairly bypassed senior workers in filling the Instrument Man B vacancies. The union requested information on the testing procedure. The company refused to furnish the actual questions, the answer sheets, and linked scores, although it did provide some more general information. The company also offered to provide scores

---

[1] *See, e.g.*, Georgetown Assocs., Inc., 235 N.L.R.B. 485 (1978) (where the Board ordered disclosure of names and addresses of striker replacements even though the replacements had been subjected to substantial harassment).

[2] 440 U.S. 301 (1979).

of any employee who would sign a waiver releasing the company psychologist from his pledge of confidentiality. The union rejected this proposal and filed an unfair labor practice charge over the company's refusal to provide all the information.

The Board ruled that the employer had acted unlawfully, and it ordered disclosure.[3] In response to the employer's concerns over confidentiality, the Board barred the union from acting in any manner that might cause the tests to fall into the hands of the workers who had taken or might take the exams.[4] The Sixth Circuit enforced.[5] In reversing the order, the Supreme Court ruled that the Board had abused its remedial discretion.[6]

The Court noted that, in the past, revelation of individual scores resulted in the harassment of some lower scoring examinees, some of whom subsequently resigned from the company.[7] In addition, publication of examination questions would force the employer to abandon use of the old tests and to have a whole new set developed.[8] Such a procedure would not only be costly but also might leave the company without any testing battery for a substantial period of time.[9] Moreover, the fear that the union would leak the test questions was deemed well founded, since unions traditionally are averse to the emphasis on test scores rather than on seniority in promotion decisions.[10]

The Court concluded that the company had a legitimate interest in avoiding publication both of linked test scores and of

---

[3] Detroit Edison Co., 218 N.L.R.B. 1024 (1975), *enforced*, 560 F.2d 722 (6th Cir. 1977), *vacated and remanded*, 440 U.S. 301 (1979).

[4] *Id.*

[5] NLRB v. Detroit Edison Co., 560 F.2d 722 (6th Cir. 1977), *vacated and remanded*, 440 U.S. 301 (1979).

[6] Detroit Edison Co. v. NLRB, 440 U.S. 301 (1979). The Court noted that it could not reverse the finding that the employer's refusal to furnish the information had violated the Act, since the employer had failed to contest that finding before the appellate court. *Id.* at 311 n.10. The Court's analysis of the remedy would, however, undoubtedly apply to future cases involving the validity of the refusal itself.

[7] *Id.* at 317.

[8] *Id.* at 313.

[9] *Id.*

[10] *Id.*; see Note, *Psychological Aptitude Tests and the Duty to Supply Information: NLRB v. Edison Co.*, 91 HARV. L. REV. 869, 875 (1978).

actual exam questions and answers.[11] The Court also concluded that, as a practical matter, the Board's remedy did not protect these interests.[12] The Court noted that the union was not a party to the appellate proceedings. Accordingly, substantial doubt existed whether the union could be the subject of a contempt citation if it ignored the Board's restrictions,[13] since section 10(c) of the Act does not expressly authorize orders against a charging party who has not been found guilty of a violation of section 8(b) of the Act. Moreover, even if the use limitation was within the authority of the Board and could be effectively enforced, the restrictive order would not remove the danger of accidental disclosure.[14] Hence, a significant probability remained that the test data might escape from the hands of the union officers.[15]

The Court concluded that the importance of maintaining the secrecy of examination questions and the danger of disclosure from the Board's order outweighed the union's interest in these data.[16] The Court modified the order to require disclosure of linked scores only upon receipt of written consent of individual employees (as the company had offered initially).[17] The actual questions and answer sheets were to remain in the company psychologist's exclusive possession.[18]

THE BOARD'S RESPONSE

Following the *Detroit Edison* decision, the NLRB General Counsel, the Board's chief enforcement officer, issued a memorandum outlining the types of circumstances in which relevant data need not be furnished.[19] The General Counsel emphasized

---

[11] Detroit Edison Co. v. NLRB, 440 U.S. 301, 319 (1979).

[12] *Id.* at 316.

[13] *Id.*

[14] *Id.*

[15] *Id.*

[16] *Id.* at 319-20.

[17] *Id.* at 320.

[18] *Id.* at 320.

[19] *Memorandum of NLRB General Counsel Irving to Field Offices on Supreme Court's Decision in Detroit Edison Co. v. NLRB*, NLRB General Counsel Memorandum 79-22 (April 9, 1979), DAILY LAB. REP. (BNA) D-1 (Apr. 13, 1979).

that establishment of relevance is not determinative in information cases.[20] If an employer refuses an information request on confidentiality grounds, a two-part test was to be performed: first, did the company have a "legitimate and substantial" interest in refusing to supply the information in the requested form; second, if such an interest exists, did the employer engage in a reasonable good faith attempt to provide the union with the desired data in an alternate form?[21] If both tests were satisfied, unfair labor practice complaints were not to be issued.[22]

These requirements are not limited to employee testing situations. Instead, they apply to all instances in which an employer claims confidentiality. Thus, if a business has a justified interest in maintaining the secrecy of certain requested data and attempts to work with the union to resolve the conflicting desires, the employer's refusal to disclose would not result in the issuance of an unfair labor practice complaint.

OTHER CONFIDENTIALITY CASES

Prior to *Detroit Edison*, an employer's interest in the confidentiality of requested data was considered to be secondary to the union's need for relevant information. Allegations of confidentiality did not usually shield the employer from the consequences of its refusal to furnish pertinent material.[23]

There were, however, circumstances in which an employer successfully asserted a confidentiality defense. In *Kroger Co. v. NLRB*,[24] the employer instituted an "operations research" program. The program was used only to help determine the total number of store employee man-hours per week. Nevertheless, the union made a broad request for any information bearing on the operations research program. The Fifth Circuit recognized that the operations research program had an effect on

---

[20] *Id.*

[21] *Id.*

[22] *Id.*

[23] *E.g.*, General Elec. Co. v. NLRB, 466 F.2d 1177 (6th Cir. 1972) (area wage surveys with participants linked with wage rates); Westinghouse Elec. Corp., 239 N.L.R.B. No. 19 (Oct. 31, 1978) (employment discrimination charges and complaints); Boston Herald-Traveler Corp., 110 N.L.R.B. 2097 (1954), *enforced*, 223 F.2d 58 (1st Cir. 1955) (salary information on unit employees).

[24] 399 F.2d 455 (6th Cir. 1968).

employee working conditions. It held, however, that, because the company had a reasonable interest in preventing dissemination of valuable managerial information, the refusal to disclose was not an unfair labor practice.[25]

Four conditions were present that convinced the court of the employer's confidentiality claim. First, the employer showed that there was a legitimate business need for keeping the requested data secret. Second, the employer demonstrated that it had been engaging in good faith bargaining and had been attempting to satisfy the union's data needs, subject to reasonable restrictions necessary to maintain secrecy. Third, the union's request was overbroad and its bargaining position inflexible. Finally, the company offered facts indicating that the union had been advised of the employer's position.

The Board now has the opportunity to rule on its first major case on confidentiality since *Detroit Edison.* In *Borden Chemical,*[26] the union requested a complete list of the raw materials and chemicals used by the business so that it could bargain about safety issues. The Administrative Law Judge ruled that the employer failed to demonstrate that the union was likely to leak the information to other businesses or to the general public or that dissemination of such data would harm the company's competitive position.[27] Accordingly, he ordered that the list be furnished to the union.[28] The Board has not yet ruled.

BAD FAITH OF REQUEST

Employers often contend that the union is acting in bad faith in demanding certain information, i.e., that the request is not motivated by the union's desire to perform its statutory duties properly and efficiently but rather by some selfish purpose. Since the union does not intend to use the desired data in a manner that will promote collective bargaining, employers argue, the employer should be excused from the obligation to supply such information.

---

[25] *Id.* at 458.

[26] No. 32-CA-551 (N.L.R.B., filed **Apr. 25, 1979**).

[27] *Id.*

[28] *Id.*

Generally, an employer is not obligated to furnish data in situations in which the requested information is obviously beyond the scope of the union's legitimate needs. If, however, the requested information includes some data that the employer is not legally required to furnish, the employer must furnish the part of the requested data that is pertinent.[29]

Moreover, to challenge a union demand for data successfully, an employer must preserve its objection by asserting either at the time the request is received or shortly thereafter that the request is excessively broad. Thus, in *Texaco, Inc. v. NLRB*,[30] an employer refusing a union application for data and alleging only that all pertinent information had been previously supplied was not permitted to cite overbreadth later as an excuse for its failure to disclose.

If a union's initial request clearly is overbroad, an employer still must supply relevant information if the workers' bargaining agent subsequently narrows the demand.[31] The second request makes the company aware of precisely what data are desired, and any deficiencies in the first request application are cured.[32]

A business is not required to furnish requested data if it can show that the union intends to use the information to harass either other workers or the employer. In *NLRB v. Robert S. Abbott Publishing Co.*,[33] the company made a claim of financial inability to grant a proposed wage increase. The employer offered to provide weekly profit and loss statements and to permit union members holding positions in the bookkeeping department to reveal financial data.

The Seventh Circuit reversed a Board finding of unfair labor practices. The court found that the information ascertained from the company's financial records would have enabled the union's auditors to confirm the plea of poverty, but it also found it apparent that the union's insistence on receipt of the company's books was not because of its desire to verify the employer's assertion but because of some other motivation, such as an attempt to publicize the employer's ailing financial condition in

---

[29] Fawcett Printing Corp., 201 N.L.R.B. 964 (1973).

[30] 407 F.2d 754 (7th Cir. 1969).

[31] *Id.*

[32] *Id.* at 757-58.

[33] 331 F.2d 209 (7th Cir. 1964).

an effort to embarrass it as well as damage its credit standing and public prestige.[34]

Use of data to inflict bodily harm upon workers and employers unsympathetic to the union also is an improper motive for an information request. If an employer is able to demonstrate that a labor organization is seeking data for a violent purpose and that a "clear and present danger" of such violence exists, disclosure is not required.

In *Shell Oil Company v. NLRB*,[35] the company asserted successfully both a violent union motivation and a high probability of physical harm resulting from disclosure. The company did so by showing that striking employees had recently engaged in violent activities, such as mass picketing at the company's gates and at the homes of employees who had worked during the strike, and that the union had refused to pledge to keep the desired data confidential. No disclosure was required.[36]

It is difficult, however, for an employer to demonstrate both the existence of a violent purpose and the imminence of danger to involved parties. In *Squillacote v. Generac Corp.*,[37] a union that had committed acts of violence two years before the present controversy but had been receiving the currently sought information for the past five months without inflicting abuse was not viewed as imposing a "clear and present danger" to the physical well-being of other employees or the employer. The previous illegal actions of the labor organization were viewed as far enough in the past to preclude consideration in the present crisis.[38]

WAIVER

By words or actions, a union may waive its right to receive company information under the Act. If it can show that the union did surrender this statutory right, the employer is re-

---

[34] *Id.* at 212.

[35] 457 F.2d 615 (9th Cir. 1972).

[36] *Id.* at 616, 619-20; *accord*, Sign & Pictorial Union, Local 1175 v. NLRB, 419 F.2d 726 (D.C. Cir. 1969) (uncontested evidence that replacements were harassed, threatened, and assaulted by strikers).

[37] 304 F. Supp. 435 (E.D. Wis. 1969).

[38] *Id.* at 439; *accord*, United Aircraft Corp. v. NLRB, 434 F.2d 1198 (2d Cir. 1970), *cert. denied*, 401 U.S. 933 (1971) (only incident of violence occurred ten years in the past).

lieved of its duty to disclose relevant data, except in situations in which the contract itself calls for the provision of certain data.[39] Such situations are rare because the courts and the Board impose high standards of proof.

A waiver of the right to receive company data must be an express waiver. The Board and the courts will not infer a waiver from the actions of the union unless the union has expressed a desire to waive the right in clear and unmistakable terms.[40] The statement of this rule is found in the *Perkins Machine Co.* case:[41]

> . . . a purported waiver will not be lightly inferred in the absence of "clear and unequivocal" language. Even when the parties consciously explore the matter during negotiations and the contract fails to touch upon it, something more is required before the union will be held to have bargained away its rights, namely, a conscious relinquishment by the union, clearly intended and expressed.[42]

Silence regarding a right will result in failure to obtain it if the benefit can only be acquired by contract provision. But the right to receive relevant information does not arise from the contract alone[43] but from implication of the terms of the Act.[44] Failure to grant a contractual right to obtain information does not constitute a waiver.[45] As the Sixth Circuit stated in *NLRB v. J. H. Allison & Co.*:[46]

> Nor do we see logical justification in the view that in entering into a collective bargaining agreement for a new year, even though the contract was silent upon a controverted matter, the union should be held to have waived any rights secured under the Act, including its right to have a say-so as to so-called merit increases.[47]

---

[39] *See* chapter VI *supra* for employer's contentions that certain contract provisions waive the union's right to information.

[40] NLRB v. Item Co., 220 F.2d 956 (5th Cir.), *cert. denied*, 350 U.S. 836 (1955) ; Hekman Furniture Co., 101 N.L.R.B. 631 (1952), *enforced per curiam*, 207 F.2d 561 (6th Cir. 1953).

[41] 141 N.L.R.B. 98 (1963), *enforced*, 326 F.2d 488 (1st Cir. 1964).

[42] *Id.* at 102 n.41.

[43] *Id.*

[44] *Id.*

[45] Timken Roller Bearing Co. v. NLRB, 325 F.2d 746 (6th Cir. 1963), *cert. denied*, 376 U.S. 971 (1964). *But see* Hearst Corp., News Service Div., 113 N.L.R.B. 1067 (1955).

[46] 165 F.2d 766 (6th Cir.), *cert. denied*, 335 U.S. 814 (1948).

[47] *Id.*

The failure of the union to obtain a disclosure clause during negotiations does not clearly and unmistakably waive the union's statutory right to information. In *NLRB v. Gulf Atlantic Warehouse Co.*,[48] the union's surrender of its demand for a seniority clause providing for the periodic disclosure of seniority lists was not deemed a waiver of the right to receive seniority data. The seniority clause ultimately agreed to specified that, in promotions, demotions, layoffs, and rehirings, both the ability and the versatility of the employee were to be of equal weight. If those two factors were of equal value, for given employees, the employees' seniority would be the determining element.

Contending that there was nothing in the contract that required it to provide seniority information, the employer refused to provide requested seniority data to the union. The employer also argued that the union's abandonment of its seniority proposal amounted to a waiver of any right to obtain seniority data. Enforcing the Board's disclosure order, the Fifth Circuit ruled that the union did not knowingly waive its right to receive seniority information by agreeing to the company's seniority provision.[49]

Even if the expired contract contained express provisions imposing on the employer an obligation to supply data, absence of them from a subsequent collective agreement will not be viewed as a waiver of the union's right to obtain information.[50]

A waiver will not be considered implied where the parties permit the contract to renew itself automatically after a complaint alleging failure to supply relevant data has been filed.[51] Similarly, an offer by the union to negotiate a matter is not a waiver of the right to obtain data bearing on that issue, nor is a contract provision explicitly reserving determination of certain subjects.[52]

---

[48] 291 F.2d 475 (5th Cir. 1961).

[49] *Id.* at 477.

[50] NLRB v. Perkins Mach. Co., 326 F.2d 488 (1st Cir. 1964).

[51] General Controls Co., 88 N.L.R.B. 1341 (1950).

[52] NLRB v. New Britain Mach. Co., 210 F.2d 61 (2d Cir. 1954).

MOOTNESS

If the requested information is no longer necessary to the union's performance of its statutory duties, the employer has argued, disclosure of that information should not be required. In *C-B Buick, Incorporated*,[53] the employer refused to substantiate a claim of inability to pay a demanded wage increase. After that refusal, the parties negotiated a contract, but the union pursued its request for data. The Board issued a standard cease and desist order and also ordered disclosure.[54] The Third Circuit enforced the cease and desist order but refused to order disclosure.[55] The court reasoned that the desired financial data were of no current relevance to the union in either negotiating a new contract or administering the present agreement.[56]

If the employer can demonstrate that it has recently supplied the labor organization with substantially the same information that is currently sought, it will not be required to furnish the data a second time. In *Old Line Life Insurance of America*,[57] the union sought an updated list of employees, their hiring dates, initial salaries, job classifications, and any merit raises or promotions received. The company refused, asserting that it had been supplying the union with basically the same information on a monthly basis since the execution of the last contract. To allay the union's fear that the information was inaccurate or incomplete, the company volunteered to check its records, but the union refused. Both the Board and the Seventh Circuit agreed that the company's earlier provision of substantially the same data now sought and its willingness to verify the validity of the previously supplied information were sufficient to satisfy its obligation to provide information.[58]

---

[53] 206 N.L.R.B. 6 (1973).

[54] *Id.*

[55] C-B Buick, Inc. v. NLRB, 506 F.2d 1086 (3d Cir. 1974).

[56] *Id.* at 1094-95.

[57] 96 N.L.R.B. 499 (1951), *affirmed sub nom.* Associated Unions v. NLRB, 200 F.2d 52 (7th Cir. 1952).

[58] *Id.* at 502; *accord*, Albany Garage, Inc., 126 N.L.R.B. 417 (1960) (where financial statements with comparative sales and profit statements had recently been furnished, the company was not required to provide additional information after claiming inability to pay). *But cf.* Rybolt Heater Co., 165 N.L.R.B. 331 (1967), *enforced*, 408 F.2d 888 (6th Cir. 1969) (financial records for year ending eight months earlier insufficient in support of claimed inability to pay).

ALTERNATIVE SOURCES OF DATA

Despite the fact that information may be obtained from other sources, an employer is not usually relieved of its obligation to disclose.[59]

If the desired data are "effortlessly available" to the union, an employer does not violate section 8(a)(5) by failing to satisfy the union's request. In *NLRB v. Clegg*,[60] the union sought the wage rate of only one employee. The record did not indicate whether this employee had refused to furnish the desired wage information to the union, and the court opined that the requested data could have been obtained by approaching the worker himself. The court concluded that the information could have been "effortlessly" obtained and that the employer's refusal to disclose was not an unfair labor practice.[61]

In *NLRB v. Milgo, Inc.*,[62] the company told the union the title of its Blue Cross/Blue Shield plan covering union employees but refused to provide a copy of the plan. The union could have obtained a copy by simply calling a Blue Cross/Blue Shield Office, and the Second Circuit held that the employer's failure to furnish the requested information was not a violation of the Act.[63] Recognizing that the company also could have phoned Blue Cross/Blue Shield to obtain a plan, the court commented: ". . . we do not applaud this type of dealing. However, one can hardly say that the union lacked 'information that is needed . . . for the proper performance of its duties' when this was so readily available to it." [64]

Another argument advanced by employers to justify a refusal to furnish data is that the desired information could have been obtained directly by questioning a substantial number of the employees. Such a contention has never been accepted by the Board or the courts. As early as 1954, the Board remarked:

---

[59] *E.g.*, NLRB v. Northwestern Publishing Co., 343 F.2d 521 (7th Cir. 1965); Globe Stores, Inc., 227 N.L.R.B. 1251 (1977); American Beef Packers, Inc., 193 N.L.R.B. 1117 (1971).

[60] 304 F.2d 168 (8th Cir. 1962).

[61] *Id.* at 176.

[62] 567 F.2d 540 (2d Cir. 1977).

[63] *Id.* at 543.

[64] *Id.* at 543-44 n.2 (citations omitted).

It is immaterial that the Union might have gathered the bulk of this needed material through a series of interviews with members and employees: It was entitled to that complete, accurate and authoritative statement of facts which only the employer was in a position to make.[65]

In *NLRB v. Northwestern Publishing Co.*,[66] the wage information was sought for upcoming negotiations, but the employer supplied only part of the information. The employer refused to provide a breakdown of compensation between commissions and auto expense allowances for one class of drivers. Rejecting the company's position that it was excused from its obligation because the desired data could be obtained directly from the drivers, the Seventh Circuit ordered the disclosure of the requested breakdown.[67]

UNAVAILABILITY OF DATA

An employer is not obligated to furnish the union with unavailable information. In *NLRB v. United Brass Works, Inc.*,[68] the company had neither job classifications nor specific wage rates for various types of work. The union requested job classification data, and the employer responded by stating that no such data existed. The Fourth Circuit, concluding that the demand was motivated by a desire to establish a system of job classifications and corresponding wage rates, held that the employer acted lawfully in failing to meet a request to furnish information that it did not possess.[69]

DISPUTE OF UNION'S MAJORITY STATUS

Numerous cases have held that an employer that refuses to disclose because it honestly feels that it is not legally obligated to do so is not relieved of its statutory responsibility to inform.

---

[65] S.H. Kress & Co., 108 N.L.R.B. 1615, 1621 (1954).

[66] 343 F.2d 521 (7th Cir. 1965).

[67] *Id.* at 525; *accord*, Texaco, Inc. v. NLRB, 407 F.2d 754 (7th Cir. 1969).

[68] 287 F.2d 689 (4th Cir. 1961).

[69] *Id.* at 696-97; *accord*, Korn Indus. v. NLRB, 389 F.2d 117 (4th Cir. 1967).

Ignorance of the law or the relevant facts is not an available defense.[70]

In particular, an employer's mistaken belief about the union's continuing status as representative of the majority of the employees in the bargaining unit, when asserted in good faith, will not protect it against an unfair labor practice charge of failing to disclose relevant data.[71] Similarly, a challenge to the validity of the Board's certification of the union seeking data does not relieve an employer of the duty to disclose.[72] Instead, the employer must provide all relevant desired information until such time as the challenge is decided against the union.[73]

POSSIBLE USE IN FUTURE LITIGATION

That relevant data arguably are being sought for use in suits against the employer under statutes other than the Act is not a valid excuse for failure to disclose. In *Westinghouse Electric Corp.*,[74] the Board noted that numerous overlapping forums and remedies exist in the field of labor relations and concluded that the possibility that the union would use or distribute the requested information for employment discrimination suits against the employer did not justify the employer's refusal to disclose statistical information and the like related to the minority and female members in its work force, nor did it justify a refusal to disclose the company's own studies of those jobs in which insufficient numbers of blacks and females were working.[75] Judicial review is pending.

EXCESSIVE REMEDIAL DISCLOSURE

In an interesting development in 1980, the Court of Appeals for the Fifth Circuit held in *Florida Steel Corp. v. NLRB*[76] that sometimes a remedial order for disclosure of information can be too much. The NLRB in that case was permitted to require a

---

[70] *E.g.*, Taylor Forge & Pipe Works v. NLRB, 234 F.2d 227 (7th Cir.), *cert. denied*, 352 U.S. 942 (1956); NLRB v. J. H. Allison & Co., 165 F.2d 766 (6th Cir.), *cert. denied*, 335 U.S. 814 (1948).

[71] Sahara-Tahoe Corp., 229 N.L.R.B. 1094 (1977).

[72] St. Elizabeth Community Hosp., 237 N.L.R.B. 849 (1978).

[73] *Id.*

[74] 239 N.L.R.B. No. 19 (Oct. 31, 1978).

[75] *Id.*

[76] 620 F.2d 79 (5th Cir. 1980).

firm that had violated the Act to mail, post, and read to employees in its *unionized* plants a statement that it would not violate the union's rights. But the Board was not permitted—with the court denying enforcement—to force the same disclosure by the firm to workers in its nonunion facilities. The court also refused to force the firm to publish notice of its noninterference in company publications that would reach customers, suppliers, and other members of the public. Such a requirement would be a penalty without benefit to making the workers "whole," for the violations. Finally, the court rejected the Board's effort to give the union paid time at nonunion plants for a thirty-minute speech to all employees. The court grudgingly saw a tenuous connection between union speeches at union plants and the firm's misconduct but saw no necessary connection between the violation and the Board's remedy.

BURDENSOMENESS OF THE REQUEST

The employer may no longer refuse to supply relevant information on the ground that compliance with the request would be unduly burdensome.[77] Instead, if the employer objects on this ground, it must notify the union of its objection and must be willing to negotiate with the union over the allocation of the work and the cost of producing the information.[78]

CONCLUSIONS ON NLRB DISCLOSURE

The preceding several chapters have discussed in detail the evolution of the present National Labor Relations Board policy on employer provision of information to employee representatives. An overview demonstrates that employee organizations have powerful means to gain access to employer records. The current thinking of the Board, led perhaps by Member Jenkins,[79] makes it very difficult for an employer to refuse information when a union requests it. The employer may be able to avoid disclosure if the union's information request is excessively expansive or very poorly stated. In general, however, disclosure to the union will be required.

---

[77] Food Employer Council, Inc., 197 N.L.R.B. 651 (1972).

[78] *Id.; accord,* General Motors Corp., 243 N.L.R.B. No. 19 (June 29, 1979) (where it was contended that compilation of requested data would require 18,000 to 20,000 man-hours, the parties were to bargain over the costs of the compilation, and if no agreement was reached, the union was to be given access to the records needed to compile the information requested).

[79] *See* chapter XVI *infra.*

PART THREE

The Privacy Issue

CHAPTER VIII

Federal Privacy Legislation and the Employer-Employee Relationship

Federal solutions to a multitude of the nation's social and environmental ills were proposed during the active legislative decade of the 1970s, and many of those solutions in turn became problems themselves as experience with their consequences clashed with the idealism of their creating and drafting sponsors. The area of privacy is perhaps typical of this political phenomenon. Hearings in Congress recorded a feeling that American citizens were concerned about their right to be left alone and about the erosion of that right by privacy invasions made in the name of government, industry, product and service sellers, and others. A federal solution was created in a compressed period of last-minute compromises to honor a retiring legislator who had a strong interest in privacy. The solution did not work as planned, and an anticipated extension into private sector records did not develop. In the context of labor relations, the likelihood of federal privacy legislation on the model of the 1974 Privacy Act seems farther and farther away as experience with legislated federal solutions proves the weakness of those cures for societal problems.

THE PRIVACY ACT OF 1974

Senator Sam Ervin of North Carolina was the leading figure in the long struggle to protect individual privacy rights through legislation. Ervin chaired a series of hearings that stretched over several years and, in search of privacy concerns, delved into virtually every aspect of modern data-collection and dissemination.[1] The Ervin hearings produced an extensive record, reflect-

---

[1] *Federal Data Banks, Computers, and the Bill of Rights: Hearings Before the Subcomm. on Constitutional Rights of the Senate Comm. on the Judiciary,* 92d Cong., 1st Sess. (1971) [hereinafter cited as *1971 Hearings*]; *Privacy:*

ing a great deal of preparation by many interested groups. The groups reflected both the liberal and conservative constituencies of privacy; the issue evoked a unique political coalition enjoying the patronage of the American Civil Liberties Union and of staunch conservative lawmakers.[2] Any legislative effort attracting such a diversity of views deserves careful study.

During the second half of the Ninety-Third Congress, while the legislative elections of 1974 were shaping political priorities for individual legislators and the Watergate scandal was shaping the priorities of the national leadership, privacy legislation did not seem likely to receive the committee and floor action time that a complex balancing statute truly deserves.[3] The difficulties of shaping a Privacy Act at all can be reflected in one large and one small issue. The large issue was whether to apply federal privacy control to all private sector activity, using as a jurisdictional base the interstate commerce clause of the Constitution. Some favored comprehensive attacks on collection and dissemination of private data from private records systems. It was argued that a solution addressing only the federal problems would cure only part of the problem.[4]

The Collection, Use, and Computerization of Personal Data: Joint Hearings on S. 3418, S. 3633, S. 3116, S. 2810, and S. 2542 Before the Ad Hoc Subcomm. on Privacy and Information Systems of the Senate Comm. on Government Operations and Before the Subcomm. on Constitutional Rights of the Senate Comm. on the Judiciary, 93d Cong., 2d Sess. (1974) [hereinafter cited as *1974 Hearings*].

[2] Senator Barry Goldwater; Congressman Barry Goldwater, Jr.; representatives of the Liberty Lobby and the American Civil Liberties Union; Professor Alan Westin of Columbia University; and various liberal groups testified at the 1974 hearings. Many commercial associations and corporations, such as IBM, submitted statements to the hearings. *1974 Hearings, supra* note 1.

[3] For a useful treatment of the politics of the bill's passage, *see* Cohen, *Justice Report/New Privacy Law to Have Major Impact on Government Data*, 7 NAT'L J. REP. 20 (1975) [hereinafter cited as Cohen, *Justice*]. *See also* Large, *Congress Finishes Work on 'Privacy' Bill But Measure Has a Number of Loopholes*, Wall St. J., Dec. 19, 1974, at 8, col. 3. In an earlier article, an unnamed private attorney at the markup of the Act said that he felt that the staff and senators "did not understand the bill and its implications" because of its "enormously complex problems." Cohen, *Justice Report/Protection of Citizens' Privacy Becomes Major Federal Concern*, 6 NAT'L J. REP. 1521, 1527, 1530 (1974) [hereinafter cited as Cohen, *Protection*].

[4] The concern with data banks and computer-retrieved personnel data was the primary focus of concern regarding private sector persons' privacy rights. *1974 Hearings, supra* note 1; *1971 Hearings, supra* note 1. Action on private systems was deferred. S. REP. No. 1183, 93d Cong., 2d Sess. 19 (1974).

Against this argument was the private sector's persistent counterargument that government did not yet know enough about the means and consequences of privacy protection statutes. If government did not fully consider the means and mechanical problems and fully study the consequences and costs of sharing and disclosing private files, it was argued, omnibus solutions would only worsen the problem. Red tape and privacy problems would increase, according to these counterpoint arguments.[5]

The chronology of passage of the Privacy Act appears in hindsight to be incredible. A major bill was introduced in May 1974.[6] Its markup session occurred during the turbulent month of August, when the Senate and House were participating in the drama surrounding the resignation of Richard Nixon as president. The bill moved swiftly onto the calendar, with a Senate report issued in late September,[7] a House report in early October,[8] easy passage through both bodies in the weeks after Election Day,[9] a reconciliation of conflicts through a written compromise paper in lieu of conference committee,[10] and passage as one of the last actions of a tired Congress on December 18, 1974.[11] Such rapid progress reflects less upon the merits of the legislation and more on the leadership's desire to honor its retiring colleague, Senator Ervin. His sponsorship of the bill was the subject of many laudatory speeches during the brief debates prior to passage. This noble parting gesture will be viewed as a flawed but sincere tribute to a pioneer on privacy rights. The flaws in the complex and poorly constructed statute, however, make it difficult to consider its adoption as a model for future laws.

---

5 Cohen, *Justice*, *supra* note 3; Cohen, *Protection*, *supra* note 3. *See* the deferral in the *Analysis of House and Senate Compromise Amendments to the Federal Privacy Act*, 120 CONG. REC. 40,881 (1974) ; S. REP. No. 1183, *supra* note 4.

6 S. 3418, 93d Cong., 2d Sess. (1974). Senator Ervin introduced this bill on May 1, 1974. 120 CONG. REC. 12,646 (1974).

7 S. REP. No. 1183, 93d Cong., 2d Sess. (1974).

8 H. REP. No. 1416, 93d Cong., 2d Sess. (1974).

9 120 CONG. REC. 36,917; 36,976 (1974) (Senate passage on Nov. 21; House passage on Nov. 20).

10 *Analysis of House and Senate Compromise Amendments*, *supra* note 5.

11 Privacy Act of 1974, Pub. L. 93-579, 88 Stat. 1896 (codified at 5 U.S.C. § 552a (1976)).

PROVISIONS AND WEAKNESSES

The Privacy Act limits some disclosures of personal information from a defined set of files [12] held by government agencies [13] and limits the means and the purposes of collection of data from individuals.[14] The Act permits access by an individual to his or her own file [15] and correction of that file in some cases,[16] unless the file is exempted under one of the permissible exemptions of the Act.[17] Some rather convoluted civil [18] and criminal [19] remedies against agencies are provided, with some exemptions from the remedies permitted to be established by some agencies.[20] So many qualifications and exemptions were poured into the rapidly evolving statute during 1974 that its provisions appear quite fine in broad overview but are quite evadable in practice.[21]

The weakened version of the Privacy Act that emerged from the compromise process has several significant flaws. First, the statute is limited to a class of files that are "individually identifiable" and in the custody of federal agencies.[22] The agencies are free to index their files according to subject matter, such as "factory inspections," "beryllium manufacturers," or the like,

---

[12] 5 U.S.C. § 552a(a)(4) (1976). The files must be maintained in a formal "system of records" for the agency to be subject to the Act. *Id.* § 552(a)(5).

[13] *Id.* §§ 552a(a)(1), 552(e).

[14] "To the greatest extent practicable," information should be collected from the individual directly. 5 U.S.C. § 552a(e)(2) (1976). Purposes cannot include exercise of First Amendment rights as a subject of collected information. *Id.* § 552a(e)(7).

[15] *Id.* § 552a(d)(1).

[16] *Id.* § 552a(d)(2). There is an appeal and disagreement-notice provision as well. *Id.* § 552a(d)(3)-(4).

[17] *Id.* § 552a(j)-(k).

[18] *Id.* § 552a(g).

[19] *Id.* § 552a(i).

[20] The Central Intelligence Agency can exempt its system of records from certain provisions of the Act. *Id.* § 552a(j)(1).

[21] *See generally* 2 J. O'REILLY, FEDERAL INFORMATION DISCLOSURE §§ 21.07-.08 (1977); Davidson, *The Privacy Act of 1974—Exceptions and Exemptions,* 34 FED. B. J. 323 (1975).

[22] If the file cannot be retrieved from the system by some personal identifier of an individual, such as a name, the file is not subject to the Act. 5 U.S.C. § 552a(a)(5) (1976).

which will remove the files from the Privacy Act's scope.[23] The Act permits some agencies to exempt their files completely from access and other rights of affected persons.[24] The Central Intelligence Agency, the Federal Bureau of Investigation, and other criminal law enforcement agencies [25] (not including some administrative agencies that have incidental powers to enforce their laws with criminal penalties [26]) have a blanket exemption of their files from the Privacy Act. Also, the Act permits agencies with some investigative roles to exempt specific files from the access provisions of the Act.[27] For example, individual charge files of the Equal Employment Opportunity Commission (EEOC) are not accessible under the Privacy Act because the EEOC has exempted them by rule from the reach of the Act.[28]

Perhaps the most important weakness from the standpoint of individuals whose files are held by agencies is the easy opportunity for an agency to disclose individual information under a "routine use" exception.[29] Each agency publishes a number of file system notices in the *Federal Register*.[30] In the fine print of each system's notice is a list of the usual reasons *why* the agency will disclose the information. These routine uses allow the agency to transfer the private information to organizations or persons outside of the holding agency.[31] A federal employee's

---

[23] And some have done so for just that reason. Interviews with Stanley Weinbrecht, Associate General Counsel, National Labor Relations Board; Soffia Petters, Associate Solicitor, Department of Labor; Constance duPre, Associate General Counsel, Equal Employment Opportunity Commission; and other agencies' counsels in Washington, D.C. (Jan. 14 and Feb. 7, 1980).

[24] 5 U.S.C. § 552a(j) (1976).

[25] To receive a blanket exemption from the Privacy Act, an agency's principal function must be criminal law enforcement, not civil action or regulation. *Id.* § 552a(j)(2).

[26] The principal function of OSHA, for example, is not criminal law enforcement, although criminal sanctions are available to the Department of Justice in prosecuting certain OSH Act violations. 29 U.S.C. § 666(e) (1976).

[27] 5 U.S.C. § 552a(k) (1976).

[28] Interview with Constance duPre, Associate General Counsel, Equal Employment Opportunity Commission, in Washington, D.C. (Feb. 7, 1980).

[29] 5 U.S.C. § 552a(a)(7) (1976).

[30] *Id.* § 552a(e)(4).

[31] *Id.* § 552a(b)(3). *Compare* Gorod v. IRS, 79-1 U.S. Tax Cas. (CCH) ¶ 9243 (D. Mass. Jan. 17, 1979) *with* Stiles v. Atlanta Gas Light Co., 453 F. Supp. 798 (N.D. Ga. 1978) *and* Burley v. United States Drug Enforcement Administration, 443 F. Supp. 619 (M.D. Tenn. 1977).

job application might, for example, be made available to an employee union representative without the consent of the individual if union access is permitted as a "routine use." [32] The individual would not know about the access.[33] When this disclosure occurrence is discovered, perhaps belatedly, the individual might try to get the agency to change its rules to limit disclosures to purposes compatible with the reason for the agency's collection of the file.[34] Strengthening of the "compatible purpose" test was recommended by a federal study group on future Privacy Act amendments.[35] A proposed new standard would require that disclosure must be consistent with the individual's "reasonable expectations of use and disclosure" of the information supplied to the agency.[36]

THE PRIVACY ACT AND THE UNIONS

The labor movement's interest in the federal privacy legislation was minimal. The hearing record for the final statute included a brief letter from one local union at a federal hospital endorsing controls over misuse of personal data by management supervisors.[37] Unlike issues that have attracted national labor attention, however, the Privacy Act lacked a direct impact on private sector activities, and its limitation to federal files was a deterrent to much union concern. Part of the legislation establishing the Privacy Act also established a Privacy Protection Study Commission, and only a small handful of union witnesses participated in that Commission's postenactment studies of the Privacy Act and its role in private sector privacy isuses.[38]

---

[32] Local 2047, Am. Fed'n of Gov't Employees v. Defense Gen. Supply Center, 423 F. Supp. 481 (E.D. Va. 1976), aff'd, 573 F.2d 184 (4th Cir. 1978).

[33] Notice is usually given except in routine-use disclosures. 5 U.S.C. § 552a(b)(3) (1976).

[34] This could be done by a petition for amendment of the final rule.

[35] *The Privacy Act of 1974: An Assessment*, in PRIVACY PROTECTION STUDY COMMISSION, PERSONAL PRIVACY IN AN INFORMATION SOCIETY, app. 4, at 61 (1977).

[36] PRIVACY PROTECTION STUDY COMMISSION, PERSONAL PRIVACY IN AN INFORMATION SOCIETY 517 (1977).

[37] *1974 Hearings, supra* note 1, at 622 (statement of National Federation of Employees).

[38] *Employment Records* in PRIVACY PROTECTION STUDY COMMISSION, PERSONAL PRIVACY IN AN INFORMATION SOCIETY, app. 3, at 65 (1977).

The early stages of implementation of the Privacy Act included thousands of notices in the *Federal Register* detailing the existence of systems of agency records considered to be subject to the Act. One of the aspects of this massive publication process that did *not* perform as the drafters expected was the public oversight role. Public comment was invited on agency notices and on their Privacy Act rules, but virtually no comments were received.[39]

Failure to comment about the proposed "routine uses" in the agency-published notices, however, was a mistake for some of the federal unions. In a 1976 Virginia case,[40] a local of the American Federation of Government Employees was surprised to learn that the Privacy Act of 1974 overrode the information disclosure provisions of a 1972 contract with the Defense General Supply Center. Under the existing contract, the employer had been obligated to provide certain information about employees to the union. When the Privacy Act's implementation date arrived, the employer notified the union that it would no longer receive six types of employee information, including nominees for pay increases and awards, referral lists for new job openings, warning letters and proposed disciplinary notices, names of employees being considered for elimination by reductions in force, etc. The union vigorously opposed the statement by the employer, and after further debate, the employer insisted that three types of information would not be disclosed and one type would be supplied with names of individuals deleted.[41] The union sued.

The employer's defense was that the Privacy Act prohibits the disclosure of certain information to *any* third person or organization without consent of the individual, absent a "routine use" consistent with the Privacy Act and with the purposes for gathering or generating the information. The union asserted that the employer could not make a unilateral change in the contract. When the employee records maintained under a set of Civil Service Commission rules were listed for "routine uses," the only routine use allowed was the name and identifying in-

---

[39] Comments were extremely rare, except on certain CIA programs where comments could unfortunately do no good because the CIA is totally exempt from the Privacy Act. 5 U.S.C. § 552a(j)(1) (1976).

[40] Local 2047, Am. Fed'n of Gov't Employees v. Defense Gen. Supply Center, 423 F. Supp. 481 (E.D. Va. 1976), *aff'd*, 573 F.2d 184 (4th Cir. 1978).

[41] *Id.* at 483.

formation concerning the individual.[42] The federal district court
determined that the Act properly excluded disclosure if the
"routine use" regulation was valid. As to whether the failure
to list the disciplinary and related files as routinely accessible
to unions was valid, the union argued that it was not equitable
for the employer to take advantage of the Privacy Act to terminate a bargained-for flow of information to the union. The
court observed:

> Neither the language of the Privacy Act nor its legislative his-
> tory indicate that Congress intended to preclude disclosure to recog-
> nized labor unions of relevant information under a negotiated collec-
> tive bargaining agreement. A recognized union may occupy a unique
> position under the Privacy Act as it is the exclusive representative
> of the employees for whom the records are maintained. Disclosing
> relevant information to recognized unions may easily be seen to
> advance the nation's federal labor-management relations policy
> by providing the union with data necessary to pursue its representa-
> tional duties.[43]

The court was sympathetic to the union but was unwilling to
find that the regulation limiting uses was inconsistent with the
personal information protections that the Privacy Act had established. Since the narrow regulation was presumptively valid
and consistent with the statutory intent of the Privacy Act, the
court upheld the rule.[44] The employer was not obligated to
supply the union with the information, and the decision was
upheld on appeal.[45] Access would thus be denied unless the union
convinced the federal government agencies responsible for the
routine use categorization of personnel files to treat the union's
desired classes of information as "routine use" items.[46]

IMPACT ON FEDERAL EMPLOYEE UNIONS

The Privacy Act has been relatively unused by federal employee unions. It has not been a major problem in recent years,
although the 1975-76 period of implementation added a great

---

[42] *Id.* at 483-84.

[43] *Id.* at 485 n. 7.

[44] *Id.* at 485-86.

[45] 573 F.2d 184 (4th Cir. 1978).

[46] If the agency changed its rule the "routine use" of union disclosure
would then be added, after notice and comment procedures had been followed.
5 U.S.C. § 552a(a)(7) (1976).

deal of paperwork for agency information-management officials while systems were established and exemptions were drafted and published as rules.

At the Labor Department, the paperwork effect of the Privacy Act has been its only major impact.[47] Reissuance once each year of lists of systems subject to the Act is regarded as an exercise of no appreciable benefit. There were only four Privacy Act-related suits pending against Labor at the beginning of 1980. Most of the sensitive files relating to departmental investigations, which would otherwise have been accessible to individual requesters, are within exempted systems under the control of the Labor Department's Inspector General. Many of these are criminal investigation matters.

The use of the Act in litigation has been rare. A dozen demands for correction or amendment of employee disability files have been made, usually seeking the correction (by deletion) of an examination report that disagreed with the claimant's view of his or her physical ailment. In one lawsuit, a union attempted to file suit under the Privacy Act as a representative of a class of individuals, each having Privacy Act rights. The case was dismissed because the union is an organization, not an "individual," [48] and because no class actions are permitted under the Privacy Act.[49]

The National Labor Relations Board has not seen any effect of the Privacy Act, other than paperwork processing of notices.[50] The charges brought by employees are filed at the Board's offices by firm or employer, not by the charging individual's name. The prefiling documents in the docket at the regions are temporarily filed by individual names, but these have not been a subject of Privacy Act problems.[51]

The Federal Mediation and Conciliation Service (FMCS) has found more individual grievants interested in obtaining their arbitration files from FMCS arbitration cases. Particularly if

---

[47] Interview with Soffia Petters, Associate Solicitor, U.S. Department of Labor, in Washington, D.C. (Jan. 14, 1980).

[48] *Id.; see* 5 U.S.C. § 552a(a)(2) (1976).

[49] Each individual is treated on a person-by-person basis. 5 U.S.C. § 552a(g) (1976).

[50] Interview with Stanley Weinbrecht, Associate General Counsel, National Labor Relations Board, in Washington, D.C. (Jan. 14, 1980).

[51] *Id.*

the reason for the arbitration is a discharge for personal misconduct, in which the individual's character is partly at issue, there may be occasional requests; however, the FMCS has not experienced a wide use of the Act.[52] Two agencies more recently established under the Civil Service Reform Act—the Office of Personnel Management (OPM) and the Federal Labor Relations Authority [53]—have likewise not found the Privacy Act to be an area of activity. The OPM's contract organization responsible for monitoring the details of the hundreds of federal employee contracts has not seen *any* contracts in which unions have bargained for specific additional rights under the Privacy Act, e.g., the establishment of new "routine use" categories to permit access by the union to additional information. If such arrangements are being made, they are outside of the contract, in the nature of political arrangements between agency policymakers and union representatives.[54]

A final item of interest that affects federal employees is the potential for individual harm from unwarranted or incorrect disclosures of personal data. Public employees have special privacy concerns not necessarily shared by private sector employees. In some cases, damages could be obtained by a federal employee for misconduct in the handling of personal data by an employer's representative, such as a supervisor. The Privacy Act provides a remedy, however, with a defined requirement of "intentional or willful" misconduct and a limitation to only "actual damages." [55] This Privacy Act remedy may be the employee's sole opportunity to obtain relief against the agency, even if the employee might have won a greater verdict against the agency prior to the passage of the Privacy Act for the same type of misconduct.[56] The real weakness of this remedy is a matter of controversy. The future lawsuits to establish liability principles will have an important effect on the willingness of victims of information misuse to resort to the courts.

---

[52] Interview with David Vaughn, General Counsel, Federal Mediation and Conciliation Service, in Washington, D.C. (Jan. 14, 1980).

[53] Interview with attorneys, Federal Labor Relations Authority, in Washington, D.C. (Feb. 7, 1980).

[54] Interview with LAIRS system manager, OPM Office of Labor-Management Relations, contracts administration group (Feb. 7, 1980).

[55] 5 U.S.C. § 552a(g) (1976).

[56] Goodman, *Remarks*, 34 FED. B. J. 316, 318 (1975).

IMPACT ON THE PRIVATE SECTOR

The Privacy Act emerged from Congress with no provision affecting the private sector, except for the establishment of a Privacy Protection Study Commission.[57] Several reasons led to the deletion of private sector records systems. First, the hearings record had not shown a significant means of controlling the many distinct questions arising about private records systems. Second, the jurisdictional basis for information control had not been well developed, for many information systems were beyond the reach of the interstate commerce powers of Congress.[58] Third, the remedies that would have to be considered to solve private sector problems would necessarily vary from the regulations and litigation systems that the federal agencies could handle under legislation affecting federal agencies alone. Finally, the weak political alliances that supported the 1974 momentum for federal privacy legislation would probably have collapsed had the bill reached into private sector practices, leaving the Congress with no bill at all for the then foreseeable future.

Expansion of the Privacy Act into the private sector was not recommended by the Privacy Protection Study Commission. Instead, the Commission decided to tailor specific recommendations to specific areas of need:

> In the private sector, the Commission specifies voluntary compliance when the present need for the recommended change is not acute enough to justify mandatory legislation, or if the organizations in an industry have shown themselves willing to cooperate voluntarily. . . . The Commission . . . relies mainly on voluntary compliance in the area of employment and personnel; though there are a few exceptions . . . the Commission prefers to rely mainly on voluntary compliance because of the complexity of the relationship between employer and employee, and the difficulty of classifying all the various records different employers maintain about their employees and the way they use these records in employment decision-

---

[57] Pub. L. No. 93-579, § 5, 88 Stat. 1897.

[58] A transcript of the colloquy in a unique markup session reveals that Senator Muskie wanted to reach the private sector but knew that he lacked a hearings basis for such action. *See* SENATE COMM. ON GOVERNMENT OPERATIONS & SUBCOMM. ON GOVERNMENT INFORMATION AND INDIVIDUAL RIGHTS, HOUSE COMM. ON GOVERNMENT OPERATIONS, 94TH CONG. 2D SESS., LEGISLATIVE HISTORY OF THE PRIVACY ACT OF 1974, S. 3418 (PUBLIC LAW 93-579) 50-51 (Joint Comm. Print 1976). Had there been an interstate commerce connection, liberal advocates of an expansive Commerce clause interpretation—as Muskie had been in the environmental area—could have rationalized the extension into the private sector.

making. For the Commission to recommend otherwise would be to recommend uniformity where variation is not only widespread but inherent in the employer-employee relationship as our society now knows it.[59]

It is doubtful that the Privacy Act will ever be expanded into the private sector employment relationship. The gap between expectation and performance has been a telling weakness of privacy legislation. The lukewarm reception of many state laws for access to private records [60] and the very marginal record of the federal agencies' performance under the federal Act would make any congressionally imposed expansion of the Privacy Act a doubtful political enterprise. It is likely instead that the privacy concept will be reflected in a variety of specific enactments governing medical,[61] personnel discipline,[62] and credit information [63] systems. Each will gradually assemble its constituency and will pass when the legislative mood again favors such privacy controls.

The federal Privacy Act has a somewhat inhibitive or deterrent effect that deserves special consideration. Some federal investigations have been hampered by the public recognition that the sources of confidential data cannot expect absolute assurance that their statements will never be released.[64] Informants read the newspapers. Publicity about files disclosed under the Privacy Act, complementing that news attention already given to the Freedom of Information Act disclosures, makes the public aware that the government cannot keep its assurances of confidential treatment. Labor-related investigations by federal agencies such as the Labor Department can be protected by Privacy Act ex-

---

[59] PRIVACY PROTECTION STUDY COMMISSION, *supra* note 36, at 34.

[60] Very few requests were received for the use of the California right of access to files, for example. A. WESTIN, COMPUTERS, PERSONNEL ADMINISTRATION AND CITIZEN RIGHTS 230 (National Bureau of Standards Special Publication No. 500-50, 1979). Ohio's Privacy Board was permitted to die by the rarity of public use, approximately one request per month. Gordon, *An End to the Privacy Board*, Cincinnati Post, Feb. 20, 1980, n.p.

[61] H.R. 3444, 96th Cong., 1st Sess. (1979).

[62] *See, e.g.*, MICH. COMP. LAWS §§ 397.1-.567 (West 1976 & Supp. 1978).

[63] H.R. 5555, 96th Cong., 1st Sess. (1979).

[64] This is a recurrent problem in many contexts, especially but not exclusively in law enforcement. It frequently occurs in the labor relations context, even within the government. Interviews with attorneys, Federal Labor Relations Authority, in Washington, D.C. (Feb. 7, 1980).

emptions and by filing in organizational (nonindividual) file systems, but some residual inhibition of informants can be expected because of concerns about official (and sometimes unofficial, i.e., leaked) disseminations.[65]

None of the interviews conducted for this text uncovered specific cases of informant inhibition, but the General Accounting Office's study of criminal law enforcement agencies suggested that there has been a strong disincentive to continue the past relationships of government investigators with their informants.[66] Whether some government inquiries have likewise been inhibited could not be determined from headquarters interviews.

The question of Privacy Act inhibition of personnel preemployment investigations is not adequately settled. A brief study done in 1977 suggested that the civil service investigations process had not been inhibited; although less of the "borderline" negative information was being received, useful comments about the individuals under investigation were still being obtained.[67] On some occasions, the potential for dissemination of the recommendation (or criticism) will not inhibit the interviewed neighbor or coworker. Experience in the criminal law area, however, suggests that wider public awareness of the government's obligation to disclose personal files to the file subjects will gradually impede many sources of sensitive information. It is unlikely to affect traditional adversary proceedings, brought by named charging parties, but it is likely to impair government-conducted inquiries. The availability of protection for the complainant under statutes is not a full solution to the disclosure-inhibition problem.[68] Experience and further study will reveal whether the inhibition in fact occurs.

USE OF THE PRIVACY ACT TO MONITOR INVESTIGATIONS

One troublesome aspect of the information and privacy issue in certain areas of employer-employee relations is the role of

---

[65] Interview with Soffia Petters, *supra* note 47.

[66] GENERAL ACCOUNTING OFFICE, IMPACT OF THE FREEDOM OF INFORMATION AND PRIVACY ACTS ON LAW ENFORCEMENT AGENCIES (1978).

[67] A. WESTIN, *supra* note 60, at 155-56.

[68] The reason is that the prospect of later relief is probably less attractive than some defined assurance of retention of the job after the complaint has been made.

individuals and government investigators in the federal monitoring of union activities. If a union is the target of a federal investigation, the investigating agency will usually file its records under an organizational rather than individual identifier system and so remove the records from the reach of the Privacy Act. The agency alternatively could transfer the records to an investigative unit (e.g., Labor's Inspector General) and claim that the records system is a specifically exempted system.[69] Or the agency could write a routine use category so narrow that it never shares the information without the consent of the individual union members. One of the recent problems with individual consent is that consent can be coerced. In an American Civil Liberties Union study of employer information practice, a government employee who was asked about employer invasions of privacy responded that she was more concerned about her union than about the employer: "To 'help' others they wanted information from me I was reluctant to give. In the end I was hurt." [70] In the medical records context, a physician specializing in medical records issues noted that there may be a danger of peer pressure to consent to access by union representatives.[71] The expert testified at Occupational Safety and Health Administration hearings that measures for the protection of free and voluntary consent should be included in any medical records provision.[72] A Justice Department unit using an informant inside a mob-dominated organization was startled to learn that the head of the criminal group had forced all of its principal members, including the government's informant, to execute Privacy Act consent forms, which would allow release of the investigative records to that leader. If Justice were to comply and deliver the files, before or after litigation occurred, the informant would be discovered and killed; if it were to refuse or comply for all but one of the individuals' records, withholding would violate the Privacy Act or would

---

[69] 5 U.S.C. § 552a(k) (1976).

[70] A. WESTIN, *supra* note 60, at 288.

[71] *Access to Employee Medical and Exposure Records: Hearings Before U.S. Occupational Safety and Health Administration*, Docket No. H-112 (Dec. 5, 1978) (testimony of Dr. Daniel Teitelbaum at 9).

[72] ". . . I am uncertain as to whether any employee who is pressured by a union representative, by management, by OSHA or by NIOSH to release his record will be able to give a freely informed consent . . . in a time of compliance activities or other stressful situations. . . ." *Id.*

pinpoint the informant.[73] Thus, although individual consent is quite desirable, it should be recognized that peer pressures and not a desire to see one's own file might be the motivation for some uses of the Privacy Act.

THE FAIR CREDIT REPORTING ACT

Federal legislation to permit access to credit-related information has had an incidental effect upon preemployment investigations. Some employers are concerned with the credit status of prospective employees. The employee has certain rights as the subject of a credit report, with rights provided under the Equal Credit Opportunity Act.[74] A rejected credit applicant is entitled to request the reasons why credit was rejected.

The Fair Credit Reporting Act gives persons who are granted credit the right to know the nature and substance of the credit bureau's file about him or her.[75] That 1971 law provides some protection for job applicants but has significant limitations. The Act requires that an employer using a credit report as the basis for an *adverse* employment decision must notify the individual who was the subject of that decision. The person can then go to the credit agency and demand to see the credit file. There is, however, no affirmative right to obtain and see a copy without a prior adverse determination and a prior request for access.[76] A report that is partially adverse and remains in the employer's file after the individual is hired may be the basis of an adverse action in the future, such as failure to obtain a promotion.

When the Privacy Protection Study Commission considered the credit-related rights of job applicants, it urged Congress to amend the Fair Credit Reporting Act to allow either applicants or employees to see and copy information in a credit agency report, regardless of the action taken on it by the employer.[77] It

---

[73] Interviews with personnel of the Department of Justice, in Washington, D.C. (Fall 1979).

[74] 15 U.S.C. § 1691-1691f (1976).

[75] 15 U.S.C. § 1681-1681t (1976).

[76] *See* the recommendations in PRIVACY PROTECTION STUDY COMMISSION, *supra* note 36 at 77.

[77] *Id.*

urged that the person also should be given rights to correct or amend or dispute the information in the report. Finally, the Commission suggested that employers must give applicants or employees copies of the report when it is received by the employer. These recommendations became part of the Administration's 1979 proposals on new privacy legislation.[78] Several related bills were pending in the Ninety-Sixth Congress, but none had passed into law as this text went to press.[79]

---

[78] H.R. 5559, 96th Cong., 2d Sess. (1979).

[79] *Id. See also* H.R. 5555, S. 1928, H.R. 345, H.R. 2630, 96th Cong., 2d Sess. (1979).

CHAPTER IX

The Private Sector: Disclosure and Employment Records Privacy

The phases of information activity in the employment con-text are similar to categories that fit all sorts of information: the acquisition of information, the use and processing of the information, and the dissemination of information and judg-ments made from it to persons outside the collecting organization. For the employment situation, these categories are roughly the period of preemployment questioning of prospective employees (and acquisition of personal information from newly hired workers), the use of individual information in making personnel management decisions, and the transfer of information from the employer's file to third persons such as law enforcement agencies, government monitors, unions, and the like.[1]

IS THERE AN EMPLOYEE PRIVACY ISSUE AT ALL?

As a matter of living in a complex society, each individual trades off some personal privacy for some group benefit.[2] Job

---

[1] Although much of modern personnel work in larger firms is automated by electronic data-collection systems, this chapter will not discuss the peculiar problems of electronic systems; general principles of records maintenance and dissemination are sufficient for the purposes of this text. The reader interested in computer-related personnel records issues is directed to A. WESTIN, COMPUTERS, PERSONNEL ADMINISTRATION AND CITIZEN RIGHTS (National Bureau of Standards Special Publication No. 500-50, 1979).

[2] For discussions of the abstract principles of privacy, see Beaney, The Right to Privacy and American Law, 31 LAW & CONTEMP. PROBS. 253 (1966); Jourard, Some Psychological Aspects of Privacy, 31 LAW & CONTEMP. PROBS. 307 (1966); Karst, The Files: Legal Controls Over the Accuracy and Accessibility of Stored Personal Data, 31 LAW & CONTEMP. PROBS. 342 (1966); O'Brien, Privacy and the Right of Access: Purposes and Paradoxes of Information Control, 30 AD. L. REV. 45 (1978); Comment, Employee Pri-vacy Rights: A Proposal, 47 FORDHAM L. REV. 155 (1978). The best discus-sion of privacy's position as a factor in modern American society is in the introductory chapter of PRIVACY PROTECTION STUDY COMMISSION, PERSONAL PRIVACY IN AN INFORMATION SOCIETY (1977).

applications require some surrender of the privacy of details of an individual's life, such as schools attended or previous employers. Privacy can be defined broadly as the right to exclude others from certain knowledge about oneself. Privacy has been defined in many ways, including the right to be left alone, the right to select those to whom sensitive information will be transferred, or the right not to be a subject of others' surveillance or communications.[3] In the employment context, the concept of privacy operates on two levels: the individual's right to maintain his or her privacy about personally sensitive information and the individual's separate expectation that an institutional holder of personal information (e.g., an employer) will not share the individually sensitive information with other institutions or persons. The second level is the one of greatest current controversy. Because each of us shares some personal data to obtain employment, advancement, benefits, licenses, etc., the institutional custodians of the information that we have shared will be making disclosure decisions that will affect our interests.

To illustrate the first level, an individual who applies for a voluntary government program may be offended to find on the application a probing question about past psychiatric treatment. The individual may decide not to seek participation in the program rather than to share the personal data. At the second level, an employee of twenty years' experience may wish the employer to share his or her salary history with prospective mortgage lenders but not with a life insurance company. The institutional privacy issue also includes the individual's opportunity to look at the institution's record about him or her and to have errors in the record corrected.

There *is* an employee privacy issue, then, which is a major issue for employees, employers, and the government. Unions have been relatively silent on privacy issues;[4] civil liberties ad-

---

[3] Tracing the concept back to its psychological roots, Jourard finds that privacy is related to "the act of concealment." It is "an outcome of a person's wish to withhold from others certain knowledge as to his past and present experience and action and his intentions for the future." Because each of us feels institutional pressures to conform to the group, the privacy of individual life must to some extent be traded for institutional benefits. Jourard, *supra* note 2, at 307.

[4] PRIVACY PROTECTION STUDY COMMISSION, *supra* note 2, at 253; *see Employment Records*, in PRIVACY PROTECTION STUDY COMMISSION, PERSONAL PRIVACY IN AN INFORMATION SOCIETY, app. 3, at 65, 69 (1977) [hereinafter cited as *Employment Records*]. The finding was based upon testimony by unions and examination of several firms' practices.

vocacy groups have taken on themselves many of the lobbying and argumentation tasks that a union would have performed had this been an economic, rather than a social, issue.[5] This chapter examines attitudes, principles, state action, and the potential for future legislation. Those portions of employment records concerning medical history are addressed in chapter X, and records of chemical exposure and related occupational health are discussed in chapter XVI.

ATTITUDES ABOUT EMPLOYEE PRIVACY

The two levels of privacy discussed above, individual selection of persons to whom privacy information will be disclosed and institutional control of records about individual employees, are perceived differently by the public. Individual privacy has been a very public matter since the late 1960s; there has been a multitude of books, articles, and seminars relating to surveillance, governmental abuses, and the like. The Privacy Act of 1974 was the major governmental response of the 1970s to privacy concerns, but it was narrowly focused on governmental actions.[6] Institutional safeguarding of privacy rights, on the other hand, has just begun to be studied in the past several years. The surrogate role of the institution as a protector of personal privacy has begun to attract studies of employee expectations. The attitudes about how well the employer and other institutions protect (and should protect) personal information are interesting.

A 1979 study [7] done for Sentry Insurance found that 70 percent of the study respondents favored a law to require that employees have rights of access to personnel files about them. Safeguarding of the information in employee medical and personnel files against disclosure to third parties was favored by 92 percent. Almost as many, 83 percent, felt it "very important" that employers notify employees prior to releasing personal information from their files, except in the cases of regular and legally required government reports. Eighty-eight percent felt

---

5 The American Civil Liberties Union has been the most active advocate of worker privacy protections. Its *Civil Liberties Review* has published several studies of workplace privacy. *See, e.g.,* Hayden, *How Much Does the Boss Need to Know?,* Civ. Lib. Rev. Aug./Sept. 1976, at 23.

6 5 U.S.C. § 552a (1976). *See* chapter VII *supra.*

7 Louis Harris poll for Sentry Insurance, *reprinted in* Business Roundtable Privacy Task Force, Fair Information Practices: A Time for Action (1980) [hereinafter cited as Roundtable Report].

that employees should see their supervisors' reports relating to employee suitability for promotion. When asked to select from a list of institutions that ask for too much personal information, 45 percent of the sample of 1,512 respondents listed finance companies, 38 percent listed insurance companies, while only 25 percent felt that employers asked for too much personal information.

The former chairman of the federal Privacy Protection Study Commission, Professor David Linowes, surveyed employers [8] and found that 76 percent of those surveyed allowed individual employees to have access to their files, and 46 percent allowed copying of the file by the employee. Only 31 percent, however, had policies on routine disclosure of personnel records to non-governmental third parties. When asked about routine disclosure of personal data to third parties, 85 percent routinely disclosed such information to credit grantors, 49 percent to landlords, and 22 percent to charitable organizations. That 1979 study also found that 83 percent of the companies surveyed verified or supplemented the background data that they collected from employees, but only 25 percent allowed individuals to see this information.

A random poll by the American Civil Liberties Union (ACLU) of 240 respondents nationwide [9] in an approximately average survey sample produced comparable responses to those of the Sentry Insurance poll. Almost 60 percent considered a right to see personnel records to be very important, and an overwhelming majority favored statutory rights of access to personnel records by employees and rights of access to employee ratings of promotability. Only 14 percent, however, said that employers had ever asked for information that the employee felt he or she should not have been required to provide. Unlike those conducting the other studies, the ACLU asked which of the personnel records was considered most sensitive. Job performance ratings were highest on the list, followed by salary, health records, psychological information, references and comments on attitudes, and personal histories. Other information, including police record, attendance, etc., was less sensitive to the sampled group.

----

[8] The University of Illinois study of corporate privacy protection policies is reported in Linowes, *Privacy and Big Business, Selected Observations of Research Survey Findings,* in ROUNDTABLE REPORT, *supra* note 7.

[9] This ACLU poll is reported in Westin, *Privacy and Personal Records: A Look at Employee Attitudes,* CIV. LIB. REV., Jan./Feb. 1978, at 28. It is discussed in detail, including methodology, in A. WESTIN, *supra* note 1, at 278-92.

The attitude surveys are an indication of the importance of the human, not merely legal and labor relations, issues in employee privacy. When privacy rights are discussed in terms of legal principles, it is important to recognize also that they have a human dimension—the feelings, fears, and expectations of individual workers about their sensitive information in the employer's files.[10] As many employers become sensitive to the privacy concern, the legal aspects of compliance, such as state laws policing the handling of personnel records, will perhaps become less important. Groups like the Business Roundtable's Privacy Task Force are performing the educational role among employers that may eventually obviate the need for government pressures to regulate private information practices.[11]

UNIONS AND PRIVACY ISSUES

Although individuals have shown great sensitivity to privacy protection principles, as discussed above, unions have not. The discussions among employers, government and legislative sponsors of privacy initiatives, and civil liberties groups have only rarely included active union participation.[12] The federal Privacy Protection Study Commission, created by Congress to study such issues as private sector employee privacy, "got the impression that unions are not very concerned about their members' access to the records employers maintain about them." [13] The United Auto Workers observed that the issue seldom comes up in collective bargaining, that member inquiries on the subject are rare, and that requests for access to or correction of employment

---

10 Employees' fears are reflected best in A. WESTIN, *supra* note 1, at 288-89, which cites some of the random sample's anonymous comments. One stated, "I'm more concerned about my professional organization/union. To 'help' others they wanted information from me I was reluctant to give. In the end I was hurt." *Id.* 288. Another said, "Lots of employers are damn nosy and are determined to stop people with ambition." *Id.* 287.

11 ROUNDTABLE REPORT, *supra* note 7. The Business Roundtable conducted seminars for discussion of fair information practices in Chicago, Houston, New York, Los Angeles, and Washington, D.C., in 1979-80.

12 For example, the discussions of the federal legislation that became the Privacy Act of 1974 did not contain union participants, and the involvement of unions in the Privacy Commission was far less than that of academics and business witnesses. The relatively slight public sector union interest in Privacy Act matters is addressed in chapter VIII on federal privacy legislation.

13 *Employment Records, supra* note 4, at 65.

records are handled informally when they occur.[14] In the communications field, the Commission learned that 41 percent of Bell System union contracts with the Communications Workers of America gave employees rights to inspect employment records, but 47 percent made no provision, and the remainder allowed periodic inspections.[15]

Employers have been uniformly consistent in saying that few if any employees ask for access to their personnel records.[16] A 16,000-employee manufacturer told the Commission that it had never had any requests.[17] General Electric found very little interest in access or correction of records, except of course for payroll checks and W-2 tax-withholding forms.[18] Where state laws allow access to records, the laws are very infrequently utilized by employees of either private or public employers.[19] Although the elaborate mechanisms for access serve a sound protective purpose in theory, people are simply not conditioned to inquire about collection of personal information by institutions, as evidenced in 1980 by Ohio's decision to phase out its state privacy office when that office found it had an average of *one* public inquiry per month.[20] Employers can reasonably doubt the need for extensive programs, given such a pattern of disinterest.

Union interest in employee privacy rights has been significant in only two areas of private sector activity. First, unions have been the major advocates of state prohibitions on the use of polygraphs or other lie-detection devices.[21] State laws banning the

---

[14] *Id.*

[15] *Id.* But the same union challenged the withholding from workers and unions of medical records, asserting that "negative information from the medical record was the source of most suspensions and dismissals." *Id.*

[16] *Id.* at 66. *See also* A. WESTIN, *supra* note 1, at 218, 230 (only 30 of 35,000 Rockwell employees in California asked for access to their files when such access was allowed under state law; Bank of America, on the other hand, had about 100 requests per month shortly after the enactment of the California access law).

[17] *Employment Records, supra* note 4, at 66.

[18] *Id.*

[19] Shell Oil had only about a one percent request rate, and Rockwell International's rate was less than one-tenth of one percent. *Id.* at 69.

[20] Gordon, *An End to the Privacy Board,* Cincinnati Post, Feb. 20, 1980, n.p.

[21] This labor movement opposition was led by the Teamsters and the Retail Clerks, with support from the headquarters of the AFL-CIO. *See* Walters & Gunn, *Appraising Retailers' Use of the Polygraph,* RETAILING, Winter

use of the polygraph on employees, or job applicants, have come to be numerous, fed by suspicions about the accuracy of the equipment and its interpreters [22] and by union beliefs that the employees are unfairly coerced to concede an important personal privacy right as a condition of continued employment.[23] Prohibitions against the polygraph have civil liberties groups' support [24] and have attracted support in the legal literature.[25]

A second aspect of union activity is to fight those privacy initiatives that inhibit unions' gathering of information. In one federal case under the Privacy Act, a union lost contractually bargained sources of information about employees when customary union access was not permitted to continue after passage of the federal Privacy Act.[26] Unions have not been shy about wishing to maintain their sources of information. In at least one company studied for a National Bureau of Standards (NBS) report on employment records privacy, unions that had formerly enjoyed free, informal access to personnel files lost that access when the employer adopted a personnel records privacy policy.[27] When the Privacy Protection Study Commis-

---

1968, at 10, 16. AFL-CIO support has been effective in a number of states. *See* Committee on Labor and Social Security Legislation, Association of the Bar of the City of New York, *The Polygraph in Employment: The Consequences of its Search for Truth*, 28 REC. A.B. CITY N.Y. 464 (1973) [hereinafter cited as *New York Bar Report*].

[22] *New York Bar Report, supra* note 21; Craver, *The Inquisitorial Process in Private Employment*, 63 CORNELL L. REV. (1977); Comment, *Employee Privacy Rights: A Proposal*, 47 FORDHAM L. REV. 155, 185 (1978).

[23] Hayden, *supra* note 5, at 38; Markson, *A Reexamination of the Role of Lie Detectors in Labor Relations*, 22 LABOR L. J. 394 (1971). The potential chilling effects and constitutional ramifications are discussed in *Employment Records, supra* note 4, at 44-45; STAFF OF SUBCOMM. ON CONSTITUTIONAL RIGHTS OF SENATE COMM. ON THE JUDICIARY, 93D CONG., 2D SESS., PRIVACY, POLYGRAPHS, AND EMPLOYMENT (Comm. Print 1974); *The Use of Polygraphs and Similar Devices by Federal Agencies: Hearings Before a Subcomm. of the House Comm. on Government Operations*, 94th Cong., 2d Sess. (1976) .

[24] Hayden, *supra* note 5; *see* A. WESTIN, PRIVACY AND FREEDOM (1967).

[25] Craver, *supra* note 22; Markson, *supra* note 23; *New York Bar Report, supra* note 21; Comment, *Privacy: The Polygraph in Employment*, 30 ARK. L. REV. (1976). Of the more than thirty states that have legislated in this field, about one-half have some type of ban on the employment use of the polygraph, while one-half require licensing of the examiner.

[26] Local 2047, Am. Fed'n of Gov't Employees v. Defense Gen. Supply Center, 423 F. Supp. 481 (E.D. Va. 1976), *aff'd*, 573 F.2d 184 (4th Cir. 1978).

[27] Cummins Engine Company at one time allowed free access by unions to personnel files; this ended when a policy of privacy protection was instituted. A. WESTIN, *supra* note 1, at 237.

sion recommended a limitation of the set of permissible recipients for personnel data, it included a provision for unions to receive personal data routinely (as stated in the contract) for unit employees.[28] Although privacy has rarely been a subject of collective bargaining, it can be expected that employer-initiated programs of limiting access to personal information will generate counterprograms by unions to continue each union's current status as a permissible recipient of that information.[29]

PRINCIPLES REGULATING EMPLOYMENT RECORDS

Under common-law principles, invasion of privacy of an individual by another individual was not a tort offense until the development in recent decades of judicially recognized rights to preserve one's privacy from unwarranted public intrusion. When an employer developed a written record about an employee, the record was the legal property of the employer, and there were no restraints on either acquisition methods or dissemination.[30] When the employee was the subject of an inquiry, the employer enjoyed an unqualified privilege to communicate adverse infor-

---

[28] PRIVACY PROTECTION STUDY COMMISSION, *supra* note 2, at 273 (Recommendation 33(f)).

[29] The UAW won personnel records access rights in 1980 from Ford, GM, and Chrysler. Presumably, only a statutory or regulation-based refusal of access to records could override the union's contractual collective bargaining right of access, but unions will have to be sensitive to both the legislative climate, adding exceptions into statutory restrictions on dissemination, and the climate of contract situations, so that access rights are maintained when privacy of personnel records becomes a management concern for the employer. It may be premature to ask whether the union's argument for its access based on no more than the collective implied consent of unionized individuals is sufficient to protect the privacy of individuals. Because unions themselves are institutions and are not above breaching individual privacy rights for some collective goal—a trait of most institutions—the employer and employee/individual may in some cases be allied against the desires of the organization which represents the workers collectively. UAW access is described in *Privacy in the Workplace: Hearings Before U.S. Department of Labor* (Mar. 6, 1980) (testimony of the United Automobile Workers).

[30] "Upon entering into employment, every individual implicitly surrenders a certain amount of 'privacy' to the employer which thereafter must be regarded as the employer's information. We do not accept as valid the contention that information about an individual is intrinsically the 'property' or 'right' of that individual." Letter from the Association of Washington Business to the Privacy Protection Study Commission, *quoted in Employment Records, supra* note 4, at 68.

mation.[31] The contents of the record could be as relevant, timely, or correct as the employer or the contracted investigators chose to make that record. A National Bureau of Standards report summarized it best:

> [T]he law does not guarantee anyone a right to work or to be retained in a job once hired. In terms of information-collection and record-keeping, it is accepted as legitimate that employers will collect and verify personal data and work history about job applicants and will maintain extensive records about employees for purposes of payroll, benefit administration, performance evaluation, security, and many other employment matters.[32]

The NBS study drew an important distinction between the privacy of records in episodic, infrequent situations, such as credit applications or licensing, and the continuing relationship of employment. Formal records are less important to the employer, given the many other aspects of total knowledge about a person that are available to the supervisors of the employee.[33] The same study noted, however, that records are frequently imposed upon the employer by law or administrative rule in such matters as occupational exposure, health programs, and equal employment opportunity. So records are both somewhat less important to the employer and somewhat more frequently retained for nonemployer reasons than is the case in credit-related recordkeeping.

When the common-law rules regarding employment records are affected by state or federal law, the result is not always a consistent or useful program. For example, an employer that chooses not to make inquiries regarding the race or national origin of employees may be forced to do so in order to comply with government-imposed reporting obligations.[34] When state

---

[31] Note, *Qualified Privilege to Defame Employees and Credit Applicants,* 12 HARV. CIV. RIGHTS CIV. LIB. L. REV. 143 (1977). The note's author attempts to undo the existing privilege in pursuit of an additional remedy for individuals by expanding upon the slim reed of a state appellate court opinion—Harrison v. Arrow Metal Prods. Corp., 20 Mich.App. 590, 174 N.W.2d 875 (1969). Despite the author's craftsmanship, the qualified privilege seems to be alive and well in most states outside of Michigan.

[32] A. WESTIN, *supra* note 1, at 294.

[33] *Id.* at 295. For example, an employer's day-to-day personal impressions count for much more than a distant credit-granting firm's paper review of a prospective borrower's credit status.

[34] For example, preparation of a Work Force Analysis is required as part of the Office of Federal Contract Compliance Programs' required monitoring reports for those contractors who are subject to Affirmative Action Plan rules. *See* 41 C.F.R. §§ 60-1.1 to 60-741.54 (1979).

laws require the disclosure of personnel records to state agencies and the records are not sufficiently protected from public disclosure or leaks to the public, then the privacy of the employee is jeopardized.[35] Limitations on the collection of arrest records by employers or prohibitions on listing of past convictions may expose the public to the risk of recurrent criminal activity by the newly hired employee who becomes a recidivist while on the job. There is, inescapably, a shifting of the cost of repeated crime from society in general to the employer and the employer's shareholders and customers when the person with a record that has been cleaned by statute proves unexpectedly to have been inclined from past conduct to criminal pursuits. The societal benefit is the rehabilitative assistance to those not inclined to repeat the earlier errors.

The principles governing employee records practices in the 1980s will be statutory, with perhaps some additional judicial creativity in the matter of common-law privacy rights.[36] As of 1980, states that require employee access to employee records include California,[37] Connecticut,[38] Maine,[39] Michigan,[40] Oregon,[41]

---

[35] Acquisition of the file by a government agency subjects the file to the potential for leaks by persons whose interests may be adverse to either the employer or particular employees. It may also subject the file to inadvertent delivery to an information requester, or to formal transfer of copies of the file to persons requesting access to the documents as a "public record." It is not clear, however, that such personal information would be accessible; disclosure and withholding rules will vary from state to state. *See* 2 J. O'REILLY, FEDERAL INFORMATION DISCLOSURE ¶¶ 27-1 to 27-18 (Supp. 1979).

[36] For example, if polygraphs are not banned by state or federal law, a court could not ban their use in employment on constitutional grounds unless it were to construct some elongated theory of state action reaching into the private employer's transactions. This constitutional approach has been considered but is unlikely to succeed. Absent a legislative approach, "one must struggle to define a remedy based on privacy which is available against a private employer." Comment, *supra* note 25, at 35, 42. Another option seems to be the extension of arbitration decisions into other grievance-arbitration systems so that successful challenges to the polygraph or to other privacy issues would have recurring impact as precedents for other employee units. This is the approach advocated in Craver, *supra* note 25.

[37] CAL. LAB. CODE § 1198.5 (West Supp. 1980).

[38] Pub. Act No. 79-264, 1979 Conn. Legis. Serv. (West).

[39] ME. REV. STAT. ANN. tit. 26, § 631 (West 1979).

[40] MICH. COMP. LAWS §§ 423.501-.512 (West Supp. 1979).

[41] OR. REV. STAT. § 652.750 (1977).

and Pennsylvania.[42] Michigan's law is the most comprehensive. Employees have rights of access and may copy their records at cost.[43] Amendment or correction can be requested, or disputing statements by the employee placed into the file. Records used in employment or disciplinary decisions are covered. Access to certain records is excluded—for example, grievance and security investigations, certain medical records elsewhere available, educational records, certain references, and certain supervisory and personnel planning records of the employer.[44]

Michigan's law incorporated some of the federal Privacy Commission's recommendations and contains a section comparable to the federal Privacy Act limitation on permissible acquisition.[45] No employer can collect certain personal information on employees without written employee consent if the information relates to nonemployment personal activity, such as associations or employee publications. Investigative files are to be kept separate from the personnel file, and employees are to be informed of the files' existence at the end of the investigation (or two years after its beginning, whichever is earlier). Files on investigations will be destroyed if no disciplinary action is taken.[46]

Pennsylvania's law and Connecticut's 1979 enactment, as well as the Michigan law, permit corrections to be made in an incorrect record, but none of the states that permit employee access give such rights to applicants who were not hired. Employees who were laid off or placed on leaves of absence are covered by the Pennsylvania law. Former employees are permitted access to their employment records in Connecticut, Maine, and Michigan (and in Oregon for a period of sixty days after termination[47]).

RECOMMENDATIONS OF THE STUDY COMMISSION

When the federal Privacy Act of 1974 was adopted, consideration of private sector employment records was deferred

---

42 PA. STAT. ANN. tit. 43, §§ 1321-24 (Purdon Supp. 1979).

43 MICH. COMP. LAWS § 423.504 (West Supp. 1979).

44 *Id.* § 423.501(c).

45 *Id.* § 423.508; *accord,* 5 U.S.C. § 552a(e)(7) (1976).

46 MICH. COMP. LAWS §§ 423.508-.509 (West Supp. 1979).

47 Oregon law requires the records to be kept and to be available for that sixty-day period. OR. REV. STAT. § 652.750(b)(3) (1977). No other state statute requires preservation of these records.

for inquiry by a group that was established to examine the potential expansion of the nonfederal provisions of the Act. The group, the Privacy Protection Study Commission, issued its final report in July 1977 and made several specific recommendations relating to employment records.[48]

First, the Commission called on employers to adopt voluntarily what it considered to be fair information practices policies.[49] Limits on collection of certain personal information were encouraged.[50] Informing workers of the types and uses of personal data collected and of the means of access to that information that would be made available to workers was strongly recommended. The Commission encouraged employers to adopt reasonable procedures to assure accuracy of the information. It also recommended that an employee have an opportunity to correct or amend files or place statements of disagreement in them if he or she believes the files to be incorrect.[51] "Open records" would be designated by the employer, and explanations of how to gain access would be distributed to employees. Among the records suggested to be open are performance evaluations, medical information and reports, insurance, credit investigations of the employee, and other personal data.[52] The employer could designate which records, such as security files, would not be open to employee review.[53]

---

[48] PRIVACY PROTECTION STUDY COMMISSION, *supra* note 2.

[49] *Id.* 237 (Recommendation 2). This fair practice policy would include limiting collection to relevant data; informing of uses to be made of the data; informing of types of records maintained; adopting reasonable procedures to assure accuracy; permitting access and copying, correction or amendment of individual records; limiting internal use and external disclosures; and regularly reviewing compliance with this policy.

[50] *Id.* 250 (Recommendation 14).

[51] *Id.* 256 (Recommendation 17).

[52] *Id.* "[A]n employer should not designate as an unavailable record any recorded evaluation it makes of an individual's employment performance, any medical record or insurance record it keeps about an individual, or any record about an individual that it obtains from a consumer-reporting agency . . . or otherwise creates about an individual in the course of an investigation related to an employment decision not involving suspicion of wrongdoing. . . ." *Id.* 256.

[53] It should be noted that the Commission was aware that unavailable records could be made available by collective bargaining. "Without a union, however, employees who complain of violations of an internal policy on employee access to records have little protection from reprisals and no right of appeal if their complaints are ignored." *Id.* 254.

The Commission recommended that insurance claims and security records receive special treatment. Insurance records would not be available for use by the employer's supervisory personnel, especially health records.[54] Security files would be stored separately, and employees would be informed if the records were transferred into the employee's personnel file [55] (this suggestion was enacted into law in the Michigan privacy statute [56]).

Specific Privacy Commission suggestions for legislation included amendments to the Fair Credit Reporting Act (FCRA) and enactment of a prohibition against employers' use of polygraphs or similar equipment for truth verification.[57] The FCRA changes would prohibit interviews under the pretext of credit application checks,[58] would require employers to use care in selecting an organization to perform the investigative checks,[59] would require notice to the subject before credit investigations are run on him or her in the employment context,[60] would permit viewing of the investigative report (more frequently than under present terms of the FCRA [61]), and would require the employee's waiver of any confidentiality rights in statements permitting other persons to have access to personal credit files to be legible, specific and narrow in purpose, scope, and expiration of the authority given to the disclosing firm.[62]

In addition to the above changes, the Commission encouraged the military services to alter their discharge report coding systems and to make efforts to undo past coding-related discrimination.[63] It suggested that law enforcement agencies tighten ac-

54 *Id.* 268 (Recommendation 30).

55 *Id.* 266 (Recommendation 27).

56 MICH. COMP. LAWS §§ 423.508-.509 (West Supp. 1979).

57 PRIVACY PROTECTION STUDY COMMISSION, *supra* note 2, at 239 (Recommendation 3).

58 *Id.* 240 (Recommendation 4).

59 *Id.* 241 (Recommendation 5).

60 *Id.* 250 (Recommendation 14).

61 *Id.* 258 (Recommendation 18).

62 *Id.* 252 (Recommendation 16).

63 *Id.* 249 (Recommendation 13). This recommendation deals with the separation papers given upon release from the military, which are coded with reasons for the release of the person, e.g., character disorders, mental instability, etc.

cess to arrest records.[64] The Commission suggested that arrest records not be used in employment or licensing decisions [65] and that only "directly relevant" convictions be placed into employment records.[66]

If the Privacy Protection Study Commission recommendations were voluntarily adopted, the Commission hoped, then there would be greater attention to the individual's expectations of privacy. The employees would be able to rely on the employer as protector of their sensitive personal data. Employers would not routinely disclose the employee's personal file information, except for narrowly permissible reasons (including the obligations of a collective bargaining contract that compels the sharing of certain information with the union).[67]

ADMINISTRATION AND PUBLIC RESPONSES

The Commission's report of July 1977 was significant for what it did not produce—it did not force a tough public debate on privacy issues and did not put before Congress a recommended federal law for private sector employee privacy rights.

It was April 1979 before the Carter Administration's privacy program was unveiled. The presidential statement said:

> The Privacy Commission recommended against Federal legislation on employment records and proposed instead that employers be asked to establish voluntary policies to protect their employees' privacy. I agree.
>
> Many employers are already adopting the standards established by the Commission. Business groups, including the Business Roundtable, the Chamber of Commerce, and the National Association of Manufacturers, are encouraging such voluntary action. I urge other employers to take similar action, and I have instructed the Secretary of Labor to work with employer and employee groups in the implementation of these standards.[68]

---

[64] *Id.* 245 (Recommendation 9).

[65] *Id.* 245 (Recommendation 10).

[66] *Id.* 246 (Recommendation 12).

[67] *Id.* 273 (Recommendation 33(f)). This recommendation would permit sharing of the information with the collective bargaining representative. *See* the Privacy Protection Study Commission's discussion of union-won concessions on employees' access to records. *Id.* 254.

[68] *President's Message to Congress on Proposals to Protect the Privacy of Individuals*, 15 WEEKLY COMP. OF PRES. DOC. 581, 584 (Apr. 2, 1979) [hereinafter cited as *President's Privacy Message*].

Each of the Commission's legislative suggestions was introduced into proposed legislation, including the prohibition on polygraphs,[69] provision for military discharge code remedies,[70] and credit investigation reforms.[71]

The Labor Department began hearings on voluntary private sector action on workplace privacy in December 1979.[72] The Department's primary effort was to ascertain the experience of business firms with the Commission's 1977 privacy policy recommendations. The essence of its "state of the art" review was the workability of the Commission's suggestions in the private business community. In its October 1979 *Federal Register* notice announcing the study, the Labor Department listed the Commission recommendations and followed them with a set of experience questions to determine how much use there had been of records access rights, how policies of privacy protection had affected business costs and employees' rights, and whether privacy recommendations of the Commission had in any cases proved impractical or too costly.[73]

PRESENT AND FUTURE CONTROVERSIES

The major controversy over employment records is whether private sector voluntary action will be sufficient to provide employees with an adequate assurance of fair information practice. Most of the arguments seem to weigh in favor of voluntary action without federal intervention. First, several states have adopted or are considering information and privacy bills, and ninety-four fair information practices bills were introduced in state legislatures in 1977-78 alone;[74] second, the diversity of

---

[69] S. 854 and H.R. 2349, 96th Cong., 1st Sess. (1979). The Administration endorsed these bills. *President's Privacy Message, supra* note 68, at 584.

[70] H.R. 759 was not part of the Administration's privacy program announced on April 2, 1979. H.R. 759, 96th Cong., 1st Sess. (1979) .

[71] H.R. 2465, H.R. 5559, 96th Cong., 1st Sess. (1979).

[72] 44 Fed. Reg. 75,755 (1979).

[73] 44 Fed. Reg. 57,537 (1979).

[74] In 1977-78, 350 privacy and freedom of information bills were introduced in thirty-six state legislatures, of which 94 were fair information practices type bills and 38 dealt with criminal records. *Right to Privacy Proposals of the Privacy Protection Study Commission: Hearings on H.R. 10076 Before the Subcomm. on Government Information and Individual Rights of the House Comm. on Government Operations*, 95th Cong., 2d Sess. 395 (1978) (statement of David Linowes, former Chairman, Privacy Protection Study Commission).

information systems and information needs in the private sector
makes any regulatory scheme a difficult drafting and enforcement task; [75] and third, the employees who have been told of
their access rights have rarely exercised them, for whatever reasons.[76] The desire for better protection of rights of individuals
might better be met by private remedies, such as the private
remedies for Privacy Act enforcement. Neither the Congress
nor the states nor the public seem to be eager to create a
privacy protection bureaucracy to enforce what should be self-
enforced rights of individuals.[77]

A second controversy will be the collection of information on
private, nonemployment activities. A union appointed a new
shop steward at a nuclear power plant construction site because
the former shop steward had off-the-job contacts with an antinuclear power group. The construction worker sued the union.
Another, in a similar situation on the same site, also has sued
the union in a case involving freedom of association with antinuclear groups.[78] There is no constitutional right to keep a job
or to dissent against substantive policies of a private employer
(absent some statutory provision protecting certain forms of
protests against unsafe working conditions or for union representation, etc.),[79] and it may never be politically or constitutionally possible for government to force a private employer
to retain an employee whose attitudes appear to the employer to
be disloyal, absent some protection of antidiscrimination laws
for the worker's ethnic or racial group. Only in a few tentative
ways, such as the recent Supreme Court decision rejecting po-

---

[75] This was one of the rationales for not regulating the private sector with
an elaborate system like the federal Privacy Act. PRIVACY PROTECTION STUDY
COMMISSION, *supra* note 2, at 27-28.

[76] A. WESTIN, *supra* note 1, at 230. Less than one-tenth of one percent of
Rockwell's 35,000 California workers had used their California statutory
rights of inspection. *Id.*

[77] Westin found that, in a survey, 62 percent opposed a government privacy
system, and one wrote in the margin: "Absolute[ly] not! If government gets
into it, I will have no privacy." *Id.* at 286.

[78] Cerra, *Con Edison Worker Sues Union In Dispute on Atom Plant Safety,*
N.Y. Times, Jan. 8, 1980, at B6, col. 1. The worker obtained an outside
speaker for an off-site meeting of workers; the union learned of the outside
speaker's antinuclear affiliation and removed the worker as shop steward. He
filed a federal suit on constitutional and Landrum-Griffin Act grounds.

[79] This is best discussed in A. WESTIN, *supra* note 1, at 294-300.

litical patronage as a condition of public employment,[80] have the federal courts accepted arguments that nonemployment activities cannot be considered in the retention of employees. In the meantime, the trend appears to be toward lessening the acquisition of information about employees' nonemployment-related activities.[81]

A third controversy may be the rights of unions to detailed personal information about members and other employees of the bargaining unit. The preceding chapters discussed this in the NLRB context. It may eventually come to a clash between workers as individuals, desiring employers to retain their files in confidence,[82] and unions as representatives of the group, demanding access to the individual's file over his or her objection. Some of the established traditions of union access to information may eventually become entangled in the controversial issue of limited access to individual information, as has already occurred in the public sector.[83] If unions are able to negotiate a position of mandatory contractual access to personnel files, as the United Auto Workers have been able to do in their 1979-80 contracts with major auto manufacturers, then these worker-privacy disagreements may be "solved for the individual" by the union's judgment on who will gain access to the records and when.[84]

---

[80] Branti v. Finkel, 48 U.S.L.W. 4331 (1980).

[81] Some employers have redrafted their application forms to avoid these areas. *See* A. WESTIN, *supra* note 1, at 227.

[82] Such as a worker offended at union use of personal information for union ends at the cost of the worker's privacy. *Id.* 288.

[83] *See* Local 2047, Am. Fed'n of Gov't Employees v. Defense Gen. Supply Center, 423 F. Supp. 481 (E.D. Va. 1976), *aff'd*, 573 F.2d 184 (4th Cir. 1978).

[84] *Privacy in the Workplace: Hearings Before U.S. Department of Labor* (Mar. 6, 1980) (statement of Alan Reuther for the United Automobile Workers). Ford alone of the "Big Three" also permitted unlimited employee access to medical records for individual employees by agreement with the UAW.

CHAPTER X

The Private Sector: Disclosure and Medical Records Privacy

The use and protection against misuse of an employee's medical and psychological records constitute one of the most sensitive issues on the current labor-management scene. For the federal government, the employer, the employee, and the union, medical records disclosure is also one of the most tangled issues with conflicting legal, ethical, political, and economic aspects.

ROOTS OF MEDICAL RECORDS PRIVACY

Privacy of medical information may be generally defined as the right of the individual subject of a health record to determine how information will be placed into the record, for what purposes it will be used, and to whom the record will be disclosed. As a concept, privacy of health information has the benefit of centuries of traditional protection. The physician takes the Hippocratic Oath, which includes a promise of preserving the patient's confidences.[1] Traditionally, legal systems have recognized certain rights not to disclose privileged secrets; in most states today, by statutory privileges, the protection of physician-patient confidential statements is assured, although the terms of the privilege vary with the terms of different state statutes.[2] Some states protect all medical files, while others

---

[1] "Whatsoever things I see or hear concerning the life of man, in any attendance on the sick or even apart therefrom which ought not to be noised about, I will keep silent thereon, counting such things to be inviolably sacred." Hippocratic oath, *quoted in* Annas, *Legal Aspects of Medical Confidentiality in the Occupational Setting*, 18 J. OCCUPATIONAL MED. 537 (1976).

[2] *See, e.g.*, OHIO REV. CODE ANN. §§ 2317.02, 4731.22 (Page Supp. 1979). States without the privilege include Texas, Vermont, South Carolina, and Rhode Island. Six more states have very limited privilege statutes. R. SMITH, PRIVACY: HOW TO PROTECT WHAT'S LEFT OF IT 133-35 (1979).

cover only embarrassing information about the patient.[3] The codes of ethics for physicians, including those of the American Medical Association,[4] expressly respect patient confidentiality. Finally, state medical licensing statutes require a physician to withhold the confidential statements of patients from public discussion, unless the patient's consent is first obtained, under penalty of license suspension.[5]

The patient-physician communication privilege reflects a societal agreement with the medical profession's self-selected system of promising secrecy. That promise is a matter of quid pro quo: the maximum amount of information should be shared with the physician, exposing the full secrets of the patient, so that medical attention can be provided to the fullest extent. The physician receives more information because the patient can rely upon the physician's nondisclosure of those confidences.

It is estimated that 95 percent of medical care provided by corporate health units may not be "occupational" medical care.[6] The means by which workers receive health care vary. Often, the minor, nonoccupational care is provided by employer-paid physicians rendering medical services to employees. Workers' colds and flu symptoms probably top the statistical list for miscellaneous medical visits. Some of the medical care paid for by employers is provided by private physicians in their own general practice offices, where the worker's job-related health examinations and treatment are part of the normal care of individual patients by the physician. This is particularly the case in small-

---

[3] Pennsylvania has the narrower, archaic provision. PA. STAT. ANN. tit. 28, § 328 (Purdon 1958).

[4] "A physician may not reveal the confidences entrusted to him in the course of medical attendance, or the deficiencies he may observe in the character of patients, unless he is required to do so by law or unless it becomes necessary in order to protect the welfare of the individual or the community." AMA Canons of Medical Ethics, *quoted in* Annas, *supra* note 1, at 537.

[5] State licensing statutes can be the basis for civil tort actions against a physician who wrongly discloses a patient's confidential medical information, Horne v. Patton, 291 Ala. 701, 287 So.2d 824 (1973).

[6] *Access to Employee Medical and Exposure Records: Hearings Before U.S. Occupational Safety and Health Administration*, Docket No. H-112 [hereinafter cited as *Employee Records Hearings*] (Dec. 1978) (testimony of Dr. Bernacki, United Technologies Corp.). OSHA witnesses at the same hearings, Drs. Teitelbaum and Whorton, agreed that many items in the medical record were not strictly occupational but included personal difficulties as well.

town, small-plant settings, in which the worker and his family
may be regular patients of the physician who also conducts
medical examinations, keeps records, and cares for job-related
conditions at the office under contract to the employer.[7] Occasionally, the occupational physician employed by the employer
plant conducts a side practice from a different medical office
that serves the personal needs of workers, their families, and
other individuals.

An important conceptual barrier must be broken before one
can discuss workplace medical records: not all, and perhaps
not even a majority, are distinct corporate files within corporate
control and prepared by corporate employees who are physicians.
There is a very mixed bag of records, and once this mixed bag
is placed in the general files of practicing physicians the problems of an employer's granting either government or union
access to the records are exacerbated.[8]

THE CLASSES OF MEDICAL RECORDS

For purposes of this discussion, health *history* records and
health *condition* records are considered separately. A health
history reveals the past status of the worker's medical condition. Alcoholism, venereal disease incidents, drug dependence
episodes, nervous conditions, and other embarrassing details of
the worker's past history are particularly sensitive items. If the
physician is to help the patient, the patient must communicate
these self-revealing admissions. Since as much as 95 percent
of medical department treatments may not be of "occupational"
ailments, much of the information contained in records will be
more relevant to personal problems or conditions than to
workplace injuries or exposure-related illnesses induced by workplace conditions. To use any such history requires great sensitivity for the patient's expectation of secrecy. Health history is
very sensitive, because some nonphysician supervisors might

---

[7] In this situation, the OSHA rule would apply to the records despite their
intermingling with personal and family records. *Employee Records Hearings,
supra* note 6 (Dec. 6, 1978) (transcript of cross-examination of Grover
Wrenn, OSHA, at 25).

[8] On the one hand, the OSHA assertion of authority reaches toward the
file, while the physician's obligation to withhold the personal portion of the
file of that individual patient, unless the patient consents, is to the contrary. The AMA vigorously attacked OSHA on this issue; Sammons, *Access to Employee Exposure and Medical Records*, 240 J. A.M.A. 2175 (1978).

wrongly assume that an individual may relapse into alcoholism or show traits of a past drug problem or weaken under stress as a result of some past episode. These items in the history file are considered highly confidential.[9]

The medical history is distinct from the present medical condition. In a current file, the patient's health condition is disclosed; the patient reveals the present status of mind and body to an extent that could either embarrass the individual (e.g., who is trying to cope with an alcohol problem) or could stigmatize him to prevent consideration for promotion or advancement. For example, a tendency toward stress-related digestive problems may be associated with the burdens an individual would face in filling some higher office within the employer's firm. Maintaining the privacy of a patient's current condition is especially important when the worker may be capable of managing a medical problem but fears that the supervisor's or manager's knowledge of that condition would impede progress in the firm, e.g., by a transfer or denial of consideration for a promotion. The employer's physician will report ineligibility recommendations but will not usually divulge the detailed basis for the recommendation without the employee's consent.[10]

Of the two types of records, medical history is perhaps more sensitive than present status for the currently healthy worker. The worker does not want conditions with which he or she is *not* presently afflicted to be part of the consideration of his or her advancement potential or of maintenance in a present assignment.[11] The worker probably wants more confidential treatment for the file of past conditions and for those ongoing conditions that require extended treatment. The current medical

---

[9] This was the consensus of both OSHA and industry physician witnesses. *Employee Records Hearings, supra* note 6.

[10] Collings, *Medical Confidentiality in the Work Environment*, 20 J. OCCUPATIONAL MED. 461 (1978) ; *see* Testimony of the American Occupational Medical Association at *Employee Records Hearings, reported in* CHEMICAL REG. REP. (BNA) 1745 (Dec. 29, 1978).

[11] This is particularly true in the currently controversial area of restricting female workers' exposure to lead or other potentially hazardous substances that could affect reproductive organs. The existence of pregnancy, at least in the early months, is a confidential matter, and some pregnant or possibly pregnant workers would not accept a requirement that they disclose their natural condition to management and accept transfers away from the workplace during pregnancy. The EEOC's response to this situation is found in 45 Fed. Reg. 7514 (1980).

condition information is also sensitive, but many healthy workers would likely object more to disclosure of the history than to disclosure of their present state of fitness for their present work. A recent poll suggested that privacy of medical records was a major concern for Americans generally.[12]

Medical records privacy in the employment situation is different from the same subject in hospital or medical institutional settings, in which the service flows directly from the health professional to the patient. In the factory or worksite situation, the physician has an additional responsibility to assure that the worker will not endanger others in the workplace by virtue of some disabling medical condition. For example, advanced heart disease in a passenger airplane pilot may become manifest in a heart attack while the pilot is at the controls of a plane during landings. The responsibility to the employer does not replace the physician's primary duty to the patient. Officials of the American Occupational Medical Association testifying at a government hearing on medical records disclosure issues stated that the "premise on which a candid, trusting employee-physician relationship is founded" is the sound practice of occupational physicians "not to disclose employee medical information to anyone, including management, unless disclosure is required legally or there is an overriding public health concern." [13]

A subsidiary issue in medical records privacy is the matter of third-party communications contained in the individual's record. If the physician's own objective observations, such as those on blood pressure, may be retained in confidence, what of subjective impressions by consulting physicians and letters received by the physician about the medical problem from relatives or insurors that are placed in the file? In general, these have enjoyed the same privileged status as the other information in the file, subject to the patient's consent.[14] A claim of privilege for *all* the contents of the medical file has generally been respected.

---

[12] A Sentry Insurance Co. poll found that 65 percent of those surveyed want a law protecting medical records privacy and 91 percent want a law requiring access by individuals to their medical records. 125 CONG. REC. H. 3538 (May 21, 1979).

[13] *Physicians Say OSHA Access Proposal Might Harm Employee-Doctor Relationship*, CHEMICAL REG. REP. (BNA) 1745 (Dec. 29, 1978).

[14] But OSHA specifically intends to give access to these items with access to the rest of the file. *Employee Records Hearings, supra* note 6 (Dec. 6, 1978) (transcript of cross-examination of Grover Wrenn, OSHA, at 25).

EMPLOYEE RIGHTS: PREDISCLOSURE CONSENT

The person who is the subject of medical records generally has, by state law, a statutory right to object on grounds of privilege to the use or introduction of those medical records into evidence.[15] In several cases, courts have awarded damages under tort law standards for the nonconsensual disclosure of personal medical information, including the records and photographs of the patient.[16] Worker-patients have similar legal rights and recourse against disclosure without consent.[17]

The first element of the right to consent is the tort law power of the patient to restrain or recover damages for disclosure. The disclosure may breach an implied contract of confidentiality between the patient and the physician.[18] The tort of intentional breach of a confidential relationship in those states that recognize the action may be a separate basis for recovery.[19] In those cases in which the worker's medical record or photo is displayed without consent to a large group of persons, the tort of unconsented publication of personal photos for some private gain might be a basis for recovery.[20]

The second element of the right to consent is the concept of invasion of privacy, both as an implied quasi-constitutional right of individuals and as a conceptual basis of tort law recovery. Many states recognize legal remedies for invasions of privacy.[21]

---

[15] *See, e.g.,* OHIO REV. CODE ANN. §§ 2317.02, 4731.22 (Page Supp. 1979).

[16] *See, e.g.,* Horne v. Patton, 291 Ala. 701, 287 So.2d 824 (1973). *See generally,* Annot., *Physician's Tort Liability, Apart from Defamation, for Disclosure of Confidential Information About Patient,* 20 A.L.R. 3d 1109, 1115 (1968); Swan, *Privacy and Record Keeping: Remedies for the Misuse of Accurate Information,* 54 N.C. L. REV. 585 (1976); Willy, *Right to Privacy in Personal Medical Information,* 1978 MED. TRIAL TECH. Q. 164 (1978). On medical photography, *see* Stevens, *Medical Photography, the Right to Privacy and Privilege,* 1978 MED. TRIAL TECH. Q. 456.

[17] Annas, *supra* note 1.

[18] Annas discusses *Horne,* which used this theory among others to establish liability. The common public understanding of confidentiality obligations of the physician was the basis for this implied contract. *Id.* (discussing Horne v. Patton, 291 Ala. 701, 287 So.2d 824 (1973)).

[19] And this was permitted in *Horne* as to a disclosure to an employer.

[20] Stevens, *supra* note 16.

[21] Privacy invasion is one of the developing areas of the law of torts; readers are directed to consider the RESTATEMENT (SECOND) OF TORTS §§ 652A-652J (Tent. Draft No. 13, 1967) for detailed analyses of current legal thinking in the area of privacy and its remedial aspects.

The Supreme Court dealt with medical records privacy concerns in the 1977 case of *Whalen v. Roe*.[22] A state statute required the reporting to the authorities of names and addresses of persons who had received certain controlled drugs. The law was a means by which the state could monitor some physicians' excessive delivery of narcotics to addict patients. A lower federal court found that there *was* an invasion of a constitutionally protected zone of privacy when the state intruded into the physician's prescribing practices for individual patients. No public dissemination of the names would occur, but the lower court held that the statute invaded patient privacy.[23]

The Supreme Court in *Whalen* upheld the state statute; it found that the disclosure to the state was not "meaningfully distinguishable from a host of other unpleasant invasions of privacy that are associated with many facets of health care." Although it was not a tort-damages suit, the special circumstances of state control in *Whalen* excused an invasion that might have been successfully challenged in some other litigation:

> [D]isclosures of private medical information to doctors, to hospital personnel, to insurance companies, and to public health agencies are often an essential part of modern medical practice even when the disclosure may reflect unfavorably on the character of the patient. Requiring such disclosures to representatives of the State having responsibility for the health of the community, does not automatically amount to an impermissible invasion of privacy.[24]

But aside from these governmental and health institutions, which can make "not impermissible" invasions, the law on invasion of privacy still covers the unconsented dissemination by a physician to third persons of a subject's medical history or condition. It may also reach to the subsequent use of the information by a recipient. Permission for the physician to use the record and photos of the patient in training interns and residents at a hospital, for instance, does not necessarily extend to publication of the private record in a journal of national distribution.[25]

---

[22] 429 U.S. 589 (1977).

[23] Roe v. Ingraham, 403 F. Supp. 931 (S.D.N.Y. 1975).

[24] Whalen v. Roe, 429 U.S. 589, 602 (1977).

[25] Stevens, *supra* note 16.

EPIDEMIOLOGY AND PEER PRESSURE

A third aspect of worker-patient rights of consent is the government's desire to obtain comprehensive information on workplace exposure and risks. The government is concerned with scientifically accurate projections that require maximum access to the records of the population to be studied. So the workers' rights to consent to disclosure will conflict with the accuracy needs of the scientific investigation. The Occupational Safety and Health Administration (OSHA) and its sister agency, the National Institute of Occupational Safety and Health (NIOSH), regard the interest of the greater number of workers—who ostensibly profit from the agencies' work—as overriding the confidentiality interests of the individual workers.[26] Beyond this balancing, in which privacy is secondary, the government asserts that it will be able to preserve the confidentiality of the records once it obtains access to them.[27]

A final aspect of worker consent to disclosure of medical records is the peer pressure upon individuals to cooperate with union development of evidence against the employer. In its adversarial position against the employer, a union could use the records for ammunition. For example, the union's hiring of a medical consultant to study the workplace may lead to a demand for access to worker medical records. The group, not the individual, would benefit, according to the union argument.

There are situations in which the workers regard the union as a source of privacy invasions.[28] Unfair peer pressure to divulge one's medical record has been opposed by physicians who work with unions, since any consent given for this sensitive disclosure should be completely voluntary.[29] Disclosure of medical records can become a political issue to enhance union strength regardless of individual members' reservations. At a

---

[26] *Employee Records Hearings, supra* note 6 (Dec. 1978) (testimony of NIOSH). *See also* Gordis & Gold, *Privacy, Confidentiality and the Use of Medical Records in Research*, 207 SCIENCE 153 (1980).

[27] OSHA asserts that adequate safeguards will preserve the confidentiality of the records and that Freedom of Information Act requests for them will be denied. 44 Fed. Reg. 3994 (1979).

[28] A. WESTIN, COMPUTERS, PERSONNEL ADMINISTRATION AND CITIZEN RIGHTS 288 (National Bureau of Standards Special Publication No. 500-50, 1979).

[29] *Employee Records Hearings, supra* note 6 (Dec. 1978) (testimony of Dr. Richard Wegman for the Occupational Safety and Health Administration at 13).

1978 OSHA hearing, when some labor speakers denounced "capitalist, international imperialist" employers who "put profit first and safety last," [30] pickets and witnesses demanded access for the unions to employee medical records:

> Labor organization members described company physicians as "hired flunkeys" doing the bidding of management and uninterested in the welfare of the workers. "Confidentiality" was described as a "myth." Privacy in a doctor-patient relationship is a "joke," they said, with medical records being used to "keep workmen's compensation rates low" and as a weapon to lay off "trouble-makers." [31]

The politicization of the consent issue intensifies the dilemma for any workers who may not wish to have their medical files exposed to review by union representatives or government officials. If the worker does not consent to dissemination of his or her records, there may be peer pressure to sign the consent forms.[32] At this point, the worker's concern will rightfully increase. The safeguards against misuse of these files vanish when nonphysicians gain access to them, because only the professional licensing statutes would provide an effective inhibition to unwarranted disclosure of the files.

EMPLOYEE RIGHTS: ACCESS TO MEDICAL RECORDS

As a matter of state law and regulation and general personnel practices, individuals are entitled to learn the contents of their medical files held by or for an employer.[33] The practice in most

---

[30] *"It's Our Right to Know," Union Reps Tell OSHA Medical Records Access Hearing,* CHEMICAL REG. REP. (BNA) 1628 (Dec. 22, 1978).

[31] *Id.*

[32] A physician testifying for OSHA stated, "I am uncertain as to whether any employee who is pressured by a union representative, by management, by OSHA or by NIOSH to release his record will be able to give a freely informed consent even for his work-related medical record in a time of compliance activities or other stressful situations . . . ." *Employee Records Hearings, supra* note 6 (Dec. 5, 1978) (testimony of Dr. Daniel Teitelbaum at 9).

[33] Several state laws already permit access when the patient is involved in litigation. *See* G. ANNAS, THE RIGHTS OF HOSPITAL PATIENTS (1975). A sound legal case can be made for *some* access to the contents of these medical records, but access to the *actual record* is not fully established by statute or case law in most states, short of litigation. A. WESTIN, A POLICY ANALYSIS OF CITIZEN RIGHTS ISSUES IN HEALTH DATA SYSTEMS 33-34 (National Bureau of Standards Special Publication No. 469, 1977) ; *see* PRIVACY PROTECTION STUDY COMMISSION, PERSONAL PRIVACY IN AN INFORMATION SOCIETY 256, 266 (1977). Definite statutory rights exist in Florida and Massachusetts. R. SMITH, *supra* note 2.

firms is to permit the worker either to review the complete file or to discuss the contents of the file with a physician employed by the firm.[34] Fewer firms are at either end of the spectrum, refusing any disclosure to workers or totally releasing the entire file for removal by the employee.[35]

State laws and licensing regulations that govern physician recordkeeping provide rights for patient access, and many require such access as a matter of patient right. Unions may also insist on that right of access for their members as a term of the collective bargaining agreement's health and welfare provisions.[36] Several states provide statutory rights for the worker to have access to his or her medical file held by the employer.[37]

Should disclosure of medical records be made to any reviewer, physician or not, who is designated by the worker?[38] Physicians generally resist disseminating patient records to persons other than the patient—who may decide to retransfer as he or she chooses—or the patient's designated physician. Transfer among physicians of medical records is routine, and the recipient is bound by the same ethical and legal constraints as the physician who created the record. Unions may prefer not to hire expensive consulting physicians if the same screening could be done by less expensive hygienists, toxicologists, or other nonphysician scien-

---

[34] *Employee Records Hearings, supra* note 6 (Dec. 15, 1978) (testimonies of Dr. M. Johnson for the Chemical Manufacturers' Association and Dr. A. McLean for the American Occupational Medical Association).

[35] Even those that would release the entire medical file may reserve the portions relating to psychological or mental impairments, which should be reviewed prior to disclosure by a physician to prevent misinterpretations, which could be harmful to the patient. OSHA witness Dr. Richard Wegman stated that dissemination of this mental information should be limited to health professionals only. *Employee Records Hearings, supra* note 6 (Dec. 1978) (testimony of Dr. Richard Wegman for the Occupational Safety and Health Administration).

[36] PRIVACY PROTECTION STUDY COMMISSION, *supra* note 33, at 254.

[37] *See, e.g.,* statutes cited in chapter IX, notes 37-42, *infra.* Medical records are exempt from disclosure under the Pennsylvania law, however. PA. STAT. ANN. tit. 43, § 1321 (Purdon Supp. 1979).

[38] This philosophical disagreement about third-party recipients was exacerbated in the OSHA medical records rulemaking by a conscious omission of any limitation on who could serve as designated observers of one's medical record. Peer pressure on the twentieth of twenty workers to join the other nineteen in passing their records to a fellow worker who chairs a unit safety committee, for example, could be coercing the surrender of an important right and would perhaps open up a potential abuse by the nonphysician recipient. *See* Sammons, *supra* note 8.

tists. However ethical these individuals may be, they do not bear the same set of sanctions and incentives shared among physicians.[39]

When the Occupational Safety and Health Administration proposed a rule in 1978 on mandatory access to medical records by workers, it included such access as a worker's right, which the worker could delegate to any representative, regardless of medical background.[40] That open-designation point was one of the most controversial issues in the OSHA proposal.[41] The final rule of May 23, 1980, did little to resolve the controversy.[42]

Access rights are also a political issue, as is consent to disclosure of the records to third parties. Access is regarded as a "right to know" provision. Some industry observers have opposed rights of access on the grounds that the information cannot be properly understood by the recipients or that it may be misunderstood despite the employer-paid physician's attempts to explain it.[43] Teamsters union officials responded with the contrary presumption that, if an employer withheld access to the information, the workers will be likely to presume that some hazard is being concealed.[44]

---

[39] An OSHA witness who works with unions testified: "Non-physician union representatives should be considered the same as non-physician management representatives; neither should have access to the individual's medical records. Physicians employed by or contracted with either unions or management are bound by the same moral, ethical and legal restrictions. Non-medical personnel do not necessarily hold the same rules of conduct." *Employee Records Hearings, supra* note 6 (Dec. 5, 1978) (testimony of Dr. Donald Whorton for the Occupational Safety and Health Administration).

[40] 43 Fed. Reg. 31,371 (1978).

[41] It attracted a great deal of negative comment both from OSHA's witnesses, such as Dr. Whorton; from academic physicians, such as Dr. Sammons; and from industry witnesses at the hearings. *Employee Records Hearings, supra* note 39; Sammons, *supra* note 8.

[42] 45 Fed. Reg. 35,211 (1980). *See* discussion *infra*, pp. 132-38.

[43] The Manufacturing Chemists Association (MCA) testimony noted that the complete medical record "contains an array of facts and information which only a licensed physician is capable of interpreting. For example, it may contain diagnoses and differential diagnoses; it may contain subjective clinical impressions or it may contain memoranda of conversations with third parties concerning the employee's personal habits or supposed shortcomings." *Employee Records Hearings, supra* note 6 (MCA Post-Hearing Brief). The author appeared as an expert witness for the MCA in the Chicago hearings on this issue.

[44] *Employee-Doctor Relationship, supra* note 13, at 1746.

A final controversial aspect is whether general rights of access will improve the quality and utility of medical recordkeeping and improve patient care. If the records are known to be subject to disclosure, the physician treating the patient might be more likely to withhold from the record a subjective comment or suspicion that, for any physician treating the patient subsequently, might be the key to a successful diagnosis of a slowly developing condition. These subjective comments will be less likely to appear because the desire for a complete record will have to be balanced against the new expectation that the entire record will eventually be read by the patient, the union, and other persons. Candor probably will suffer, and successful but subjective means of therapy could suffer as well.[45]

EMPLOYEE RIGHTS: USE OF MEDICAL DATA

The use of medical information to affect a patient's job or self-confidence adversely is an issue of sizzling controversy. When a worker is statistically likely to develop an incurable disease and the disease resulted from an exposure that is no longer present in the work environment, should the worker be told of the now unavoidable potential for suffering an eventual, painful death?[46] That is an information transfer problem. When a worker's genetic makeup makes him or her susceptible to some genetic disorder, which is triggered by exposure to a possible mutagenic chemical, should the worker be barred from that workplace or instead be allowed to accept risks of unknown dimension?[47]

The first aspect of use of medical information is the easiest to explain. Occupational physicians have a duty to use the medical information received to safeguard other workers by alerting

---

[45] Knowledge of the oversight by third persons will likely inhibit long-shot, exploratory suspicions but will probably not affect the more objective observations made by the physician.

[46] Kolata, *Genes and Cancer: The Story of Wilms Tumor*, 207 SCIENCE 970, 971 (1980). This article contains one physician's comment: "A lot of people say that telling people they might have a disease when they may never get it is worse than the disease itself."

[47] "Those most susceptible to cancer might be denied employment or given jobs only in areas where they would not be exposed to the chemicals. . . . [S]ome people may resent the tests because they could shut them out of lucrative jobs." Kolata, *Testing for Cancer Risk*, 207 SCIENCE 967, 969 (1980).

the employer to the possible consequences of the illness or condition. But as an ethical matter, occupational physicians segregate their files from general corporate files and do not provide supervisors with the detailed medical records of individual workers.[48] A government witness in the OSHA hearings on access to employee medical records testified that a breach of occupational physician ethics, such as disclosure of medical confidential files to a worker's supervisor, is rare today.[49] For most firms, files are accessible only to a limited number of the health unit employees who bear a professional responsibility for maintenance of the secrecy of the records.[50]

The second aspect of use of files is preemployment screening. The decision not to hire may turn upon a preexisting medical condition that disables the prospective employee from carrying out the duties of the job. The physician screening job applicants has a duty to make known the ineligibility of the worker, and the applicant has no grounds for objection about the communication of that ineligibility to the employer's personnel staff.

Preemployment screening is different from most of the physician-patient contacts, however, because it is temporary, conditional, and noncommittal about prospects for a longer relationship. It is unlikely that the screening physician is preemployment physicals would be held to the same duty of confidence in the usual physician-patient communications.[51]

The third aspect of use of medical information is the most controversial one. Some workplace exposures to chemicals cannot be reduced to zero exposure; if the substance is to be used at all, some workers will inevitably be exposed to the substance. Our knowledge of risks is very limited for certain chronic hazards, such as multigeneration genetic damage through chromosome alteration. The causes of cancer are not well understood; genetic mutations and the promotion of birth defects in future children (teratogenicity) may be caused by exposure to some chemicals. Sterility caused by chemical exposure has

---

[48] *See, e.g.,* Collings, *supra* note 10.

[49] *Employee Records Hearings, supra* note 6 (Dec. 5, 1978) (testimony of Dr. Donald Whorton for the Occupational Safety and Health Administration).

[50] *Employee Records Hearings, supra* note 6 (Dec. 15, 1978) (testimony of Dr. A. McLean for the American Occupational Medical Association).

[51] Annas, *supra* note 1.

been alleged by a chemical union against a pesticides manufacturer.[52] But the *how* and *why* factors are not clear.

One of the frontier ideas under discussion among some industrial hygienists and medical researchers is that the genetic characteristics of each individual play a role in susceptibility to certain chronic hazards.[53] This oversimplification of a complex scientific theory is offered to show that science *may* find in the future that our personal propensities toward certain illnesses are as important as the hazard in the items to which we are exposed. If receptivity is important, then the less receptive the people exposed, the less the damage that will occur. The chemical industry has devoted extensive funding to genetic research, because susceptibility of workers to chemical hazards may have critical importance to the industry's future workplace safety.[54]

If a worker is believed to be susceptible to risk and the production of the substance is needed to serve some societal function, e.g., a medicinal gas or military-missile component, then the worker must move, the worker must accept the risk, or the processing of the material must change. In past years, the worker merely accepted the little-understood risk, if the risk was known at all, just as coal miners have accepted the risks of black lung disease from coal dust inhalation in the mines.[55] Today, susceptible workers can be moved out of the hazardous position if there are sufficient alternate positions available and if the workers are willing to transfer. But haste alienates the transferees. Some female workers of childbearing age sued a chemical firm during 1980 and alleged that the firm had given them a choice of either leaving the profitable workplace assignments they had held or having themselves sterilized to avoid risks to future children from the chemicals with which they

---

[52] This situation, of DBCP pesticides connected to worker sterility, was discussed in *Employee Records Hearings, supra* note 6 (Dec. 5, 1978) (testimony of Dr. Donald Whorton for the Occupational Safety and Health Administration).

[53] *See, e.g.*, Kolata, *supra* note 46.

[54] Severo, *Screening of Blacks by DuPont Sharpens Debate on Gene Tests*, N.Y. Times, Feb. 4, 1980, at A1, col. 5.

[55] Coal miners, however, also have a federal compensation system that pays benefits with relatively slight evidence of individual causal connection, so there has been a societal shifting of costs from the workers and firms to the taxpayer to compensate for the inevitable lung effects of the necessary occupation of coal mining. 30 U.S.C. § 901 (Supp. II 1978).

were working.[56] In attacking the transfer policy, the union claimed that the workplace should be made safe for all workers, not maintained in a hazardous status quo while "susceptible" production workers were screened away from their jobs.[57] The Equal Employment Opportunity Commission also launched an attack on worker-reassignment actions by employers, which the EEOC considered a discriminatory action against females or selected groups of employees.[58] If potential fetal defects would harm pregnant women, it was felt, then prospective fathers' sperm may also be affected. The *New York Times* contributed to the debate with a three-part series on genetic screening of employees,[59] which in turn led to proposed New York legislation to ban the practice of genetic screening while it is still in its infancy.[60]

If an employee is selected or rejected for a job because of a medical condition, the employer must be prepared to defend the rationality of that decision in the event of a grievance, an unfair labor practice charge, or a discrimination charge. Because the scientific aspects of genetic damage, behavioral disorders, and cancer causation are still open to speculation, the employer has a dilemma brought on by the information. If the employer has the information and wishes to act on it by transfers, the consequences will be subject to challenge from either the persons to be protected by the withdrawal action (workers) or the persons supposedly protecting the workers (antidiscrimination agencies and unions).[61] If, however, the employer learns of a risk to the employees and does not act, it may breach its general duty under the Occupational Safety and Health Act to

---

[56] *Sex Bias Suit Filed by 13 Women At American Cyanamid Company*, N.Y. Times, Feb. 3, 1980, at 37, col. 3.

[57] Severo, *Genetic Tests by Industry Raises Basic Questions of the Rights of Workers*, N.Y. Times, Feb. 3, 1980, at 1, 36.

[58] *Interpretive Guidelines on Employment Discrimination and Reproductive Hazards*, 45 Fed. Reg. 7514 (1980).

[59] Severo, *supra* note 54; Severo, *supra* note 57; Severo, *Dispute Arises Over Dow Studies on Genetic Damage in Workers*, N.Y. Times, Feb. 5, 1980, at A1, col. 1.

[60] *Bill is Offered in Albany to Outlaw Gene Tests*, N.Y. Times, Feb. 6, 1980, at A17, col. 1.

[61] The EEOC, for example, would probably challenge the action under its proposed new guidelines. 45 Fed. Reg. 7514 (1980).

protect the workers from unsafe conditions.[62] The employer may or may not have the option to close down the process and redesign it to satisfy OSHA that it has eliminated exposure.

The manufacturer may not be able to close down a process for redesign and retooling if foreign competitors would seize the market irretrievably (and without regard for their workers' levels of exposure)[63] or if the material is such that no engineering controls system could eliminate all exposure or if the material meets a national defense need that cannot be postponed to suit the needs of the production employees.

The redesign of the system might also be an expensive proposition relative to the cost of transferring production workers or paying them higher wages for lesser assignments. The usual rule of thumb is that the last 5 percent of exposure potential is more expensive to eliminate than was the other 95 percent, because absolute elimination is much more difficult than the mere construction of an isolation system in general. Unless the material that is potentially hazardous has an accepted permissible exposure level,[64] the unions and the government may not be satisfied with continued exposure of workers to small amounts of the material.

One of the current regulatory system's weaknesses is the absence of a mechanism to force decisions on the acceptability of risk. No regulatory agency is required to decide that a chemical has been controlled to a sufficient but not absolute level X percent usage. Exposure elimination, while a valuable ideal, is often *not* a practical goal in light of the costs which that ideal would impose on the manufacturer, consumers, and the workers. If the workplace closes down for economic reasons in response to union and government demands for elimination of *any* risk, then the workers achieve a Pyrrhic victory—safety assurance and unemployment insurance. If there were a central consensus on the acceptability of threshold risks, limits of acceptable exposure risk, and other undecided scientific questions that have such important legal ramifications, then the workers might be

---

[62] 29 U.S.C. § 654(a) (1976). This section requires the employer to furnish its employees with a place of employment free from "recognized hazards."

[63] The OSHA standards have no legal effect in foreign nations.

[64] The toxicological debate over levels of exposure and the no-threshold theory are beyond the scope of this subject. *See generally* the current National Cancer Institute view in Gori, *The Regulation of Carcinogenic Hazards*, 208 SCIENCE 256 (1980).

able to assume intelligently *some* risks of the unknown in return for continued employment.

THREE DIFFICULT CASES

When the National Institute of Occupational Safety and Health determined to obtain access to individual employee medical records, it began with the assumption that the government would easily win access because of the government's fine record of public health monitoring and sound reputation for protection of confidential data. It has won two and lost one as this book goes to press, but NIOSH strategists could not have been farther off target.

The first litigated decision, *E. I. duPont* v. *Finklea*,[65] was a vigorous challenge to the government's taking of medical records without consent. DuPont had polled the *subjects* of the medical records, and 631 persons refused to consent to governmental access. The government sued DuPont to force the delivery of the records of the 631 persons against their will. The court found that the OSH Act allowed inspection of the records, but that the mere assertion of intent to protect was not enough. First, the court specifically ordered the government not to disclose the information to anyone and not to copy the information. This effectively removed NIOSH's scope of discretion under the Freedom of Information Act [66] to make permissive disclosure of the information to FOI Act requesters. Next, the court imposed specific security procedures for the handling of the information within NIOSH's control, and return of the records was required.[67] Also, NIOSH use was limited to "qualified and trained" health professionals having a "demonstrable need" to utilize that information. If NIOSH breached the court's re-

---

[65] 442 F. Supp. 821 (S.D.W.V. 1977).

[66] A federal agency has a general discretionary power to disclose documents from its files if no other statute exists to bar the disclosure. Chrysler Corp. v. Brown, 441 U.S. 281 (1979).

[67] The return of documents was seen as a major achievement because most agencies refuse to return documents once they are in their formal control. This leads firms to refuse agency personnel the power of physical control over the records, which denies them the FOIA obligation to disclose the records. *See* Forsham v. Harris, 100 S.Ct. 978 (1980). Sometimes statutory amendments require the return of agency-obtained documents, a desired course of action. *See* Federal Trade Commission Improvements Act of 1980, Pub. L. No. 96-252, 84 Stat. 374 (1980).

quirements, it could be held in contempt of court, and its officials could be penalized.

The next litigation, *General Motors Corp. v. NIOSH,*[68] raised the identical issue of governmental access to employee medical records. The court read the Ohio physician-patient privilege statute[69] as controlling upon the claimed federal right of access. Physicians' claims of privilege were aided by the court's comment. The court ordered the deletion of names and identifying details from the employee records before they were released to NIOSH.[70] Although this may not be suitable in some cases (e.g., a record showing alcoholism tendencies of a 6'8" power tool operator whose name is omitted), the deletion and the court-imposed security precautions would generally be satisfactory.

NIOSH had much more luck on its third try. A newly appointed federal judge in Pittsburgh who apparently had not dealt with federal agencies in the past gave NIOSH a platitudinous endorsement as a responsible delegate of the Congress and as an exceptional defender of the public health. Because the agency had promised confidential treatment, impressing the court, and because the Pennsylvania physician-patient privilege statute is archaic, covering only disclosures tending to disgrace the patient,[71] the judge in *United States v. Westinghouse Electric Corp.* gave the agency *all* the access it had wanted with *no* additional reservations.[72] Had Westinghouse received a judge more familiar with either government disclosure issues or the propensities of agencies to leak information, the case would presumably have emerged from the judicial process with restrictions similar to those of the *GM* case on NIOSH's use of the data.

The issue of disclosure and limitations on disclosure will probably reach the appellate courts within the next two years. It is predicted that legal authority for the inspection of medical records will be upheld but that personal identifiers and names will have to be deleted from any files obtained by the agencies from employer records. If OHSA's harsh disdain for the *General Motors* case, aired in the *Federal Register*, is accepted, then the

---

[68] 459 F. Supp. 235 (S.D. Ohio 1978).

[69] *See* Hammonds v. Aetna Cas. & Sur. Co., 237 F. Supp. 96 (N.D. Ohio 1965); Ohio Rev. Code Ann. §§ 2317.02, 4731.22 (Page Supp. 1979).

[70] Identity deletion is controversial. *See, e.g.,* Gordis & Gold, *supra* note 26.

[71] Pa. Stat. Ann. tit. 28, § 328 (Purdon 1958) (repealed 1978).

[72] 483 F. Supp. 1265 (W.D. Pa. 1980).

courts and OSHA will have discarded an important privacy right of individual employees and discarded a series of past statutory and traditional assumptions about notice and access.[73]

OSHA'S MEDICAL RECORDS RULE

The preceding portions of this chapter lay the groundwork for the most massive medical records involvement of the federal government at any time of the nation's experience. The Occupational Safety and Health Administration's final rule on medical and exposure records access, issued May 23, 1980, as a new 29 C.F.R. § 1910.20,[74] eliminated most preconceptions of workplace privacy and thrust a federalized cure on a poorly defined "problem" of medical records retention. The agency's predeliction to cure with an ax rather than a probing scalpel may leave commentators puzzling for years to come whether there *is* any medical records privacy expectation any more.

The essential requirements of the OSHA rule are as follows:

1. When a medical record subject to the rule is retained by an employer or a private physician acting in conjunction with an employer, the employer is under a legal duty (punishable by civil and possibly criminal sanctions) to deliver the original or a copy of the medical record either to the employee or to the employee's designated representative.[75]

2. A designated representative may be anyone at all, regardless of status, training, education, etc.[76]

3. Very few specific cases could be imagined in which a medical record would not be delivered to an employee; in each case, it must then be delivered totally to the designated representative, who may then do anything with it, including delivering it to the employee.[77]

---

[73] OSHA criticized *GM*, but its critique was so self-serving that it was wholly unpersuasive. It spoke not at all of Pennsylvania's peculiar and archaic medical records privilege law but stated that *GM*'s outcome was the product of the unusual nature of Ohio's law. Ohio's is the more commonplace national model, with Pennsylvania the aberration. R. SMITH, *supra* note 2; 45 Fed. Reg. 35,211; 35,252 (1980).

[74] 45 Fed. Reg. 35,211; 35,277 (1980) (to be codified in 29 C.F.R. § 1910.20).

[75] *Id.* 35,279 (to be codified in 29 C.F.R. § 1910.20 (e) (2)).

[76] *Id.* 35,277 (to be codified in 29 C.F.R. §1910.20 (e) (2)).

[77] *Id.* 35,279 (to be codified in 29 C.F.R. § 1910.20 (e) (ii) (D)).

4. Access rights extend to all employees with two general exceptions—employees who have held only office or general positions which never could or did involve contact with chemicals or with potentially harmful work environments [78] and employees whose exposures have not included any materials which the rule's sweeping four-part definition would consider "harmful." [79]

5. Prompt disclosure, within fifteen days of request, is required for employee access or the access of designated representatives.[80] Each employer's access program must begin in August 1980,[81] and education of workers about access rights must begin in October 1980 [82] (unless the rule is stayed by a federal appellate court pending review).

6. NIOSH is not covered, apparently because of internecine disputes at the working level [83] and the difficulty of adapting OSHA access to NIOSH study needs.[84]

7. Last but not least, OSHA asserts that it must be given total rights of access to all employee medical records and exposure records covered by the rule.[85] OSHA reneged on granting advance notice to individual workers [86] and belatedly asserts that it will be flexible rather than stringent in safeguarding workers' privacy rights when sharing the records within its staff and with its contractors.[87]

The May 1980 publication of the final rule in almost one hundred pages of *Federal Register* type proved to industry observers

---

[78] *Id.* 35,277 (to be codified in 29 C.F.R. §§ 1910.20(b)(1), 1910.20(c)(4)).

[79] *Id.* 35,277-78 (to be codified in 29 C.F.R. §§ 1910.20(b)(2), 1910.20(c)(11)).

[80] *Id.* 35,278-79 (to be codified in 29 C.F.R. § 1910.20(e)(1)(i)).

[81] The effective date of the rule was August 21, 1980. *Id.* 35,280 (to be codified in 29 C.F.R. § 1910.20(j)).

[82] Sixty days after the effective date, education must begin. *Id.*

[83] During the hearings to produce the OSHA rule, NIOSH's testimony was sometimes more extreme than OSHA's, and it was apparent that NIOSH policies differed on a number of points from the plans of OSHA. *Employee Records Hearings, supra* note 6.

[84] 45 Fed. Reg. 35,211; 35,256 (1980).

[85] *Id.* 35,277 (to be codified in 29 C.F.R. § 1910.20(e)(3)).

[86] *Id.* 35,289.

[87] *Id.* 35,289-90; 35,296 (to be codified in 29 C.F.R. § 1913.10(e)).

that political exigencies mattered more to the OSHA rulemaking staff than the weight of testimony at the hearings. OSHA's own witnesses, with a distinct distance between them and industrial experience, favored an extreme view.[88] Their positions were cited widely in support of the agency's initial conclusions, sometimes going farther in demands for records than the original 1978 proposal had attempted to go.[89] Skeptical of witnesses with dozens of years of medical experience in occupational medicine,[90] though supportive of advocacy groups' positions generated for this particular proceeding,[91] OSHA's preamble to the final rule is an essay in rationalization for a politically attractive solution. Its primary failure is the lack of definition of the "problem" that medical records disclosure "cures." If there is a problem in the long term, it will be government itself because the agency carefully backed away from self-proposed guidelines which would have structured, limited, and channeled the handling of personal medical records.[92] Government agency "flexibility" was accorded

---

[88] The Supplementary Information provided by OSHA in the *Federal Register* contains many references to OSHA witnesses Wegman and Weiner (a physician and state employee-attorney), which suggests that they were the principal, most frequent sources relied upon by the Labor Department. *Id.* 35,211-77. Hearing statements by both witnesses were inordinately critical of trade secret protection of chemical constituents of mixtures.

[89] 43 Fed. Reg. 31,371 (1978).

[90] Many of the industry witnesses were occupational physicians, medical department directors, academic and professional society members, and the like.

[91] Analysis of OSHA's Supplementary Information published in the *Federal Register* suggests that ad hoc spokesmen and international union spokesmen who favor more government regulation of the medical records access issue supplied the predominant support for the agency's final rule. Although the selection of sources for final rules in a large record is a matter within the agency's discretion, the history of this proceeding suggests that private sector witnesses not supportive of OSHA received short shrift notwithstanding expertise.

[92] Erosion of the guidelines is excused by a need for greater "flexibility," although personal medical records will thereby be easier for more people to obtain from their employers with fewer safeguards than in the 1978 guidelines. The fact that OSHA used the draft guidelines to parry industry criticism of the rule itself and then magically caused the protective safeguards to disappear in the final rule leaves one skeptical of the agency's good faith in presenting a fair opportunity for dialogue and comment on its proposals. Had an SEC-regulated corporation proposed to its shareholders a certain safeguarding system and then adopted one as weak as OSHA's final rule, the rule-writers would likely serve jail terms for materially misleading proxy recipients to their detriment. For OSHA, however, the tactic was quite effective in achieving the agency's political goals.

more weight than medical privacy interests. Worker groups who in 1978-79 hearings criticized exploitation by "capitalist, international imperialists" [93] may be back in 1988-89 protesting the casual dissemination by bureaucrats of files taken without anyone's consent [94] from workplace medical departments. Time will measure the wisdom of OSHA's political solution.

EMPLOYER RIGHTS AFTER THE OSHA RULE

If the OSHA medical records rule is not vacated on appeal, employers will have a significant compliance burden. First, each employer must annually conduct an education and information program to advise workers of the right to obtain access to the medical files. [95] Second, the employer must—if it opts not to give access to all employees—define for its own work force the class of workers whose office assignment or other duties have not, do not, and (as far as predictable) will not expose them to chemicals or to certain physiological hazards. [96] An extreme example might be an oil tanker company whose office manager may be assigned to ride aboard a tanker, where motion sickness (covered by the rule) [97] may befall the normally land-bound worker. A more frequent case would be the worker in receiving or shipping functions, or one about to transfer into those posts, [98] who may

---

[93] *"It's Our Right to Know," supra* note 30.

[94] The employer cannot object because of the threat of penalties from OSHA. 29 U.S.C. § 658(a) (1976); 43 Fed. Reg. 35,211; 35,279-80 (1980) (to be codified in 29 C.F.R. § 1910.20(e)(3)). OSHA refuses to give employees an advance right to consent to the dissemination of their personal medical records. 45 Fed. Reg. 35,289-90; 35,296 (1980) (to be codified in 29 C.F.R. § 1913.10(e)). OSHA considered personal notice was felt "often unnecessary and overly burdensome." *Id.* 35,289. Yet the Carter Administration had previously loudly touted its commitments to personal privacy protection and individual choice before losses of confidentiality. *See President's Message to Congress on Proposals to Protect the Privacy of Individuals*, 15 WEEKLY COMP. OF PRES. DOC. 581 (Apr. 2, 1979).

[95] 45 Fed. Reg. 35,211; 35,280 (1980) (to be codified in 29 C.F.R. § 1910.20 (g)).

[96] *Id.* 35,277 (to be codified in 29 C.F.R. §§ 1910.20(b)(2), 1910.20(c)(4)).

[97] Vibration and repetitive motion are harmful for this rule's definitional purposes. *Id.* 35,278 (to be codified in 29 C.F.R. § 1910.20(c)(11)).

[98] A future assignment to such a position is enough to merit a review of existing exposure records. *Id.* 35,277 (to be codified in 29 C.F.R. § 1910.20 (c)(4)).

have accidental exposure through predictable spills and leakage of chemical products.[99]

Third, the class of workers who have rights under the rule will be able to demand access to existing medical files, whenever created,[100] and so access must be provided within fifteen days after the request is received.[101] The employer need not pay for the time spent examining the records,[102] but the opportunity to examine the records must be convenient for the worker. Copies must be provided free for the asking (except that a charge can be made for repeated requests for the same material).[103] As has been discussed elsewhere in this text, the Freedom of Information Act forces disclosure of government documents to requesting persons within ten days, but the government suffers little or no penalty for delay, and its responses frequently consume weeks or months beyond the statutory deadline.[104] For OSHA's rule-enforcement functions, however, the passage of this information from one private person (employer) to another (employee or designated representative) must comply with the rule's deadline of fifteen days.[105]

Fourth, the employer must be prepared for access demands by a "designated representative" of the employee. For exposure records relating to monitoring of individual workers' chemical exposures, unions are automatically designated representatives without prior consent of employees.[106] For medical records, unions or any other person or group can be given the individual employee's rights if the individual signs the medical records access consent form specified by OSHA's appendix to the regulation.[107]

---

[99] *Id.; see id.* 35,265.

[100] The rule is expressly retroactive in scope, covering all preexisting medical and exposure records.

[101] 45 Fed. Reg. 35,211; 35,278-79 (1980) (to be codified in 29 C.F.R. § 1910.20(e)(1)(i)).

[102] *Id.* 35,271.

[103] *Id.* 35,278 (to be codified in 29 C.F.R. § 1910.20(e)(1)(iii)).

[104] *See generally* 1 J. O'REILLY, FEDERAL INFORMATION DISCLOSURE § 7.02 (Supp. 1979).

[105] 45 Fed. Reg. 35,211; 35,278-79 (1980) (to be codified in 29 C.F.R. § 1910.20(e)(1)).

[106] *Id.* 35,277 (to be codified in 29 C.F.R. § 1910.20(c)(3)).

[107] *Id.* 35,280 (to be codified in 29 C.F.R. § 1910.20 app. A).

Fifth, the employer must be aware of the limited rights to withhold information. For medical records, deletion of sources of sensitive information is permitted if the source's identity would be in some way sensitive ("John's wife reports that he attempted suicide in 1978 . . ."), but only if the source has no business relationship to the individual.[108] For specific diagnoses of psychiatric conditions or terminal illnesses, an employer's physician may refuse to tell the employee directly but then must tell the union steward or other "designated representative" the very information withheld from the employee.[109]

For commercially sensitive information that has been included in past medical records and exposure records, the employer will have to disclose the information if it does not fit into several very narrow categories.[110] Even if it does so fit, alternative descriptions would be appropriate.[111] OSHA, however, made a small concession on chemical identities and required identity of the chemical in an exposure record to be disclosed only if there is no Material Safety Data Sheet or other exposure test result available to provide the worker with the necessary safety data.[112] For future records, the secret identities of chemical substances will have to be disclosed only if the employer mistakenly included the secret in the disclosure-bound records.[113] The burden will be on the employer to change its ways.

Sixth, the employer needs to tie the exposure records' existing trade secrets into a protectable package before disclosure. As was just discussed, the commercially sensitive data must be made available to workers or other "designated representatives"; and for unions, OSHA defines a collective bargaining representative as a designated representative per se without need for individual

---

[108] *Id.* 35,279 (to be codified in 29 C.F.R. § 1910.20(e)(2)(ii)(E)).

[109] *Id.* 35,279 (to be codified in 29 C.F.R. § 1910.20(e)(2)(ii)(D)).

[110] *Id.* 35,279 (to be codified in 29 C.F.R. § 1910.20(f)).

[111] *Id.* For example, an alternative description could be the "machine closest to the office" instead of the "automatic left-handed widget drive machine" if the machine is a secret.

[112] *Id.* 35,277 (to be codified in 29 C.F.R. § 1910.20(c)(5)(i)-(iv)).

[113] The rule does not require that the trade secrets be listed, but if they are, they are vulnerable to access demands of the rule.

workers' consents.[114] Employers must design a trade secret non-disclosure agreement that fits the bounds of the OSHA rule.[115] Nonemployee union agents, contractors of unions, and others might be designated to receive sensitive secret information. The employer must draft an appropriate form warning the recipient of penalties for dissemination of the secret data.[116] If the data are not shielded by such a warning form, their subsequent disclosure would be without any legal penalties and perhaps would be construed in the civil courts as a waiver of rights. The results for the employer could be disastrous.

Finally, an employer must decide whether to go on collecting as much and as detailed information as had been the case before. An industrial hygiene program's output will now have to be seen as a potentially public output from the company to employees and to designated nonemployee recipients. Reexamination of what is collected and why and in what detail will be essential to the employer's successful coexistence with the new rule.[117]

FUTURE DIRECTIONS

An indication of future directions in the medical records issue is the 1980 contract between the United Auto Workers (UAW) and the Ford Motor Company. Ford reached an agreement with the UAW to provide contractual rights of access by all Ford

---

[114] 45 Fed. Reg. 35,211; 35,277 (1980) (to be codified in 29 C.F.R. §1910.20 (c)(3)).

[115] *Id.* 35,280 (to be codified in 29 C.F.R. § 1910.20(f)(3)). Note, however, that the rule's purported prohibition of damages clauses would never successfully be supported in court and that a prudent firm must either demand a warrant (and fight the access order in court) when OSHA seeks access or refuse to deliver the secret information and fight out the details of an acceptable confidentiality agreement in the OSHA and OSHRC tribunals. The OSHRC view on an acceptable contractual clause would then be taken to the appellate courts. No employer should enter the drafting of such an agreement with the naiveté about such contractual promises as was exhibited by the authors of the OSHA rule. Damages clauses are appropriate and should be used where needed.

[116] Despite OSHA's effort to override state trade secret laws with a specious claim of preemption, the multiplant firm is advised to list all or the most applicable state prohibitions on a single universal form for use in all disclosures of its secrets. Then state prosecutions could be brought, and the appropriate notice (where needed) will have been uniformly given.

[117] Reexamination is an urgent need for those firms with high technology and limited past control of the contents of such records.

workers to their occupational medical records, held by or for Ford.[118] And OSHA perceived its medical and exposure records rule to be a minimum standard with greater access rights obtainable through bargaining.[119]

Congress is considering medical records privacy legislation that is much tighter in safeguards than OSHA's 1980 rules, but the federal legislation, apparently for political reasons, avoided any coverage of occupational medical records and focused only on hospital and nursing home health-care providers.[120]

---

[118] *Privacy in the Workplace: Hearings Before U.S. Department of Labor* (Mar. 6, 1980) (statement of Alan Reuther for the United Automobile Workers).

[119] 45 Fed. Reg. 35,212-77 (1980).

[120] H.R. 3444, 96th Cong., 1st Sess. (1979).

PART FOUR

The Freedom of Information Act

CHAPTER XI

Information Policy and the Freedom of Information Act

The Freedom of Information Act, a 1966 federal statute [1] amended later in 1974 [2] and 1976,[3] has become widely known to the general public as a source for disclosure of "secret files." There have been many news reports that begin, "Newly disclosed files released under the Freedom of Information Act today revealed that . . ." The Act merits attention in the labor field for its impact on the flow of information that is sensitive but not wholly "secret," including information that might be sensitive to one side in a negotiation or that might be concealed by the National Labor Relations Board's counsel to be sprung against an employer-respondent in the midst of a controverted hearing.[4] Every labor attorney has a stake in the accessibility of information controlled by federal agencies such as the NLRB.

BACKGROUND

The Freedom of Information Act, an independent portion of the Administrative Procedure Act,[5] is a charter of rights under which members of the public can obtain access to governmental information. Extensive treatments of the Act's history and its

---

[1] Pub. L. No. 89-487, 80 Stat. 250 (1966) (codified at 5 U.S.C. § 552 (1976)).

[2] Pub. L. No. 93-502, 88 Stat. 1561 (1974).

[3] Pub. L. No. 94-409, 90 Stat. 1241 (1976) (codified at 5 U.S.C. § 552b).

[4] See chapter XIII infra, regarding the use of the Freedom of Information Act in NLRB hearings.

[5] Administrative Procedure Act, ch. 324, 60 Stat. 237 (1946) (codified in scattered sections of 5 U.S.C.).

operation have been published elsewhere.[6] This chapter is limited to the Act's statutory policies and to basic information relating to the labor-management use of the Act.

Provisions of the 1947 Administrative Procedure Act required that agencies issuing regulations must make them available to the public and that agencies adopting interpretations or staff guidance documents affecting members of the public must make those types of information available for easy access by the public. The 1947 Act also had a narrow provision permitting an agency to disclose from its files certain information to requesting persons who were properly and directly concerned with the subject of the information if the agency chose to do so.[7] This set of provisions allowed the agencies to decide to whom its files would be disclosed, if and when it was in the agency's interest to do so. There was also no effective sanction to compel agencies to disclose publicly their rules, guidelines, and other undisclosed operating rules.

The 1960-66 period was one of increasing public concern about the abuses of secrecy within government. A major effort was mounted by newspaper groups to force government agencies to accept the principle of "openness" and accountability to public and press oversight. Many agencies vigorously resisted, asserting that disclosure of their files to members of the public would harm their ability to operate, would distract their staff from the administration of the existing substantive laws, and would imperil their ability to investigate wrongdoing. Some government agencies, such as the Treasury and Defense Departments, made a major effort to shape the legislation to serve their needs.[8]

---

[6] *See, e.g.,* 1 J. O'REILLY, FEDERAL INFORMATION DISCLOSURE (1977 & Supp. 1979); Saloschin, Newkirk, & Gavin, *A Short Guide to the Freedom of Information Act,* OFFICE OF INFORMATION LAW & POLICY, U.S. DEP'T OF JUSTICE, FREEDOM OF INFORMATION CASE LIST i (1980). There are, in addition, about four other guidebooks and more than a hundred published articles discussing the Act.

[7] Administrative Procedure Act, ch. 324, § 3, 60 Stat. 237 (1946). This section was really ineffectual as an access statute and was of little value to the public during the period of its existence, 1947-66.

[8] The principal justification for the commercial confidential information protections, which are found in current law at 5 U.S.C. § 552(b)(4), was the testimony of the Treasury Department that any system of public access to government documents should not displace existing expectations of confidential government handling of sensitive business data. *See* the discussion in National Parks & Conservation Ass'n v. Morton, 498 F.2d 765 (D.C. Cir. 1974).

As the Freedom of Information (FOI) Act developed, its text was expanded to include a defined set of exclusions, which reflected a set of compromises with the general philosophy of openness. Under the FOI Act, information was to be presumed public upon request. Other precedential types of information were to be published in the *Federal Register* [9] or made public by dissemination through public reading rooms,[10] where the useful documents would be readily available. Agencies would be entitled, however, to withhold certain types of information from *any* such disclosure. The types were carefully specified in nine exemptions,[11] which resulted from extensive negotiations between the agencies and the congressional advocates of public disclosure.

As the new law took shape, most of the agencies obtained their desired exemptions in the hearing process or in the subsequent informal negotiations. Apparently, the NLRB failed to recognize what had been shaped without its participation. The Senate passed the FOI Act in 1964 without any amendment that might be used to protect NLRB witnesses from the disclosure of statements prior to Board hearings. That omission would have had a major impact on the Board's processes by remedying long-criticized methods of "trial by ambush." [12] Extraordinary consequences must have called for extraordinary measures by the Board. Three days after the Act was passed by the Senate, on July 28, 1964, Senator Humphrey used a rare procedural maneuver to call the Act back for reconsideration.[13] The Board, and perhaps the AFL-CIO, was quite interested in reconsideration of the investigations point, but unfortunately, history does not record the motivations underlying Senator Humphrey's action.

Humphrey engaged in what appears to have been a prearranged colloquy with the primary sponsor of the FOI Act, Senator Long of Missouri. Humphrey directly called for protection of NLRB witness statements, and he offered a belated amendment to keep all investigative files confidential. Long wanted

---

9 5 U.S.C. § 552(a)(1) (1976).

10 *Id.* § 552(a)(2).

11 *Id.* § 552(b)(1)-(9).

12 "Trial by ambush" was the unflattering term applied to the Board's refusal of prehearing discovery regarding the Board's case. Changes to that system have been rare and grudgingly adopted. *See* NLRB v. Adhesive Prods. Corp., 258 F.2d 403 (2d Cir. 1958); Alleyne, *The "Jencks Rule" in NLRB Proceedings*, 9 B.C. INDUS. & COM. L. REV. 891 (1968).

13 110 CONG. REC. 17,666 (1964).

labor support for his bill in the House. Humphrey wanted the statements of prospective witnesses for the NLRB to be subject to withholding until the witnesses had testified—a provision comparable to federal criminal practice under the Jencks Act. Senator Long promised that an accommodation would be made to meet Humphrey's concerns.[14] The bill was repassed.

The final Freedom of Information Act was adopted in 1966, after further Senate passage, Administration pressure for modifications, and a rather perfunctory House debate. The NLRB's witnesses were covered with the protection that Senator Humphrey had desired. Witness statements of a civil enforcement agency were not required to be made public if they were not "available by law to a party other than an agency," [15] i.e., they could be withheld from the public if they were not subject to a discovery motion in a court case against the agency.[16]

The exemption remained in this form during 1966-74, until the Act was amended. The Board was able to cite both the general discovery limitations on what was "available," and the historical intent of the Humphrey amendment as reasons for not disclosing the NLRB's witness statements.[17] In 1974, the Act was amended to eliminate this language and to substitute for it a narrow class of reasons for the withholding of investigative files.[18] That alteration of the Act and its controversial consequences are discussed in chapter XIII.

The exemption provisions permitting the withholding of personal privacy information [19] and agency internal memoranda [20]

---

[14] The accommodation promise was easily made because the House had not yet acted and passage was impossible until the House acted. Thus, redrafting could occur during the long election recess into 1965, by which time Vice President Humphrey was in an admirable position to work with Senator Long on an appropriate phrasing of the revised exemption.

[15] Pub. L. No. 90-23, § 552(b)(7), 81 Stat. 54 (1967).

[16] *See, e.g.,* Williams v. IRS, 345 F. Supp. 591 (D. Del. 1972), *aff'd,* 479 F.2d 317 (3d Cir. 1973), *cert. denied,* 414 U.S. 1024 (1973).

[17] *See, e.g.,* Wellman Indus. v. NLRB, 490 F.2d 427 (4th Cir.), *cert. denied,* 419 U.S. 834 (1974); Barceloneta Shoe Corp. v. Compton, 271 F. Supp. 591 (D. P.R. 1967). The latter was both the first case under the Act and the first challenge to Board discovery using the Act.

[18] Pub. L. No. 93-502, § 2(b), 88 Stat. 1561 (1974) (codified at 5 U.S.C. § 552(b)(7)(A)-(F) (1976)).

[19] 5 U.S.C. § 552(b)(6) (1976).

[20] *Id.* § 552(b)(5).

have remained unchanged since their original adoption in 1966. In addition, the Act's requirement for dissemination and indexing of guidelines, rules, and precedential opinions, which were the first two segments of the Freedom of Information Act,[21] have remained unchanged from the origins of the Act to the present time.

STRUCTURE OF THE ACT

There are three classes of public information governed by the Freedom of Information Act. The first class consists of agency rules of procedure, "substantive rules of general applicability," and "statements of general policy or interpretations" adopted by an agency. These must be published in the *Federal Register*.[22] The NLRB has published its procedural rules, including its very sparse provisions for prehearing discovery. The Board rarely if ever adopts substantive rules; the Board instead operates by adjudication of litigated precedents since it has historically preferred adjudication of specific cases over the adoption of rules [23] as a means of molding its law.

A second category of information affected by the FOI Act is the set of opinion and guidance information required to be made available for copying, with appropriate indexing.[24] This information usually is not published but is indexed and made available in agency reading rooms. It includes final opinions of the agency, staff manuals and instructions to agency staff *if* they affect members of the public, and those adopted statements of policy that have not been published by the agency.

The third class of information is the largest and most controversial. Any record within the control of any federal agency is accessible upon request of any person.[25] That expansive statement has a few exceptions. First, the request should reasonably specify the desired information, and requesters are subject to reasonable search and copying fees.[26] Second, the agency has the discretion, if it chooses to do so, to withhold data within one of nine ex-

---

21 *Id.* §§ 552(a)(1)-(2).

22 *Id.* § 552(a)(1).

23 *See, e.g.,* NLRB v. Bell Aerospace Co., 416 U.S. 267 (1974).

24 5 U.S.C. § 552(a)(2) (1976).

25 *Id.* § 552(a)(3).

26 *Id.* § 552(a)(4)(A).

empt classes of documents.[27] Third, if the agency and a reviewing court agree that the material is within a class of information that *could* be withheld because it is within one of the nine exemptions, then the court cannot override the agency's discretion to withhold it.[28] Finally, the person who has submitted to the government agency information appearing in the federal file may, when that file is requested under the FOI Act, have some rights to demand that the agency withhold the document. This latter issue is dealt with later as a "reverse-disclosure" problem.[29]

The structure of the third portion of the Act is relatively simple. An agency has a record in print or tape or other physical form. A person requests that the record be disclosed. The person need not explain why, or for whom, the information is sought.[30] The law treats all requesters alike and requires disclosure unless the information is exempt. For example, convicts about to be released from jail can ask the federal prosecutor for the addresses of the witnesses who testified against them. The agency should respond within ten days to the request for disclosure.[31] In some cases, the agency will ignore the time limits of the Act; in some cases, it will explain its delay and ask additional time; and in some cases, it will punctually respond to the request (although mere response is sufficient and actual delivery of records may take longer).

When the agency and the requesting person disagree about the release of the documents, the agency will respond in writing, denying the request, and the agency must cite the statutory exemption permitting the agency to refuse the request for disclosure. At that point, the requesting person may appeal within the agency.[32] If the agency continues to refuse disclosure, the person may receive a complete *de novo* reexamination of the legal status of the documents by suing the agency to enjoin

---

[27] *Id.* § 552(b) (1)-(9). *See* Chrysler Corp. v. Brown, 441 U.S. 281 (1979).

[28] Thus, the major question becomes not whether the exercise of the option was correct but whether the definition in the exemption covered the document at issue.

[29] *See* chapter XV *infra.*

[30] "Any person" is entitled to access. 5 U.S.C. § 552(a)(3) (1976).

[31] The 1974 amendments instituted a ten-day rule, which is usually ignored by the agencies. *Id.* § 552(a)(6)(A)(i); *see* 1 J. O'REILLY, FEDERAL INFORMATION DISCLOSURE § 7.02 (Oct. 1979).

[32] 5 U.S.C. § 552(a)(6)(A)(ii) (1976).

withholding.[33] If the requesting person wins, the court will order disclosure. It may also award attorneys fees and costs for the requester who has "substantially prevailed" against the agency.[34] If the court wishes, it may examine the records *in camera* to determine the correctness of the agency's legal claims. Each case is to be considered with the burden on the agency to support its claim of exemption.[35]

The structure of the FOI Act is almost identical at each of the federal agencies operating in the labor field. A processing office receives requests and farms them out to the substantive task organizations within the agency for that group to locate the documents; then the processing group determines whether that set of information about the agency or its activities (or about some third person investigated by the agency) can be withheld. If the program office wishes the records to be withheld and the request-processing office concurs, then a legal decision is reached within the agency, and the records are not disclosed. A responsible official, who faces individual penalties against any arbitrary action,[36] must concur in the agency's denial. Each of these steps is institutionalized within the agencies to comply with the Act's short deadlines for handling incoming requests.

Some labor agencies, such as the NLRB, do not even bother to treat routinely requested and routinely disclosed information as subject to the FOI Act.[37] For example, the Federal Mediation and Conciliation Service routinely sends out requested copies of forms prior to labor disputes by contracting unions and em-

---

[33] *Id.* § 552(a)(4)(B). The procedural "deck was stacked" against the agencies by the 1974 amendments to rectify what many liberal groups felt was the delaying and obstructive tactics of government agencies. Thus, the burden is on the agency, the case may be expedited, and the court may decide the merits *de novo*.

[34] *Id.* § 552(a)(4)(E). Unions, individuals, or small businesses are likely to win their fees and costs if successful; larger firms are less likely to ask for or receive such awards, although the awards may be made to them at the court's discretion.

[35] *Id.* § 552(a)(4)(B). If the agency fails to show that the material withheld was all within one of the exemptions (or several of them), the agency loses.

[36] *Id.* § 552(a)(4)(F). An "arbitrary" withholding decision may, upon request of a federal court, be reviewed by the Merit Systems Protection Board and disciplinary action taken against the employee. This has rarely been tried and is unlikely to be favored by courts or the personnel agencies.

[37] Interview with Stanley Weinbrecht, Associate General Counsel, National Labor Relations Board, in Washington, D.C. (Jan. 14, 1980).

ployers.[38] Since no agency has exclusive administrative control
over the decentralized operation of the Freedom of Information
Act process, each agency may use slightly variable procedures
to hasten the flow of records out to the public.

Each agency must reconcile its FOI Act procedures with the
needs of its own substantive programs and with the defined set of
procedural rights in the Act. When an agency is pulled between
the requirements of openness under the FOI Act and the needs
for administrative secrecy, which may or may not be covered by
the exemptions, then a tension develops. Courts will have to
unravel the results of the disputes. The case of the NLRB and
its investigative files is one of the most interesting of the FOI
Act's many tangled stories of conflict.[39]

FACTORS IN INFORMATION POLICY

[The conflict between openness, based on the desire for *accountable* government, and the Freedom of Information Act's exemptions, based on the desire for *efficient* government, has had a
significant effect on the information policy of the federal labor
agencies.] The ability to investigate fraudulent conduct by a
union, which might be prosecuted, is an important federal power.
When done objectively and correctly, such government work is
a benefit to all of society. Confidentiality can help. Some observers might consequently feel, however, that the Labor Department acts too infrequently or has been unduly influenced not
to prosecute vigorously.[40] A document rebutting such observations helps the Department's image, and a disclosure request
would be readily granted. Other observers may feel that improper
motives had led the Department into some of its investigations
and that these motives should be publicized to call congressional

---

[38] Interview with David Vaughn, General Counsel, Federal Mediation and
Conciliation Service, in Washington, D.C. (Jan. 14, 1980).

[39] *See* chapter XIII *infra.*

[40] For example, a press inquiry into abuses of workmen's compensation
benefits was scuttled when the Department refused to disclose the files of
certain employee claims, asserting that the individuals whose misuse of the
compensation system was claimed had a privacy right not to have the files
disseminated. The Department won. Ironically, the workers were among
those assigned to the Labor Department group in charge of workmen's compensation! Plain Dealer Publishing Co. v. United States Dep't of Labor, 471
F. Supp. 1023 (D. D.C. 1979). Release could have spared the Department
some embarrassment about the misconduct, but the Department placed the
privacy value above the public oversight value of disclosure.

oversight attention to a bureaucratic vendetta in a particular case. A record in the agency's file may inferentially indicate an improper motive or illegal method, and its disclosure could deter government misconduct in some future case.

Balanced against the openness policy's benefits are its inhibitions against efficient government. A "chilling effect" analysis might be applied: investigative witnesses might be chilled and deterred from freely telling government agents of law violations in some cases.[41] This chill may be especially felt at the NLRB, whose proceedings cannot begin until some individual volunteers to bring a complaint.[42] Another chill from records disclosure might befall agency policymaking employees and their subordinates. The reasons given for agency actions, as stated in internal memos, would be less freely expressed and perhaps less creative if all the memos were placed on the public record.[43] Finally, some agency files contain submitted information that is either confidential business data or personal privacy information, shared with the government under expectations that it will be kept in confidencce. A threat of full disclosure chills that relationship of trust between the government and the party sharing the confidential information. To avoid that ill effect, the discretionary exemptions are invoked.[44]

An agency that considers itself "above the law" in information matters often finds itself litigating more cases than it can handle from challengers asserting rights under the Freedom of Information Act.[45] This was the case, historically, with the NLRB's

---

[41] This is poignantly illustrated by the convicts who testified in several 1979 hearings that convicted criminals compared their files, obtained under the FOI Act, to identify informants by piecing together clues to their identities. The informants are no longer informing, having been "terminated with extreme prejudice." For other instances, *see* GENERAL ACCOUNTING OFFICE, IMPACT OF THE FREEDOM OF INFORMATION AND PRIVACY ACTS IN LAW ENFORCEMENT AGENCIES (1978).

[42] This is one of the underlying concerns in the Board's vigorous defense of witness statements. Interview with Stanley Weinbrecht, *supra* note 37.

[43] This is the primary rationale for exempting intraagency memoranda from disclosure. 5 U.S.C. § 552(b)(5) (1976); *see* 2 J. O'REILLY, FEDERAL INFORMATION DISCLOSURE § 15.02 (1977, Supp. 1979).

[44] The exemption, contained in 5 U.S.C. § 552(b)(5), was invoked 4,992 times in 1977. The third heaviest user was the Labor Department (475 denials), followed by the NLRB (318 denials).

[45] Whether or not the agency indeed presumes itself to be untouched by the law, its attraction of too many suits indicates both an attitudinal and legal problem. The NLRB has had more FOIA suits brought against it than any

posture, since the Board fought vigorously on two fronts—
against disclosure of its precedential Advice and Appeals Memoranda [46] and against prehearing disclosure of its witness statements.[47] The Board won partial victories in both cases. The
Board's policy still firmly ignores the FOI Act's presumptions
of openness where that policy clashes with Board operations. The
less active federal labor agencies have had somewhat less of a
problem with managing the FOI Act's administration.[48] Their
choices have more frequently been in favor of disclosure than
have the Board's. By 1980, it is fair to say that a matured
policy in most of the agencies routinely disclosed most of the
information that the Act had intended to be disclosed. Only in one
area, that of witness statements, is there still a simmering
controversy.[49]

THE ROLE OF CONGRESS AND THE COURTS

Except for one brief episode in 1964 (the Humphrey amendment
described above), the Freedom of Information Act has evolved
without any comment or complaint from the National Labor
Relations Board to the Congress. A sister agency, the Federal
Mediation and Conciliation Service, was able to have a protective
interpretation written into the Act's legislative history.[50] For the
most part, however, the labor community (both the federal agencies and their constituencies) have been silent on the issue of
information disclosure. Congress has therefore remained out of
the labor field in its revisions of the Freedom of Information Act.

Perhaps the only relevant change to the law was the inclusion of many multimember agencies, including the NLRB, in the

---

other agency; for a time, it had one suit a day coming in from a federal
court litigant in one of the district courts.

[46] *See* chapter XII *infra.*

[47] *See* chapter XIII *infra.*

[48] The Federal Labor Relations Authority, Federal Mediation and Conciliation Service, the EEOC, and the Department of Labor's non-OSHA units
have had relatively few problems. Interviews with Elizabeth Medaglia,
Deputy Solicitor, FLRA; David Vaughn, General Counsel, FMCS; Constance
duPre, Associate General Counsel, EEOC; Soffia Petters, Associate General
Counsel, U.S. Department of Labor, in Washington, D.C. (Jan. 14, 1980).

[49] *See* chapter XIII *infra.*

[50] 5 U.S.C. § 552(b)(4) (1976); *see* H.R. REP. No. 1497, 89th Cong., 2d
Sess. (1966).

1976 Government in the Sunshine Act.[51] The statute required the multimember agencies to make their decisions in open public meetings, unless the agency acted under one of the "Sunshine exemptions"[52] or unless the agency chose to resolve its disputed cases by circulation of draft written opinions to all members.[53] With the exception of that tangential change, Congress has been remarkably uninterested in altering the disclosure and nondisclosure policies of the Freedom of Information Act as they apply to the NLRB.

The congressional inaction has been well balanced by more activity in the courts. The NLRB has independent litigating authority in federal courts. Its attorneys from Washington have fought more than one hundred Freedom of Information Act cases in dozens of federal courts.[54] Labor issues have been involved in dozens of appellate cases, many with comparable factual issues achieving different results in the different courts of appeals.[55] The Supreme Court has dealt with two major NLRB cases, the *Sears*[56] and *Robbins*[57] decisions and, in at least two other cases, has dealt with personnel information of a type similar to that experienced in labor practice, the *Chrysler*[58] affirmative action statistics and the *Rose*[59] disciplinary reports cases.

Information policy for the agencies in the labor field has been relatively simple. At agencies other than the NLRB, much of

---

[51] 5 U.S.C. § 552b (1976).

[52] *Id.* § 552b(c).

[53] And thereby avoided a "meeting"; the Sunshine Act applies if there is a meeting of the agency members but not if they act by written circulations of proposed opinions. *See id.* § 552b(a)(2).

[54] For a listing of all the cases, *see* OFFICE OF INFORMATION LAW & POLICY, U.S. DEP'T OF JUSTICE, FREEDOM OF INFORMATION CASE LIST (1979).

[55] *Compare* Robbins Tire & Rubber Co. v. NLRB, 563 F.2d 724 (5th Cir. 1977), *rev'd*, 437 U.S. 214 (1978), *with* Title Guarantee Co. v. NLRB, 407 F. Supp. 498 (S.D.N.Y. 1975), *rev'd and remanded*, 534 F.2d 484 (2d Cir. 1976), *cert. denied*, 429 U.S. 834 (1976).

[56] NLRB v. Sears, Roebuck & Co., 421 U.S. 132 (1975).

[57] NLRB v. Robbins Tire & Rubber Co., 437 U.S. 214 (1978).

[58] Chrysler Corp. v. Brown, 441 U.S. 281 (1979).

[59] United States Dep't of the Air Force v. Rose, 425 U.S. 352 (1976).

the information is available; relatively few exemptions are claimed.[60] For the NLRB, there are several classes of information. One large body of information is routinely disclosed without need for an FOI request.[61] Some other information, including advice memoranda prepared by Board headquarters attorneys and election/representation files, are sometimes disclosed and sometimes withheld. The class of documents including prospective witnesses in NLRB hearings, however, is protected by blanket confidentiality treatment and almost always is withheld by the Board.[62] Knowledge of this firm stance has reduced disclosure requests for these types of documents to a relative handful.[63]

EFFECTS OF INFORMATION POLICY ON THE FEDERAL AGENCIES REGULATING LABOR MATTERS

In the course of preparing this text, officials of several agencies with FOI Act duties agreed to participate in interviews. The success enjoyed by the National Labor Relations Board in defending its witness statements before the Supreme Court delighted the other agencies' counsels who were interviewed. The Federal Labor Relations Authority, a new adjudicative body created by the Civil Service Act, has modeled its positions on issues of public disclosure upon those of the NLRB.[64] Although the requesting person in some of its cases is another federal agency and cannot therefore be a "person" for Freedom of Information Act requests, the Federal Labor Relations Authority has received "FOI requests" from agencies. It applies the NLRB approach and refuses to disclose the witness statements until after the

---

[60] Interviews, *supra* note 48.

[61] The Board received about 1,500 inquiries which it considered "requests" in 1979. Many more requests for documents were satisfied simply by handing out the information with no recording or formal processing. These larger numbers of literal requests were not considered statutory "requests."

[62] Interview with Stanley Weinbrecht, *supra* note 37.

[63] *Id.* Some make the request but soon learn that it is fruitless; the staff usually does not hear from these requesters again after its firm denials.

[64] Staff attorneys for the Board and those for the Authority share the common prosecutorial desire to keep their case secret until it is presented; for the Authority, it is a case of one federal employee (prosecutor) keeping the statement of another (witness) away from a third (the agency's representative) so that one agency (FLRA) can enforce against another federal agency. Nonfederal observers may find the whole thing a compounding of absurdities.

proceeding has closed and no further action upon it can be taken.[65] That cooling-off period after file closure serves the Authority's needs.

The Federal Mediation and Conciliation Service (FMCS), which has many active mediation cases, considers the commercial secrets exemption to be most important, because legislative history during development of the FOI Act included an explicit reference that the commercial exemption would protect mediation files.[66] If the FMCS finds a requester is fishing in the files for a mediation officials' interpretation of the pending case, then the agency's lawyers claim *both* the commercial confidentiality exemption to disclosure and the provision exempting internal agency memoranda.[67] Because the FMCS has not been sued, its withholding policies have remained consistent.[68] Much of the routine information it discloses, including Form F-7 filings recording potential strike situations, is not even considered to be Freedom of Information Act material.[69]

The Equal Employment Opportunity Commission also found the NLRB's Supreme Court victory protecting witness statements to be a very pleasing turn in the case law. With the NLRB precedent in hand, the EEOC has been able to defend more readily its own witness statements.[70]

Finally, the Labor Department's investigations range into many different areas, including the only criminal enforcement authority of the relevant federal agencies.[71] Labor's withholding of information requested under the Freedom of Information Act is predominantly the safeguarding of Occupational Safety and

---

[65] To date, the Authority's attorneys state that they have not been challenged on legal grounds, although an agency is not a "person" and could never bring an FOI Act suit against another agency. *See* 5 U.S.C. §§ 551(2), 552(a)(3) (1976).

[66] H.R. REP. No. 1497, 89th Cong., 2d Sess. (1966).

[67] Interview with David Vaughn, *supra* note 38.

[68] *Id.* An unrelated but comparable agency, the National Mediation Board, has, however, been sued for disclosure of labor union authorization cards. American Airlines, Inc. v. National Mediation Bd., 588 F.2d 863 (2d Cir. 1978).

[69] Interview with David Vaughn, *supra* note 38.

[70] Interview with Constance duPre, Associate General Counsel, Equal Employment Opportunity Commission, in Washington, D.C. (Feb. 7, 1980).

[71] The Labor Department prosecutes fraud cases and violations of the Labor-Management Reporting and Disclosure Act and similar statutes.

Health Administration (OSHA) files from the disclosure requests of the investigated firms and of plaintiffs' attorneys.[72] OSHA comprises the bulk of Labor's FOI Act caseload.[73] As a result of those investigative files conflicts, Labor was a large user of the FOI Act's law enforcement exemptions, notwithstanding its policy of making many items of information subject to free disclosure without need for an FOI request.[74]

USERS OF THE ACT

The Labor Department cannot keep track of its many thousands of requests for information, but it estimates that perhaps 10 percent of FOI requests come from unions, a large percentage from employers, and a large percentage from private attorneys who use Labor information in litigation. Relatively few requests are received from individuals for their own files.[75] Because of OSHA's direct relationship with evidence useful in liability lawsuits, many of its requests can be attributed to extrajudicial discovery and supplementation of discovery.[76]

The National Labor Relations Board finds that approximately one-half of all incoming requests come from parties to a proceeding, often requesting the Advice Memoranda that justified the dismissal of a charge without further action by the Board.[77] In the last year for which statistics are available,[78] the Board received more than 650 requests from persons who were actually parties to a Board proceeding. The Board has seen wide variations of the numbers of pending requests, depending on current case law, although the 1978 Supreme Court decision protecting witness statements virtually eliminated overnight the Board's

---

[72] Interview with Soffia Petters, Associate General Counsel, U.S. Department of Labor, in Washington, D.C. (Jan. 14, 1980).

[73] *Id.* The OSHA load is 60 percent or more.

[74] Few of the requests received by the Bureau of Labor Statistics or the Pension Plans (ERISA) group are treated as FOIA requests. *Id.*

[75] *Id.*

[76] *Id.; see, e.g.*, Pilar v. S.S. Hess Petrol, 55 F.R.D. 159 (D. Md. 1972).

[77] Interview with Stanley Weinbrecht, *supra* note 37.

[78] *Id.* This was 1977.

considerable burden of pending FOI lawsuits and appeals.[79] The
burden of such cases has declined, although unfair labor practice
charges are still the focal point of about 90 percent of all NLRB
information disclosure requests.

The Equal Employment Opportunity Commission's accounting
of requests and requesting persons is incomplete, since the Commission ceased to chronicle the identities or interests of the FOI
requesters several years ago as an economy measure.[80] In 1975-
76, a study found that 45 percent of requesters were either
charging parties or respondent-employer representatives who were
engaged in proceedings before the Commission.[81] Unions have
rarely used the Act at the EEOC. A specific provision in Title
VII, however, governs the rights of charging parties and respondents to obtain information on EEOC cases.[82] Thus, the
general public has more limited rights of access to the Commission's data than do participants. This factor increases the number of requests attributed to active parties in Commission charge-
resolution proceedings. The requests proceed under the FOI Act
but exercise the statutory Title VII access rights.

The strangest users of all are federal agencies themselves,
which ask the Federal Labor Relations Authority to release
FLRA files under the Freedom of Information Act, although an
agency is not considered to be a person for the exercise of FOI
Act rights.[83] The Authority is relatively new, and one of its own
priorities has been to set up a decision system for the handling
of pending FOI requests when these are received from unions
or members of the public.[84]

A related agency, the Merit Systems Protection Board, has a
set of special regulations governing "whistle-blower" employees,
whose disclosure of misconduct leads to some investigation of

---

[79] The Board went from 94 pending cases and 410 pending appeals to a
mere handful after NLRB v. Robbins Tire & Rubber Co., 437 U.S. 214 (1978).
Interview with Stanley Weinbrecht, *supra* note 37.

[80] Interview with Constance duPre, *supra* note 70.

[81] *Id.*

[82] *Id.;* *see* Civil Rights Act of 1964, §§ 706, 709, 42 U.S.C. §§ 2000e-5,
2000e-8 (1976).

[83] 5 U.S.C. §§ 551(1)-(2), 552(a)(3) (1976).

[84] Interview with Elizabeth Medaglia, Deputy Solicitor, Federal Labor
Relations Authority, in Washington, D.C. (Feb. 7, 1980). *See* the FLRA's
information policy, 45 Fed. Reg. 3482 (1980) (to be codified at 5 C.F.R.
§ 2411.3).

waste or abuse in government.[85] It is likely that many of the requests for that information may come from the press or from persons actively seeking to discredit an agency's programs. The MSP Board is, however, too recently constituted to permit a historical assessment of its disclosure policies.

Use of the Act also varies among business groups. The employer who seeks information from the NLRB staff's file may be doing so to assist in a particular case. Another firm's request to the Bureau of Labor Statistics for certain data will assist in its economic forecasting. And a third firm may be interested in identifying an informant to OSHA.

It is relatively rare that the press, original sponsors of the FOI Act, use the Act to gain useful information. Instead, the press relies on traditional news sources. Occasional use of the FOI Act by the press has on some occasions been extremely *un*helpful; in a Labor Department case in which excessive compensation claims were allegedly asserted by workers charged with administering a compensation system, the privacy of the workers was held to override the public's interest in the misconduct allegations.

IS THE FREEDOM OF INFORMATION ACT WORTH THE TROUBLE?

More information comes out of the United States government under legal rights of access as well as under publication programs than from any other government, perhaps in the history of governments. The Freedom of Information Act's exposure of the internal workings of government has been a major political science phenomenon for democratic ideals of citizen oversight of government. Wrongdoing and mismanagement have occasionally been exposed from government-released documents forced into public view by the FOI Act.

The costs, however, have ranged in the millions of dollars, many thousands of professional staff hours diverted to respond to FOI requests, and some disruption in public confidence in government. This last factor may be the net long-term loss of greatest importance. The short-term losses, in programs delayed and costs incurred, can be dealt with by increasing administrative overhead funds of the agencies, but the doubt that many

---

[85] 44 Fed. Reg. 75,913; 75,922 (1979) (to be codified at 5 C.F.R. pt. 1261 app.).

people feel about the government's ability to keep a secret is fraught with complications. As long as the NLRB succeeds in protection of witness statements, it may do better in retaining confidence than the Federal Bureau of Investigation or the Central Intelligence Agency has done.[86]

Ultimately, whether disclosure or public access statutes are worth the trouble is a societal decision. For the NLRB, Supreme Court endorsement of its withholding of investigative files reduced a flood of requests to a trickle.[87] As a result, deterrence of programs is slight, if felt at all. The public has, however, gained more knowledge of how the process works, of how decisions are made, and of what the labor bureaucracy's plans and directions will be. From that perspective, Freedom of Information has been a success. The Act has, however, created disincentives to commercial firms' voluntary cooperation with some federal agencies.[88] From that perspective, the Act has done significant harm to administrative agency cooperation with the business community.

---

[86] *See, e.g.,* GENERAL ACCOUNTING OFFICE, *supra* note 41.

[87] Interview with Stanley Weinbrecht, *supra* note 37.

[88] *See* chapter XVI *infra.*

CHAPTER XII

The Freedom of Information Act: A Tool for Opening Up the NLRB

The National Labor Relations Board's policymaking functions operate outside the mainstream of federal agency rulemaking. The Board uses the adjudicative model of individual case precedents established on certain facts, with policies altered as the facts of a particular case warrant a change and, more importantly, as the Board's membership and political philosophy change.[1] The adjudicative approach makes it important that potential litigating parties understand which cases the Board is likely to consider, and why, and which philosophies underlie the present Board's adjudicative decisions.[2] The Freedom of Information Act has had a profound effect in opening up the processes and reasoning of the Board and in forcing the dissemination of more data about the Board's decisional processes.

THE STATUTORY RULE

The first two sections of the Freedom of Information Act prohibit agencies from maintaining "secret law"—nonpublic rules of action or procedure that affect private litigants.[3] An agency such as the NLRB cannot use a rule that adversely affects the

---

[1] For a good description of the development of majority views within the Board, see E. MILLER, AN ADMINISTRATIVE APPRAISAL OF THE NLRB (Labor Relations and Public Policy Series No. 16, 2d ed. 1978). The Board enjoys great freedom to alter its direction, because it is not subject to mandatory rulemaking as long as it chooses to make its policy determinations by adjudication. See NLRB v. Bell Aerospace Co., 416 U.S. 267 (1974).

[2] Because so much discretion is delegated, regional opinions and communications between regions and Board headquarters are very important. In other agencies, the only decisions may be made in Washington.

[3] For a discussion of the "secret law" issue in detail, see 1 J. O'REILLY, FEDERAL INFORMATION DISCLOSURE ¶¶ 6-1 to 6-33 (1977 & Supp. 1979).

rights of a litigant without first assuring public availability [4] (and in some cases publication) [5] of that rule. These duties are independent of the general document-request provisions [6] of the Act.

The Freedom of Information Act requires *Federal Register* publication for four types of information:

1. Organization of the agency, including means by which the agency can be petitioned or addresses to which requests can be made;

2. Statements of the agency's procedures;

3. Statements of the rules for the agency's procedural and reporting requirements; and

4. Substantive rules of general applicability and statements of policy or interpretations that have been adopted as agency policy by the agency. [7]

A separate class of information need not be published in the *Federal Register* but must be affirmatively available, indexed, and accessible to the public (e.g., by reading rooms). This class of information includes final opinions of the agency in adjudications (which are promptly published and accessible under normal NLRB practice), statements of policy or interpretations adopted by the agency but not published in the *Federal Register*, and "administrative staff manuals and instructions to staff that affect a member of the public." [8] Agencies commonly put these on display in a reading room. "Affirmative" availability means that the agency makes special efforts to open files to visitors, without requests.

This administrative scheme is slightly expanded from the comparable section in the 1947 Administrative Procedure Act, which gave virtually the same directives to the federal agencies. One of the differences instituted by the 1966 law is the addition of a clause prohibiting an agency from relying on, citing, or using documents against a member of the public unless those

---

[4] The minimal availability includes indexing and a public reading room area. 5 U.S.C. § 552(a)(2) (1976).

[5] *Id.* § 552(a)(1).

[6] *Id.* § 552(a)(3); *see* chapter XI of this text for a discussion of that access procedure.

[7] 5 U.S.C. § 552(a)(1) (1976).

[8] *Id.* § 552(a)(2).

documents have been made available to the public in accordance with the Act's formal access procedures.[9] If the employer in a labor case could show that the Board has informally adopted a policy of rejecting employer exceptions written on green paper, for example, and the Board rejected its litigation filings without first publishing a formal notice or making available a procedural rule regarding the "green paper prohibition," *then* the employer would be able to challenge the Board's action successfully. The thrust of the availability-and-indexing provision is to prohibit use of secret law by an agency to the detriment of someone outside the agency.[10]

Board decisions are published and available for sale, and persons wishing them may subscribe to them through the Government Printing Office or by reading the decisions in the Board's public reading room at the Executive Secretary's Office in Washington. The Board rarely uses the *Federal Register*.

Because the Freedom of Information Act was intended to strike at the use of "secret law" by the agencies, it was considered important to define *which* of the Board's practices would be most vulnerable to disclosure under the key provision in the Act. Items that were *adopted* (i.e., substantively assented to by the Members), have the effect of a final decision for the Board, and have adverse decisional impact on a private person must be accessible.[11] Other nonindexed information may be available upon request.[12] The litigation over NLRB policies has developed in two directions; some information was required to be affirmatively available, and some other information (including opinion letters) was available on request because the courts refused to allow

---

[9] *Id.* § 552(a)(1) (last paragraph), (a)(2) (last sentence).

[10] Agencies are presumed to have satisfied this requirement if they can show that a particular party received actual notice. A prior warning against the use of green paper, for example, would permit the Board, using that hypothetical above, to strike a later submission.

[11] For the definition of "adoption" of a policy, *see* 1 J. O'REILLY, FEDERAL INFORMATION DISCLOSURE § 6.03 (1977 & Supp. 1979). In the broadest terms, adoption occurs when the agency management approves, relies on, or promulgates the rule or policy described.

[12] General access can be used even for publicly available documents if a requester chooses to write in for them, 5 U.S.C. § 552(a)(3) (1976), but the converse is not true. The mere fact that someone could write to the Board and request a document under general access rules does not excuse the Board's failure to index it and make it accessible under (a)(2). *Appalachian Power Co. v. Train*, 566 F.2d 451 (4th Cir. 1977).

withholding that information under a Freedom of Information Act exemption.[13]

THE BATTLE OVER "SECRET LAW"

The failure to act can be as much a policy decision as an action itself. The decision not to pursue a charge into the NLRB complaint process is a final decision against the charging party by the General Counsel of the Board. If the person asserting a violation of the Act is unable to convince the General Counsel to bring a complaint, then there will be no Board proceeding at all. That exercise of complaint authority is unreviewable under the case law.[14]

Procedurally, the Regional Directors acting for the General Counsel have the first level of discretionary authority.[15] If the Regional Director believes a charge should be pursued, the Regional Director files a charge. If that Director determines not to file a charge, the letter rejecting the charging party's assertions is accompanied by a statement that the charging party may appeal to the General Counsel in Washington. The odds for reversing that Regional Director's decision are quite low.[16] In the most controversial cases, or those of novel interest, the Advice Branch of the General Counsel's Office will issue an Advice Memorandum to the Regional Director before the decision to reject the charge is made.[17]

There is a very great chance that "secret law" or unannounced agency policies affecting private persons could emerge from this process of internal decision-making communications within the Board hierarchy. The reasons for the denial of the complaint may help the union or the employer in future cases in which

---

[13] For the investigative materials cases, see chapter XIII *infra*.

[14] Vaca v. Sipes, 386 U.S. 171 (1967); 29 U.S.C. § 153(d) (1976).

[15] 29 C.F.R. §§ 101.6, 101.8, 102.15, 102.19 (1979). The role of the Regional Director was examined in the disclosure context by the Supreme Court in 1975. NLRB v. Sears, Roebuck & Co., 421 U.S. 132 (1975).

[16] The system is described effectively in NLRB v. Sears, Roebuck & Co., 421 U.S. 132 (1975). The procedures are detailed in the Board's procedural rules, 29 C.F.R. § 101.6 (1979). See Division 1267, Amalgamated Ass'n of St., Elec. Ry, & Motor Coach Employees v. Ordman, 320 F.2d 729 (D.C. Cir. 1963).

[17] NLRB v. Sears, Roebuck & Co., 421 U.S. 132 (1975); see 29 C.F.R. § 101.8 (1979).

similar conduct is alleged; the drafting or the collection of evidence or the quantum of proof presented in subsequent cases will be affected by knowledge of the reasons why the General Counsel or the Regional Director issued a denial of a charge in a particular case.

The essence of a prodisclosure argument asserting "secret law" in an agency proceeding is the assertion that a final disposition of a case, adverse to a party, can be made by an agency official.[18] That final disposition is a law-making power in that the official establishes what the rule of law for that type of case shall be.[19] If the information is not affirmatively made available to the public, this line of argument then holds that the agency has utilized "secret law" to decide the case and that the Freedom of Information Act has been violated.[20]

In 1970, an American Bar Association (ABA) committee report criticized the NLRB's refusal to disclose the lower-level decisions that disposed of many cases without formal proceedings. The ABA group noted that the Board made decisions to dispose of some cases through litigated hearings but that other cases were also of precedential value because no action had been taken on them: "It [the problem] is in all the remaining cases, however, where the General Counsel either through the Advice Branch or through the Office of Appeals determines that issuance of complaint *is not warranted,* and that such determination constitutes final agency action of precedential import." [21]

THE SEARS CASE

Sears, Roebuck & Co. sought access to certain Advice and Appeals Memoranda of the NLRB and relied on the precedential value of the documents as support for its argument that the Freedom of Information Act required their availability. The Board argued that the Memoranda rejecting a charge were not final opinions of the agency and that, even if they were, they were exempt as internal agency memoranda used in policy-

---

[18] *See* the rationale discussed in NLRB v. Sears, Roebuck & Co., 421 U.S. 132 (1975).

[19] This was the situation in *Sears* because of the rarity of any override of the General Counsel's Advice Memoranda.

[20] 5 U.S.C. § 552(a) (2) (1976).

[21] 2 ABA LABOR RELATIONS LAW SECTION 7 (1970), *quoted in* NLRB v. Sears, Roebuck & Co., 421 U.S. 132, 156-57 (1975).

making. Sears won in the District of Columbia district and appellate courts, and the Board sought and received certiorari from the Supreme Court.[22]

Before the Supreme Court, Sears argued in the alternative that the memoranda disposing of cases were *either* "secret law" required to be made accessible or were nonexempt agency records, which could be requested from the agency by any person, including the employer. The Board responded that the opinions which it was required to publish under the Act did not include this class of memoranda. Even if they could be requested and were agency records, without benefit of affirmative accessibility, the Board argued that they were exempt from required disclosure.[23]

The Supreme Court's analysis treated separately the issues of exemption from requested disclosure and required availability to the public. As to individual requests, the internal agency memoranda exemption to the Freedom of Information Act[24] incorporates into the withholding powers of an agency the litigation privilege concepts of the federal discovery rules. If a document were normally privileged in civil discovery, it would not have to be disclosed under the Freedom of Information Act.[25] The exemption covered such categories of withholding in civil litigation as the executive privilege for internal agency predecisional documents,[26] the work product privilege,[27] and the attorney-client

---

[22] Sears, Roebuck & Co. v. NLRB, 346 F. Supp. 751 (D. D.C. 1972), *aff'd*, 480 F.2d 1195 (D.C. Cir. 1973), *aff'd in part, rev'd in part, and remanded*, 421 U.S. 132 (1975).

[23] The primary position was that the material was not under 5 U.S.C. § 552(a)(2); the fallback position was that, even if it was so required to be available, the access provisions of (a) did not apply because the material was exempted by 5 U.S.C. § 552(b)(5).

[24] 5 U.S.C. § 552(b)(5) (1976).

[25] The civil discovery privileges were placed into the Act's disclosure requirements in recognition of its potential use as an alternate means of discovery. *See* 2 J. O'REILLY, FEDERAL INFORMATION DISCLOSURE § 15.03 (1977 & Supp. 1979).

[26] Renegotiation Board v. Grumman Aircraft Eng'r Corp., 421 U.S. 168 (1975).

[27] Because of the exemption, nothing in the FOI Act "would override normal privileges dealing with the work product." 110 CONG. REC. 17,667 (1964) (remarks of sponsor, Sen. Long). *See also* Mead Data Central, Inc. v. United States Dep't of the Air Force, 566 F.2d 242 (D.C. Cir. 1977). The work product privilege has been held to apply to the NLRB nonattorney investigators who work under the general instructions of Board attorneys

communications privilege.[28] According to the Court, postdecisional explanations could *not* be withheld, and the agency documents that state reasons for an adopted decision must be released. Final opinion documents of an agency could never enjoy the traditional *pre*decisional privilege because they dispose of the matter that was before the agency, usually with an explanation of the agency's rationale. Therefore, the Court held, they could not be covered by the predecisional documents protection of the internal memoranda exemption.[29]

The Supreme Court's conclusion from this analysis was that the set of NLRB Advice and Appeals Memoranda, which acted as a final disposition by deciding that no complaint would be filed, could not be exempted from requests for disclosure. Those memoranda, however, that merely open the process of hearing the case by directing the filing of a complaint are *pre*decisional and so remain exempt from required disclosure.[30] The Court reasoned that those findings by NLRB officials that do dispose of charges "are precisely the kind of agency law in which the public is so vitally interested and which Congress sought to prevent the Agency from keeping secret."[31] It went on to the next step, determining that the memoranda were final opinions made in the adjudication of cases by the General Counsel. Therefore, the memoranda in the cases dismissed by the General Counsel must be made affirmatively available to the public, with an index as required by the Freedom of Information Act.[32] *Sears* was a landmark case for the Board.[33]

For that large body of cases in which the Board proceeds into hearings and adjudication, the memoranda are not final dispositions.[34] They are part of the prehearing ammunition of the

---

in preparing cases. Associated Dry Goods Corp. v. NLRB, 455 F. Supp. 802 (S.D.N.Y. 1978). *But see* Poss v. NLRB, 565 F.2d 654 (10th Cir. 1977).

[28] Hickman v. Taylor, 329 U.S. 495 (1947), *cited in* NLRB v. Sears, Roebuck & Co., 421 U.S. 132, 149 n.16 (1975).

[29] NLRB v. Sears, Roebuck & Co., 421 U.S. 132, 153-54 (1975).

[30] *Id.* at 132.

[31] *Id.*

[32] The index requirement applies because of the affirmative availability requirements of 5 U.S.C. § 552(a)(2) (1976).

[33] Interview with Stanley Weinbrecht, Associate General Counsel, National Labor Relations Board, in Washington, D.C. (Jan. 14, 1980).

[34] That is, the memoranda are part of a continuing policy/adjudicative development process rather than an epitaph for the proceedings.

Board's trial attorney and constitute a form of "work product." Therefore, they qualify like other types of work product materials for the internal memoranda exemption from required FOI Act disclosure.[35]

The "secret law" problem of hidden precedents does not occur when the NLRB procedures lead to a hearing rather than dismissal of the charge. This is because the decision shifts to the Board and away from the General Counsel's organization. The precedent, if any, will be set by the Board, and the legal value of the General Counsel's memoranda is limited to the value of any advocate's submission of argument on a contested case.

Precedential value can be, and is, avoided by the Board in those cases in which the Advice and Appeals Memoranda are limited to "the circumstances of this case" as the sole explanation of the dismissal of the charge. When the agency limits its explanation to that, the Freedom of Information Act does not compel the agency to go any farther and explain its decision.[36]

A document that may be underlying a dismissal of a charge may be shielded from disclosure when the memorandum author carefully avoids an express reliance on that document. Implicit reliance is not covered by the obligation to disclose, as the Court in *Sears* obliquely decided: [37] "if an agency chooses *expressly* to adopt or incorporate by reference an intraagency memorandum," then it waives the protection of the document under the intraagency exemption and must instead rely on some other FOI Act exemption.[38] Because so many memoranda are routinely requested and disclosed, authors of the memoranda are well aware of the need to be circumspect if they wish to protect a certain statement or document from disclosure with or after the memorandum.[39]

---

[35] NLRB v. Sears, Roebuck & Co., 421 U.S. 132 (1975). The content of the General Counsel document remains the same, but its legal status shifts from final decision (if a no-complaint decision) to temporary adversarial position of the "prosecutor" in a case to be decided by a neutral set of NLRB Member "judges."

[36] *See* 1 J. O'REILLY, FEDERAL INFORMATION DISCLOSURE § 9.04 (1977 & Supp. 1979).

[37] NLRB v. Sears, Roebuck & Co., 421 U.S. 132, 161 (1975). Note that the Court italicized "expressly" to exclude a theory of implicit reliance as a basis for disclosure.

[38] For example, an ongoing law enforcement proceeding may be involved that may be protected by the exemption at 5 U.S.C. § 552(b)(7). *See* NLRB v. Robbins Tire & Rubber Co., 437 U.S. 214 (1978).

[39] Interview with Stanley Weinbrecht, *supra* note 33.

INFORMAL NOTES DIRECTING DISMISSALS

Sears provided the guiding case law for the later Fifth Circuit opinion in *Kent Corp.* v. *NLRB*.[40] The Regional Director's staff meeting about a charge produced a staff report with marginal notations about dismissal, which were scribbled by the Director as those views emerged in the conversation among the staff. The Fifth Circuit rejected imposition of any obligation on the Regional Director to prepare formal explanations of a decision not to bring charges.[41] It also found that notations not formally transcribed into an opinion could not be considered to be the institutional view of the Regional Director, acting as a delegate of the General Counsel. Had it instead been an institutional view, adopted by the agent of the General Counsel in dismissing the case, it would have fallen under the *Sears* ruling for disclosure of "secret law." [42] In the *Kent* situation, however, mere notations were held not to be disclosable.[43] Although the employer also argued that the affirmative availability requirements of the Act had not been met, the *Kent* court ruled that internal predecisional memos were not covered by the mandatory availability requirement.[44] Instead, the instructions to the agency staff, which officials would usually be required to make available to the public, could be exempted from any disclosure when (and only when) the standards of the internal memoranda exemption had been satisfied.[45]

---

[40] 530 F.2d 612 (5th Cir.), *cert. denied*, 429 U.S. 920 (1976).

[41] Because "no document in controversy purports to explain why the Regional Director decided not to issue a complaint," the court would have had to piece together scraps of comments or alternatively force the agency to create an explanation of its decision. *Id.* at 619. But an agency need not do such creation. Renegotiation Board v. Grumman Aircraft Eng'r Corp., 421 U.S. 168, 192 (1975).

[42] Kent Corp. v. NLRB, 530 F.2d 612, 620 n.16 (5th Cir.), *cert. denied*, 429 U.S. 920 (1976).

[43] *Id.* at 620-21.

[44] 5 U.S.C. § 552(a)(2) requires that an agency's instructions to staff be affirmatively available for the public's review without formal request, but the documents here were a scribbled hodgepodge, and the court refused to order them be made available. Kent Corp. v. NLRB, 530 F.2d 612, 621-22 (5th Cir.), *cert. denied*, 429 U.S. 920 (1976).

[45] " 'Predecisional' processes will quite regularly involve instructions to staff in the literal sense . . . and yet disclosure of those instructions would obviously tend to impinge on the deliberative process." *Id.* at 622 (5th Cir.), *cert. denied*, 429 U.S. 920 (1976).

ATTORNEYS' ADVICE AND THE FOI ACT EXEMPTION

The National Labor Relations Board attorneys who prepare memoranda in support of future proceedings, including those charges that will be pursued to a Board hearing, are able to claim the benefits of the internal memoranda exemption.[46] That exemption covers privileges transplanted into the Freedom of Information Act from civil litigation, including attorney-client communications and the attorney work product material prepared in anticipation of litigation.[47]

In the *Sears* case, the Supreme Court held that the attorney-prepared material could be withheld, citing the Senate report as a basis for interpreting the Act's original exemptions.[48] "Whatever the outer boundaries of the attorney work product rule are," the Court declared, "the rule clearly applies to memoranda prepared by an attorney in contemplation of litigation which set forth the attorney's theory of the case and his litigation strategy."[49] Because the official who makes the decision in an Advice or Appeals Memorandum is also the active litigating party before the Board, as General Counsel bringing the complaint, there is a special concern that the General Counsel's memoranda preceding the introduction of the complaint *not* be disclosed at the early stages of the proceeding.[50]

In the later *Kent* case, the Fifth Circuit noted that the major role of the General Counsel and his delegate the Regional Director is to prosecute violations of the Act.[51] Attorneys working for the Regional Director therefore merited exempt status for their comments preceding the disposition of the cases: "Their written

---

[46] 5 U.S.C. § 552(b)(5) (1976).

[47] NLRB v. Sears, Roebuck & Co., 421 U.S. 132 (1975). *See* 2 J. O'REILLY, FEDERAL INFORMATION DISCLOSURE §§ 15.07, .11, .12 (1977 & Supp. 1979).

[48] S. REP. No. 813, 89th Cong., 1st Sess. 2 (1965), *quoted in* NLRB v. Sears, Roebuck & Co., 421 U.S. 132, 154 (1975). It is historically important to note that Senator Hubert Humphrey, perhaps acting with the advice of the NLRB, used an unusual procedural maneuver after the FOI Act legislation had passed the Senate to change the scope of the (b)(5) exemption. Humphrey wanted "fact, law or policy" summaries to be exempt, since otherwise summaries of facts or evaluations of witness credibility would be exposed to public view. He won a change in the compromise bill, which appeared and passed in 1965. *See* 110 CONG. REC. 17,666 (1964).

[49] 421 U.S. 132, 154 (1975).

[50] *Id.* at 132.

[51] 530 F.2d 612, 623 (5th Cir. 1976).

evaluations of the evidence necessarily were founded on the assumption that any given charge *might* become enmeshed in litigation. Insofar as the privilege is meant to promote candid expressions of an attorney's theories and perspectives, it cannot properly be made to turn on whether litigation actually ensued." [52]

Therefore, the attorney who drafts theories of the case and sifts relevant factual materials in preparation of a case can receive work product protection for his or her materials. The *Kent* court left open the potential that, in some cases in the future, a showing might be made that disclosure would not offend the policy of the work product exemption.[53] Short of that exemption's being overcome, government attorneys whose cases will be pursued to hearing do enjoy the internal agency memoranda exemption to protect their documents from disclosure.

GOVERNMENT ATTORNEYS' REACTIONS

Federal attorneys interviewed for this text were each aware of the significance of the *Sears* decision for their agencies. The most telling point in the interviews was that, after *Sears,* the closing or dismissal of a charge means that some interested person who knows of the case will invariably ask for the advice memorandum that underlies the dismissal.[54] Sophisticated users of the labor statutes picked up on this availability of useful data, and they view it as a means of overseeing the work of the agency counsel. On the other hand, the agency attorney who avoids referencing of agency documents or internal memos avoids their disclosure to the adversary parties. The cost of avoiding a potentially harmful effect of disclosure is the withholding of some element of cogent presentation in the staff's recommendation document. If the reader, such as a member of the Board itself, read the recommendation without needed cross-references, the clarity and detail of a persuasive presentation might be lessened when the author of the recommendation must "look over the other shoulder" while drafting the document to avoid opening up public access to any nonpublic documents.

---

[52] *Id.*

[53] *Id.* at 624.

[54] Interview with Stanley Weinbrecht, *supra* note 33.

CHAPTER XIII

Labor Investigative Files: Access under the Freedom of Information Act

After several years of legal wrangling and intensive judicial debate, a firm rule of law now affects the National Labor Relations Board's investigative witness statements, such as the witness statements presented at unfair labor practice hearings. *If* the hearing or enforcement proceeding is still pending and has not been concluded and *if* a witness statement was received from an employee or other person with some business relationship to an employer, *then* the NLRB will not disclose—and is not required to disclose—the contents of the affidavit. If the Board refuses to disclose copies of the witness statements, then the courts will uphold the Board's refusal.

How that rule of disclosure and withholding developed is a fascinating chapter in the history of the NLRB, and one which has important consequences for the eventual reform of the Board's discovery procedures. It also has a great deal of importance for less well-known labor agencies, which utilize similar witness statements as the major source of evidence in their own proceedings.

LEGISLATION PROTECTING WITNESS STATEMENTS

Under the original Freedom of Information (FOI) Act, in effect from 1966 to 1974, an agency could choose to withhold from disclosure any law enforcement files "except to the extent available by law to a party other than an agency." [1] The Freedom of Information Act's original text was amended in 1974 because of congressional dissatisfaction with a series of cases interpreting the law enforcement exemption in a very broad manner. As with other classic confrontations between the judicial

---

[1] Pub. L. No. 90-23, § 552(b)(7), 81 Stat. 54 (1967).

interpreters and the legislative creators of statutes, the law enforcement exemption problem began with the courts giving an interpretation of the exemption that was too protective of the agency information, although such a reading was required by the literal words of the statute.[2] The next step was pressure by the losing litigants to amend the law, since they felt that the law could not have meant what the courts said it did.[3] Congress then, in a display of pique against the way in which the statute was being read (and without acknowledgment of its poor initial draftsmanship), changed the law. In retrospect, it may have gone too far toward a "correction" of the withholding problem.

A floor amendment was added to the general revision of the Freedom of Information Act, which was underway in the summer of 1974.[4] The floor amendment had its roots in an earlier American Bar Association proposal,[5] and it served to narrow the exemption to a defined set of enforcement information. The Senate adopted the amendment as a means of restricting the past court interpretations of the law enforcement exemption.[6] By doing so, it assured that the exemption's coverage would be significantly limited. This limitation was in line with the general desire of the 1974 "Watergate Congress" to ban future abuses of agency withholding powers.

The law enforcement exemption to the Act has stated since 1974 that law enforcement investigative records that otherwise

---

[2] The court cases that led to the amendment were Center for National Policy Review on Race & Urban Issues v. Weinberger, 502 F.2d 370 (D.C. Cir. 1974); Ditlow v. Brinegar, 494 F.2d 1073 (D.C. Cir. 1974); Aspin v. United States Dep't of Defense, 491 F.2d 24 (D.C. Cir. 1973); Weisberg v. United States Dep't of Justice, 489 F.2d 1195 (D.C. Cir. 1973), *cert. denied*, 416 U.S. 993 (1974). A prepared colloquy listed these as cases to be overturned by the amendment of 5 U.S.C. § 552(b)(7). 120 CONG. REC. 17,039-40 (1974) (remarks of Sens. Kennedy and Hart).

[3] Much of the 1974 lobbying was carried by the active groups on consumer and civil rights issues, with very little help from labor. Kennedy's remarks reflect this constituency. 120 CONG. REC. 17,039-40 (1974).

[4] The Hart amendment was added on the floor. *See id.* 17,040-41.

[5] *Executive Privilege, Secrecy in Government, Freedom of Information: Hearings Before the Subcomms. on Administrative Practice and Procedure, and Separation of Powers of the Senate Comm. on the Judiciary and the Subcomm. on Intergovernmental Relations of the Senate Comm. on Government Operations*, 93d Cong., 1st Sess. 154 (1973) (statement of John T. Miller, Jr., Chairman, Section of Administrative Law of the American Bar Association).

[6] 120 CONG. REC. 17,039-40 (1974) (remarks of Sens. Kennedy and Hart).

would be subject to mandatory disclosure need not be disclosed if disclosure

1. would interfere with enforcement proceedings;

2. would deprive a person of a right to a fair trial or impartial hearing;

3. would constitute an unwarranted invasion of privacy of a person;

4. would disclose the identity of a confidential source (or, for criminal or intelligence agencies, would reveal information furnished only by the source);

5. would disclose nonpublic investigative techniques and procedures; or

6. would endanger the life or physical safety of law enforcement personnel.[7]

Prior to the amendment, the law enforcement exemption had been used only very sparingly in noncriminal cases. The Federal Bureau of Investigation, related law enforcement agencies, and the custodians of the Warren Commission files were the principal recipients of requests for access to law enforcement files. The NLRB had little occasion to use the law enforcement power prior to 1974 as a rationale for its withholding.[8]

After the amendment, more NLRB cases have invoked section (b)(7) than virtually any other type of case. Although six grounds are available for withholding, the primary activity in the labor field has focused on enforcement proceedings—exemption (b)(7)(A) of the Freedom of Information Act.

WHY WITHHOLD INVESTIGATIVE FILES?

Traditionally, federal law enforcement agencies have enjoyed a privilege to withhold their investigative files from public disclosure. The dramatic narrowing of this right in the 1966 and 1974 statutes resulted in a much more cautious agency approach to the access or withholding decision. This caution was heightened by the provision that an incorrect decision would subject

---

[7] 5 U.S.C. § 552(b)(7)(A)-(F) (1976).

[8] Its three § 552(b)(7) cases were Wellman Indus. v. NLRB, 490 F.2d 427 (4th Cir.), *cert. denied*, 419 U.S. 834 (1974); Clement Bros. v. NLRB, 407 F.2d 1027 (5th Cir. 1969); Barceloneta Shoe Corp. v. Compton, 271 F. Supp. 591 (D. P.R. 1967) (the first FOI Act decision ever reported).

an agency official to both agency sanctions—the loss of a court action and the forced payment of attorneys' fees and costs [9]— and individual sanctions, since individual officials whose denials are found to be arbitrary can now be punished for their withholding of documents.[10] But *why* withhold an investigative file in the labor field at all?

There are basically two reasons given for withholding labor investigative records such as NLRB witness statements. The first reason is the prospect of intimidation and coercion of the witness whose participation in the hearing, in support of a certain point of view, becomes well known before the hearing. Since the government agency cannot file its own complaints but must await the charging of a law violation by some other party or organization, the agency is fully dependent on "volunteers" for its enforcement activities.[11] The ability to gather volunteers and to obtain information from prospective witnesses depends in large measure on the ability to protect the witnesses against retribution. The single most telling argument in favor of nondisclosure of NLRB witness statements is the fear factor—that the information disclosed will jeopardize a person's job status, promotability, or future employment prospects. The more unfavorable the testimony or the more critical that individual is as a key charging party witness, the more likely it seems that coercive effects would damage the statutory process. The Supreme Court and many lower courts have accepted this rationale.[12] As a basis for withholding, they have cited the delicate nature of the employment relationship and the potential injury to the worker and ultimately to the statutory system. Other courts, while accepting the general rule, discount the potential for coercion when the person who gives the statement happens to be a former employee no longer under the employer's control or is a person employed by a separate organization, such as an international union involved in

---

[9] 5 U.S.C. § 552(a)(4)(E) (1976).

[10] *Id.* § 552(a)(4)(F).

[11] NLRB v. Robbins Tire & Rubber Co., 437 U.S. 214 (1978). This is a major consideration for the Board's personnel who work to protect the witness statements. Interview with Stan Weinbrecht, Associate General Counsel, National Labor Relations Board, in Washington, D.C. (Jan. 14, 1980).

[12] The Court in *Robbins* noted that "the possibility of deterrence arising from *post hoc* disciplinary action is no substitute for a prophylactic rule that prevents the harm to a pending enforcement proceeding which flows from a witness having been intimidated." NLRB v. Robbins Tire & Rubber Co., 437 U.S. 214, 239-40 (1978).

an unfair labor practice case.[13] And the employer's identity is not determinate of its potential to coerce the employees, for even federal agencies as employers may be susceptible to this conduct.[14]

So the first rationale, potential intimidation of witnesses, is generally accepted as an article of fact. In a particular case, an employer might be able to demonstrate the absence of a coercive atmosphere or the absence of intimidation, but proving a negative of noncoercion is always a difficult chore.

The second rationale for withholding is the desire to allow the National Labor Relations Board to present its best case in court. This theory is somewhat more tenuous and depends upon the reader's perspective. Of course, any good advocate would prefer to preserve the secrecy of the anticipated "key witness" against the other side for as long as possible. If the Board is a defender of one's interests, then premature release of its key evidence enables the opposing side to fabricate a defense and frustrate the statutory purpose of the National Labor Relations Act.[15] If one disagrees with the charge brought by the Board, one faces what has been widely described as "trial by ambush." Advance knowledge of the Board's evidence eliminates the ambush potential and enhances the quality of one's presentation so that the real issues can be met quickly and head-on.[16] Good arguments on both sides can be made, depending on one's perspective.

Presenting the Board's best case in court is comparable to the Jencks Act rationale for permitting prosecutors to withhold witness statements until after criminal trial witnesses have given

---

[13] Nemacolin Mines Corp. v. NLRB, 467 F. Supp. 521 (W.D. Pa. 1979); Associated Dry Goods Corp. v. NLRB, 455 F. Supp. 802 (S.D.N.Y. 1978).

[14] The legal counsel for the Federal Labor Relations Authority, an agency with jurisdiction over federal employee complaints and representation issues, regard the likelihood of employee intimidation as being just as great in federal job environments as in private sector ones. Interviews with attorneys, Federal Labor Relations Authority in Washington, D.C. (Feb. 7, 1980).

[15] Fabrication of a defense by constructing an explanation for the conduct observed by the witness is the primary concern here.

[16] But note that challenges to the lack of NLRB discovery, premised on notions of procedural due process, have generally failed. *See, e.g.,* NLRB v. Valley Mold Co., 530 F.2d 693, 695 (6th Cir.), *cert. denied,* 429 U.S. 824 (1976); Comment, *NLRB Discovery Practice,* 1976 B.Y. L. REV. 845. And disdain for the Board's "trial by ambush" is not enough to beat the Board. Capital Cities Communications, Inc. v. NLRB, 409 F. Supp. 971 (N.D. Cal. 1976).

their testimony.[17] The effectiveness of the government case in both settings rests with surprise, and surprise means an absence of deterrence to the witnesses' testimony by the opponent. It is a historical irony that the 1964 Humphrey amendment to the law enforcement exemption, which installed a Jencks Act system of withholding for the Board and similar civil investigative agencies,[18] was eliminated by the Congress [19] *four years before the Supreme Court found it to be implicitly still present in the FOI Act.*[20] The "trial by ambush" approach was endorsed by the Court in the 1978 *Robbins Tire* [21] decision. So for the future and until the FOI Act is amended yet again, the Board's witness statements will be preserved from premature dissemination.

There are additional reasons for withholding investigative files. Some bureaucratic organizations prefer secrecy as a means of deploying relatively small forces in a battlefield of relatively large combatants. The Federal Mediation and Conciliation Service (FMCS), a small agency by federal standards, maintains confidential status to preserve maximum flexibility for arbitrators and mediators.[22] The labor disputes with which the FMCS deals are vulnerable to many unexpected problems, and secrecy enhances the goal of the FMCS to reach near-term agreements to problems that otherwise would be prolonged for an excessive period of time. Other agencies use the blanket protection of witness statements as a means of bargaining to achieve a negotiated victory, since the other side does not "see their hand" during the competition. The Equal Employment Opportunity Commission (EEOC), for example, watched carefully as the *Robbins Tire* case proceeded. Although the EEOC holds no hearings of its own, its management was delighted when *Robbins* provided Supreme Court assurances of blanket protection for witness state-

---

[17] 18 U.S.C. § 3500 (1976).

[18] *See* chapter XI *supra.*

[19] The reference to discovery practice was eliminated when 5 U.S.C. § 552(b)(7) was amended and divided into six subsections. Pub. L. No. 93-502, § 2(b), 88 Stat. 1561 (1974) (codified in 5 U.S.C. § 552(b)(7)(A)-(F) (1976)).

[20] NLRB v. Robbins Tire & Rubber Co., 437 U.S. 214 (1978).

[21] *Id.*

[22] Interview with David Vaughn, General Counsel, Federal Mediation and Conciliation Service, in Washington, D.C. (Jan. 14, 1980).

ments under most circumstances.[23] The inability to get information about anticipated witness testimony, the content of which might be of tactical and strategic benefit to the investigating agency, is one of the factors that may motivate some firms to settle EEOC charges without publicized litigation.[24]

Finally, some agencies want to protect witness investigative files because screening them is a bother, an administrative headache, and rigorous review of the file by unions or management will turn up possibly embarrassing information about the agency.[25] An investigative process that produces sloppy results in an overly lengthy period of study of a case can be damaging to the image and prestige of the agency before the press, Congress, and the public. Many agencies noticed an improvement in the file information, a new benefit of the fear of later disclosure, when their investigators became aware that file contents might be exposed to public review at some future time. Quality control by fear of oversight is an interesting, and probably unanticipated, benefit to agency management.[26]

THE BATTLE FOR
LABOR INVESTIGATIVE INFORMATION

The 1974 amendments to the Freedom of Information Act precipitated a number of lawsuits seeking access to NLRB investigative documents. Those amendments eliminated the protection for "files" and replaced it with the individual protection of "records." [27] As discussed above, they also removed the stilted

---

[23] Interview with Constance duPre, Associate General Counsel, Equal Employment Opportunity Commission, in Washington, D.C. (Feb. 7, 1980).

[24] *See, e.g.,* Charlotte-Mecklenburg Hosp. Authority v. Perry, 571 F.2d 195 (4th Cir. 1978).

[25] And the time burdens are, of course, an important distraction from labor law enforcement duties for the professionals who must review and delete the information. Congress has been very reluctant to give the additional funds needed to provide this FOI Act service to the public

[26] This improvement in reports was consistently mentioned by agency officials in interviews as a beneficial effect of the disclosure of investigative files. When the Privacy Act of 1974 imposed a new duty on agencies to maintain only the relevant, accurate, and timely information about individuals, that new duty and the new awareness of file-subject oversight added considerably to the quality of the input information.

[27] Pub. L. No. 93-502, § 2(b), 88 Stat. 1561 (1974). Thus, an entire file could not be exempted; the material would have to be segregated, and the disclosable portions would have to be disclosed.

language of the Humphrey amendment and its Jencks Act provision protecting records not available to a litigating party.[28] This was replaced with a very definite set of limited circumstances, including interference with an enforcement proceeding, under which withholding of a law enforcement record could be justified. Shortly after the amendments became law, the NLRB began to receive more requests than it had previously been receiving for the disclosure of investigative records.[29] The Board's rejection of those requests, which came predominantly from employer respondents in unfair labor practice proceedings, asserted the NLRB view that amendment of the law enforcement exemption had made no change in the legal authority for the Board's withholding policy.[30]

In the view of the National Labor Relations Board, as of 1975, nothing had changed in the operation of the Freedom of Information Act's law enforcement exemption, so all requests for disclosure of witness statements would be denied. The Board encountered a swelling number of lawsuits demanding disclosure and an increasing progression of district court opinions that disagreed with the Board. In the leading 1975 case, Judge Gagliardi of the Southern District of New York held in *Title Guarantee Co. v. NLRB*[31] that the Board's witness statements were no longer exempt from disclosure unless the Board could make a showing that particular withheld documents would interfere with particular proceedings. The court reviewed the information *in camera* and found specifically that its release would neither "block further information of the same type from similar sources nor . . . stifle effective preparation of the case."[32] Instead, the benefit would be in management's learning whether or not the witness statements supported its point of view on the contested issues. "This value is precisely that which is contemplated by the Freedom of Information Act and is not restricted by the exemptions to the Act."[33]

---

[28] The "except to the extent available by law to a party other than an agency" language was removed, and the present subsections were inserted. *Id.*

[29] Interview with Stanley Weinbrecht, *supra* note 11.

[30] The Board's legal position is well recapitulated in NLRB v. Robbins Tire & Rubber Co., 437 U.S. 214 (1978).

[31] 407 F. Supp. 498 (S.D.N.Y. 1975), *rev'd,* 534 F.2d 484 (2d Cir. 1976).

[32] *Id.* at 505.

[33] *Id.*

Several other district courts began to agree that disclosure should be ordered under the amended law enforcement exemption.[34] The Board counterattacked at the appellate level [35] and used the implicit threat of dragging federal courts into labor cases' routine discovery disputes as a subtle influence on the eventual outcome. The Second Circuit, in a lengthy opinion by Judge Oakes, reversed the *Title Guarantee* court and found that the employer could not obtain the requested information.[36] The Second Circuit opinion was then used by the Board to convince other appellate courts of the wisdom of blanket exemption coverage for witness statements.[37] The employer's arguments in *Title Guarantee* had been impressive and had "almost persuaded" the Second Circuit, but the employer could not rebut the assertion that Congress had not meant to change Board discovery rules.[38] The Second Circuit observed: "[W]e think that Congress would be very reluctant to change the rather carefully arrived at limitations and procedures for discovery in unfair labor practice proceedings by way of an act which, while dealing with disclosure generally, does not purport to affect such discovery." [39] The reader can choose whether or not to see between the lines a judicial disinclination to get trapped in the

---

[34] NLRB v. Hardeman Garment Corp., 406 F. Supp. 510 (W.D. Tenn. 1976), was the first of many cases affected by the district court's opinion in *Title Guarantee.* The psychological effect of such a precedent on the Board is discussed in Note, *Backdooring the NLRB: Use and Abuse of the Amended FOIA for Administrative Discovery,* 8 LOY. L. J. 145, 167 (1976). *See also* Maremont Corp. v. NLRB, 91 L.R.R.M. 2805 (W.D. Okla.), *rev'd,* 79 Lab. Cas. ¶ 11,790 (10th Cir. 1976).

[35] The Board's appellate arguments made a special effort to expedite each of the pending district court cases, and the Board gave up none of the witness statements pending appeal.

[36] Title Guarantee Co. v. NLRB, 534 F.2d 484 (2d Cir.), *cert. denied,* 429 U.S. 834 (1976).

[37] Abrahamson Chrysler-Plymouth, Inc. v. NLRB, 561 F.2d 63 (7th Cir. 1977); NLRB v. Hardeman Garment Corp., 557 F.2d 559 (6th Cir. 1977); New Eng. Med. Center Hosp. v. NLRB, 548 F.2d 377 (1st Cir. 1976); Harvey's Wagon Wheel, Inc. v. NLRB, 550 F.2d 1139 (9th Cir. 1976); Roger J. Au & Son v. NLRB, 538 F.2d 80 (3d Cir. 1976); Climax Molybdenum Co. v. NLRB, 539 F.2d 63 (10th Cir. 1976).

[38] Title Guarantee Co. v. NLRB, 534 F.2d 484, 492 (2d Cir.), *cert. denied,* 429 U.S. 834 (1976). The employer's grasp and interpretation of the FOI Act amendments were persuasive, but the appellate court hesitated to open up unfair labor practice issues on the basis of the amendments.

[39] *Id.*

swamp of petty discovery disputes in NLRB administrative hearings.

Other courts generally agreed with the Board's view.[40] But then the Fifth Circuit, rejecting the *Title Guarantee* appellate construction of the amended exemption, wrote a well-reasoned contrary opinion in the *Robbins Tire* case.[41] The decision could have been a major historic blow to the federal investigative agencies.

THE ROBBINS TIRE CASE

Robbins Tire [42] was a combined representation and unfair labor practice case. The employer won a district court Freedom of Information Act decision which held that the employer was entitled to receive at least five days prior to the Board's hearing copies of the witness statements to be used by the Board. An appeal for a stay was denied by the Fifth Circuit. Since the Board would have to disclose the witness statements at least five days before its hearing, the Board merely postponed the hearing, for over a year,[43] in order to await the contested appeal.

The Board argued vigorously in the Fifth Circuit for Judge Oakes' Second Circuit position—that classes of interference could generally be found under which the class of witness statements would be exempted from required disclosure. The comparative discovery argument was used; with the present Board rules, there was virtually no discovery, but if the FOI Act were allowed to be used, there would be a means of avoiding that barrier so that many more firms would obtain discovery through the FOI Act.[44] That was apparently the wrong tack to take before the Fifth Circuit, which had in five cases endorsed NLRB discovery rights of respondents [45] (albeit without any lasting

---

[40] *See* cases cited in note 37 *supra.*

[41] Robbins Tire & Rubber Co. v. NLRB, 563 F.2d 724 (5th Cir. 1977), *rev'd*, 437 U.S. 214 (1978).

[42] *Id.*

[43] *Id.* at 727.

[44] Comment, *supra* note 16; Note, *supra* note 34. The Fifth Circuit's view of that discovery situation was first that discovery should be permitted by the Board and second that "it is questionable whether FOIA disclosure would result in an increase in discovery rights in this court." 563 F.2d 724, 729 (1977), *rev'd*, 437 U.S. 214 (1978).

[45] NLRB v. Rex Disposables, 494 F.2d 588 (5th Cir. 1974); NLRB v. Miami Coca-Cola Bottling Co., 403 F.2d 994 (5th Cir. 1968); NLRB v.

effect on the Board's attitudes). The comparative discovery approach also contravened the intention to allow requests under the FOI Act by "any person" regardless of legal status.[46] Finally, the argument about faster or easier discovery made it possible for the Board to evade the clear directive of the amendments that *specific* harms in *specific* cases be considered.[47] This blanket approach was rejected.

Robbins Tire at the Fifth Circuit contains a lengthy discussion of the intimidation issue as well. If the Board had been able to show intimidation or coercion, it might have won sympathy, especially if the history of employer-employee relations or the witnesses' job positions or the nature of anticipated testimony made intimidation likely. The Board had no evidence of coercion, and the court could not infer that any would occur. The per se coercive approach to disclosure was rejected by the court.[48]

Finally, the court also rejected arguments that the privacy of employees would be invaded, since there was nothing personal or private about the testimony to be given.[49] A claim of the exemption protecting confidential law enforcement sources was rejected,

---

Safway Steel Scaffolds Co., 383 F.2d 273 (5th Cir. 1967), *cert. denied*, 390 U.S. 955 (1968). *See also* NLRB v. W. R. Bean & Son, 450 F.2d 93 (5th Cir. 1971), *cert. denied*, 409 U.S. 849 (1972) ; NLRB v. Schill Steel Prods. Inc., 408 F.2d 803 (5th Cir. 1969).

[46] 5 U.S.C. § 552(a)(3) (1976).

[47] The specificity was the necessary complement to the congressional rejection of blanket confidentiality assertions of the law enforcement agencies. 120 CONG. REC. 17,038-41 (1974) (remarks of Sens. Kennedy and Hart). The change meant that some specific harm would have to be shown. *See* Deering Milliken, Inc. v. Irving, 548 F.2d 1131 (4th Cir. 1977). So the directive in the amendments that nondisclosure be allowed "only to the extent that . . . production . . . would . . . interfere" must be given some meaning, the Fifth Circuit held in *Robbins*, by requiring a specific showing. 563 F.2d 724, 730 (5th Cir. 1977), *rev'd*, 437 U.S. 214 (1978).

[48] Because none of the informants would be confidential and each would appear at the hearing, the Board's "sweeping assumption of intimidation is inappropriate here." 563 F.2d 724, 731 (5th Cir. 1977), *rev'd*, 437 U.S. 214 (1978). The criteria that the Fifth Circuit suggested included historical events which make later intimidation foreseeable; vulnerability of the witness's job to some penalty (e.g., a record of marginal performance in which an intimidating suggestion would have an effect against testifying) ; and the nature of the testimony which the affiants would give. *Id.* at 732 (5th Cir. 1977), *rev'd* 437 U.S. 214 (1978).

[49] Only if there were some unusual family or personal details would the exemption under § 552(b)(7)(C) apply. *Id.* at 733 (5th Cir. 1977), *rev'd*, 437 U.S. 214 (1978).

since the identities would be disclosed routinely at the hearing shortly after the disclosure of the witness statements.[50]

Publicity about the NLRB's loss of the Fifth Circuit *Robbins* decision had immediate effects. The Board was swamped with requests.[51] The number of FOI Act suits filed against the NLRB grew to one per day, a rate never heard of before or since at any agency.[52] In the two months following the decision, 116 administrative appeals were filed from the Board's refusals to disclose witness statements. Those two months produced more appeals and more court actions than in all of the preceding year.[53] Calendar year 1977 administrative appeals had been 111; the post-*Robbins* period, in calendar 1978, produced 410. The Board set a Freedom of Information Act record, with 94 lawsuits seeking disclosure pending against the Board in a single month.[54]

The thrust of the NLRB argument to the Supreme Court on its appeal of *Robbins* was that the law enforcement exemption retained the benefits of the Humphrey provision even after its 1974 amendment. The Board asserted that particularized, case-by-case decisions whether enforcement would be inhibited by "interference" from disclosure were too difficult a chore. Showing interference with each particular hearing was "neither required nor practical," it argued.[55] On the appellee's side, it was argued that the 1974 amendments had indeed changed the standard for the protection of law enforcement files and that claims of continued blanket exemption were impossible after the amendments.[56]

THE SUPREME COURT DECISION

The Court's decision, in June 1978, gave the Board a total victory. Witness statements given in NLRB proceedings were held to be confidential per se before the Board hearing is con-

---

50 *Id.*

51 Interview with Stanley Weinbrecht, *supra* note 11.

52 This volume of litigation even exceeds that of the Federal Bureau of Investigation, which has at times had more than fifty suits pending for disclosure.

53 Interview with Stanley Weinbrecht, *supra* note 11.

54 *Id.*

55 437 U.S. 214 (1978).

56 *Id.* at 222-23.

ducted.[57] The only disclosable items were statements from closed hearing files, after all proceedings were terminated, and statements made to the Board by nonemployee witnesses.

Justice Marshall, writing for a Court which split 4-3-2 on the issue (3 concurred with a different view of the law enforcement exemption than that offered by Marshall),[58] determined that the law enforcement exemption had treated the "interference with proceedings" reason for withholding differently than it had the other reasons for withholding. Within the law enforcement exemption, as amended in 1974, there were six separate grounds on which files could be protected. The first of the six was different in style than the others, Marshall said, and the case-by-case determination of law enforcement exemptability that would be made for five of the six grounds of exemption need not be made for the "interference with enforcement" rationale.[59] A blanket protection of information to be used in unfair labor practices hearings was justified by the general, nonspecific phrasing of the "interference with enforcement" exemption and by the special needs of the NLRB, according to the Court.[60]

The Court accepted an unusual view of the 1974 amendments, one which held that Congress was interested in disclosure of old, closed cases but wished to preserve the blanket confidential treatment of information for use in currently pending proceedings. The Board took advantage of this interpretation in its argument, and the Court accepted the Board's view.[61] From the time of the 1966 Act through the *Barceloneta* [62] and *Clement Brothers* [63] cases and the *Wellman* [64] case, courts have preserved the secrecy of the Board's affidavits. The "delicate balance" in Board proceedings would be upset if now disclosure were to occur prior

---

[57] *Id.* at 236.

[58] Justices Marshall, White, Stewart, and Blackmun constituted the majority; Stevens, Burger, and Rehnquist concurred; Powell and Brennan dissented.

[59] 437 U.S. 214 (1978).

[60] *Id.* at 233-37.

[61] *Id.* at 226.

[62] Barceloneta Shoe Corp. v. Compton, 271 F. Supp. 591 (D. P.R. 1967).

[63] Clement Bros. v. NLRB, 282 F. Supp. 540 (N.D. Ga. 1968), *aff'd,* 407 F.2d 1027 (5th Cir. 1969).

[64] Wellman Indus. v. NLRB, 490 F.2d 427 (4th Cir.), *cert. denied,* 419 U.S. 834 (1974).

to hearings. Delay would result; coercion and chilling effects on witnesses were likely; and the Board's adjudicative methods would be restructured by a decision in favor of a case-by-case exemptive system.[65] So the Board prevailed.

In dissent, Justices Powell and Brennan criticized the broad reading of interference. They would have retained particularized review of each case to determine whether interference is likely.[66] This would apply in all cases *except* those in which unfavorable statements by present employees were concerned.[67] As to those, a general presumption of confidential exempt status could be found. The concurring Justices—Stevens, Rehnquist, and Burger —held that any enforcement proceeding would be interfered with and thus its witness statements withheld if the access by Freedom of Information Act means would be greater than discovery procedures already allowed for that proceeding under agency rules.[68] Their views would have expanded a blanket protection beyond NLRB unfair labor practice hearings to virtually any administrative hearing to which discovery procedures are applicable.

Robbins Tire is not a high point in Supreme Court jurisprudence. Even before the criticisms of the Court's, and especially Marshall's, opinion-drafting process appeared in print in 1979 in *The Brethren,*[69] it seemed apparent from the face of the *Robbins Tire* opinion that the principal author of the opinion was motivated much more by a desire to salvage NLRB secrecy than by any devotion to statutory construction or legislative history. The Court's means followed its end and weakened the Freedom of Information Act in the process.

Marshall's 1978 view of what Congress had intended to do with the law enforcement exemption certainly varies from the mood and expressions that prevailed in the 1974 period of reform. Any active observer of the FOI amendments of that year and anyone attuned to the Watergate problems that the revision of the law enforcement exemption was intended to address cannot accept at face value the Supreme Court's interpretation of the

---

[65] NLRB v. Robbins Tire & Rubber Co., 437 U.S. 214 (1978).

[66] *Id.* at 244-45.

[67] *Id.* at 245.

[68] *Id.* at 243.

[69] B. WOODWARD & S. ARMSTRONG, THE BRETHREN (1979).

amendments.[70] That interpretation could be considered a rationalization, whether one agrees that the Board deserved to maintain secrecy of its witness statements. In other FOI Act cases, the Court has flatly pointed out the problems that the Act has created and has invited Congress to change the statutory text to solve the problem.[71] *Robbins Tire* was a shift toward straining the Act's text to cover something barely that the Court deemed worthy, on policy grounds, of protection.

The philosophical roots of *Robbins Tire* are doubtful or nonexistent. In 1974, when the law enforcement exemption's amendment was propelled like a cannonball against the wall of law enforcement secrecy, it shattered the exemption's former presumptions of secrecy. The Court in *Robbins Tire* figuratively walked to the remains of that wall, picked up the brick marked "NLRB," and then decided that Congress *may* have meant to hit the wall but surely *did not* intend to hit that particular brick.

EFFECT OF ROBBINS TIRE

The Supreme Court opinion in *Robbins Tire* gave the National Labor Relations Board an easy means of disposing of the hundred or more pending FOI Act cases. The Board spent much of the summer of 1978 making form-letter filings of its motion to dismiss in the dozens of courts in which disclosure cases were pending. The Board had not given up a single witness statement during the whole fight, although it had postponed some hearings because of the pendency of its appeals.[72] The employer litigants had won delays but had lost the central argument that access to witness statements is a matter of statutory right.

For the NLRB's Freedom of Information staff, *Robbins Tire* solved the short-term problem of backlogged cases and the long-term problem of an abundance of requests. Today, fewer requests come in, usually from the uninformed new to the field,

---

[70] The 1974 milieu in which the agencies' former blanket protection for investigative statements was changed is chronicled in the Senate debates, the reading of which leaves one doubtful about the legislative intent arguments available to the majority in *Robbins*. *See* 120 CONG. REC. 17,014-47 (1974).

[71] *See, e.g.,* Chrysler Corp. v. Brown, 441 U.S. 281 (1979); and EPA v. Mink, 410 U.S. 73 (1973).

[72] Interview with Stanley Weinbrecht, *supra* note 11.

and they are quickly deterred from attempting to use the FOI Act.[73]

For other government agencies that hold similar proceedings, *Robbins Tire* was viewed as a blessing. The EEOC, which does not have hearings, was pleased to have the Supreme Court opinion as support for confidentiality of its investigative witness statements.[74] The Federal Labor Relations Authority (FLRA), which began operations at about the time *Robbins Tire* was decided, adopted the NLRB approach to witness statements as part of its selective package of adoption of board procedures.[75] The FLRA has consistently refused to disclose witness statements to the employing federal agencies prior to its hearings on federal employee labor disputes.

Robbins Tire was determinative of several important issues and replaced the *Title Guarantee*[76] case and its counterparts in other appellate courts as the leading opinion on unfair labor practice proceedings statements. The Supreme Court had, however, left open the matter of closed cases and other Board hearings, such as representation and backpay cases.

CLOSED CASES

Witness statements in closed cases, in which no enforcement proceedings are pending, can be subject to disclosure. The "interference with enforcement proceedings" exception is not available after the close of the proceedings.[77] The statements could be

---

[73] *Id.* The subtlety noted by Mr. Weinbrecht was that counsel seeking disclosure often withdrew their suits because (a) the legal issue had been decided and (b) they would have to continue working with the NLRB in the future, so that persisting in a losing cause for the sake of delay would have foreseeable long-term negative consequences in some situations for that counsel.

[74] The EEOC uses its information in negotiating settlements of charges and in litigating in federal court. The *Robbins* case was of great value to the Commission. The Supreme Court in *Robbins*, 437 U.S. at 219 n.5, noted that *Robbins* had a parallel EEOC case: Charlotte-Mecklenburg Hosp. Authority v. Perry, 571 F.2d 195 (4th Cir. 1978). *Robbins* was viewed as a success by the EEOC. Interview with Constance duPre, *supra* note 23.

[75] Interview with attorneys, *supra* note 14.

[76] 534 F.2d 484 (2d Cir.), *cert. denied*, 429 U.S. 834 (1976).

[77] Nemacolin Mines Corp. v. NLRB, 467 F. Supp. 521 (W.D. Pa. 1979); Associated Dry Goods Corp. v. NLRB, 455 F. Supp. 802 (S.D.N.Y. 1978). *Cf.* Clements Wire & Mfg. Co. v. NLRB, 589 F.2d 894 (5th Cir. 1979). *See generally* Poss v. NLRB, 565 F.2d 654, 657 (10th Cir. 1977) (charging party as individual suing for the closed file on the charge).

withheld on a case-by-case basis if the government were able to satisfy a federal court that they fall within one of the particular reasons for justifiable withholding, such as identifying a confidential source.[78]

In *Nemacolin Mines Corp. v. NLRB*,[79] the Board process and all enforcement proceedings had been concluded before the employer sought access to the Board's witness statements. The Board argued that witness statements were still confidential because of their precedential value. If the affidavits given by witnesses in any case were disclosed, that would have a collateral effect on the future ability of the Board to promise confidential treatment to other witnesses in other cases.[80] The court, however, ruled against the NLRB's arguments. First, the enforcement exemption for proceedings required a definite prospect of a proceeding and could not be used after all such proceedings on a particular case were concluded. No proceeding, no interference.[81]

As a second point, the court held that the confidential source exemption could not be validly claimed. Although the Board had previously won elsewhere with this argument,[82] the *Nemacolin* court held that good faith discretion is required in the agency's use of a confidentiality promise.[83] The Board was required to apply promises of confidential treatment to particular witnesses with due regard for circumstances of the case. A broad promise given to every witness in every case that the Board would never disclose the statements made by the witness was unacceptable

---

[78] 5 U.S.C. § 552(b)(7)(C) (1976). The court in *Poss* held: "To produce the files . . . certainly would not result in any 'premature disclosure' and thereby prevent the NLRB from bringing its 'strongest case in court.' There isn't going to be *any* 'case in court.'" 565 F.2d 654, 657 (10th Cir. 1977).

[79] 467 F. Supp. 521 (W.D. Pa. 1979).

[80] *Id.* at 524.

[81] *Id.*

[82] The "all interviewees may be witnesses someday" argument had been accepted in T.V. Tower, Inc. v. Marshall, 444 F. Supp. 1233 (D. D.C. 1978), but was rejected in *Nemacolin*. 467 F. Supp. 521, 525 (W.D. Pa. 1979).

[83] "If the NLRB granted confidentiality to declarants when necessary in their discretion, based on the facts of each case, a different question would be presented. . . . [E]xemption 7(D) requires the grant of confidentiality to be made on the basis of good faith discretion, not on the basis of arbitrary rule, as the grant was made in this case." 467 F. Supp. 521, 525 (W.D. Pa. 1979).

as a basis for exempt status.[84] The court discussed the conditional nature of Board confidentiality promises. If the promises are made on every witness statement, even though the Board knows it must hand over the statements immediately after the witness testifies at a Board hearing, then the confidentiality is only a conditional promise, and the Board cannot really expect to give a valid assurance.[85]

Another district court, in *Associated Dry Goods Corp. v. NLRB*,[86] further limited the Board's exemption for confidential sources. Even if the name and identifying features of the source can be withheld by the NLRB, it is obligated to disclose the content of the statement. The Board argued that the privacy of the witness would be invaded by disclosure. The *Associated Dry Goods* decision described the classes of information that might have personal privacy connotations: health records, discharge and reprimand files, applications for employment, union membership, rate of pay, and severance files.[87] Apart from these, the personal privacy interest is rarely, if ever, present in NLRB evidence. Other courts, such as the Tenth Circuit in the *Poss v. NLRB*[88] decision, have opined that the record stating a reason for termination "looks away from confidentiality" and cannot be treated as exempt from required disclosure after the hearing.

BACKPAY PROCEEDINGS

In backpay proceedings before the NLRB, the entire file is made available to the public as soon as the specification is issued by the Board.[89] This was a change in NLRB policy made as a result of the Fourth Circuit decision in *Deering Milliken, Inc. v. NLRB* in 1977.[90] The Fourth Circuit distinguished between unfair labor practice cases and backpay matters because a backpay determination is largely objective, involves no coercion or con-

---

[84] *Id.*

[85] *Id.*

[86] 455 F. Supp. 802 (S.D.N.Y. 1978).

[87] *Id.* at 815.

[88] 565 F.2d 654 (10th Cir. 1977); *accord, Gerico, Inc. v. NLRB*, 92 L.R.R.M. 2713 (D. Colo. 1976); *Kaminer v. NLRB*, 78 Lab. Cas. ¶ 11,272 (S.D. Miss. 1975).

[89] Interview with Stanley Weinbrecht, *supra* note 11.

[90] 548 F.2d 1131 (4th Cir. 1977).

troversy regarding unfairness, and cannot really be subjected to interference by discovery. Discovery of the Board's backpay case also does not permit the construction of a better defense by the respondent. In the exceptional case in which a backpay file contains truly personal and private information about the claiming individual, then the Board could segregate and withhold that information under the personal privacy exemptions for the Freedom of Information Act.[91]

USE OF THE LAW ENFORCEMENT EXEMPTION BY OTHER AGENCIES

The Equal Employment Opportunity Commission is the only one of the federal labor relations agencies that does not have hearings, but the *Robbins Tire* case was of great interest to the EEOC because that agency needed to assure protection of the witness statements that it uses in determining the outcome of charges of discrimination.[92] *Robbins* was "very helpful" to the Commission in protecting witness statements and will eventually be of greater help as the Commission begins to exercise its newly received jurisdiction over the Equal Pay Act and the Age Discrimination in Employment Act. These latter statutes do not have the specific confidentiality safeguards that Congress imposed in Title VII of the Civil Rights Act for the protection of investigative files. Title VII acts as a specific exemption from disclosure for most EEOC files, but the added protection of the law enforcement exemption will be needed for pay and age cases to be handled by the Commission.[93]

At the Department of Labor, the Wage and Hour Division is an active user of the law enforcement exemption. Its philosophical position is that protection of the complaining employee is the most important element of enforcement.[94] The Labor Department's enforcement depends to a large extent upon volunteered information. This view is shared by Labor's Occupational Safety and Health Administration as well. "We have very few hard and fast rules," Labor's lead counsel for disclosure cases

---

[91] 5 U.S.C. § 552(b)(6) (1976).

[92] Interview with Constance duPre, *supra* note 23.

[93] *Id.*

[94] Interview with Soffia Petters, Associate General Counsel, U.S. Department of Labor, in Washington, D.C. (Jan. 14, 1980).

stated, "but protection of witness identities is one of them." [95]
Reprisals, often subtle but allegedly perceptible, are the danger
which the Department's policy seeks to avoid.

Labor's investigative exemption also can be used against
unions. In some cases, a dissident union person can complain to
the Department and also ask about the Department's files on the
union. The union then may ask the Department to release the
dissident's identity. Although usually the identity of the people
making disclosure requests is public, there are cases in which
the dissident needs to be protected under the "confidential source"
portion of the law enforcement exemption. On two occasions, the
Department has used the law enforcement exemption to avoid
the risk to an informant's life or health from union retaliation.
Retaliation concerns at the Department of Labor, however, are
predominantly related to the employer's economic sanctions
against the complaining witness.[96]

In several litigated FOI Act cases, the Department has supplied the information requested or has been upheld in its ability
to subpoena needed information because of the opportunity of
the information holder to obtain confidential treatment. OSHA's
ability to gather information for use in its enforcement hearings
has been the subject of some litigation, with the Department
usually prevailing in its defense of confidentiality.[97]

The Federal Labor Relations Authority (FLRA) applied the
confidential protection of witness statements to its new policies
as soon as it became operational. *Robbins Tire* assisted the new
agency in withholding witness investigative statements, even if
the "employer" seeking access to the statements was another
federal agency.[98] The FLRA policy of nondisclosure of witness
statements has not been challenged in court as yet. Unlike the
NLRB, which had many suits from employers requesting Freedom of Information Act access rights, the FLRA's employer

---

[95] *Id.*

[96] *Id.* These economic concerns are not always met by the existence of an
employee-protective statute, since the subsequent reinstatement as a remedy
may be an insufficient deterrent in any particular case to protect a needed
informant.

[97] Moore-McCormack Lines, Inc. v. I.T.O. Corp., 508 F.2d 945 (4th Cir.
1974); Pilar v. S.S. Hess Petrol, 55 F.R.D. 159 (D. Md. 1972).

[98] Interview with attorneys, *supra* note 14.

group is outside of the FOI Act because each is an "agency" rather than an FOI-eligible person.[99]

OTHER REASONS FOR WITHHOLDING THE FILES

On some occasions, two other Freedom of Information Act exemptions are also used to defend information that a federal labor agency wishes to preserve as confidential. These include the commercial confidential data exemption and the personal privacy exemption.

Commercial data that are not public and are obtained by the agency from a private person (with or without an advance promise of confidential treatment) may be withheld from disclosure under the fourth exemption of the Freedom of Information Act.[100] The burden is on the agency to demonstrate, usually with the help of the financially interested party, that the information is either "trade secret" in nature or is commercial data whose disclosure would cause some harm to the submitting person's competitive position. The most vigorously contested area of information law under this exemption has been the matter of EEO files, obtained by government contract compliance/affirmative action monitoring bodies such as the Labor Department's Office of Federal Contract Compliance Programs. If those personnel data are claimed to be confidential, the owner of the data usually will be afforded a right to seek administrative and judicial review prior to any dissemination of the data to a competitor.[101]

In a very unusual 1978 case, the first one asserting the commercial confidentiality defense in a purely labor relations context, a union won a federal appellate court decision to the effect that unions have commercial confidentiality rights to withhold organizing campaign signature cards, which if disclosed would reveal the union's competitive position vis-à-vis competing unions in the same bargaining unit. The expanded commercial confidentiality exemption in *American Airlines, Inc. v. National Mediation Board*[102] suggests that a union would be able to make valid

---

[99] *See* 1 J. O'REILLY, FEDERAL INFORMATION DISCLOSURE §§ 5.01-.07 (1977 & Supp. 1979). *Compare* 5 U.S.C. § 551(1) (1976), *with* § 552(a)(3).

[100] 5 U.S.C. § 552(b)(4) (1976).

[101] *See* chapter XVI *infra.*

[102] 588 F.2d 863 (2d Cir. 1978).

claims of commercial secrecy for union-submitted information before the Board. Employers are already able to make such claims and to obtain protective orders for Board proceedings under conditions of protection discussed in chapter XVI.

The commercial confidentiality standard in use by most courts in 1980 measures whether a piece of information would, if disclosed, cause substantial harm to the competitive position of the information owner.[103] That standard is linked to the separate "trade secret" category within the same exemption.[104] If an item of information is within the "trade secret" category, then the showing of degrees of injury is not necessary and the material is per se exempt from required disclosure. In 1979, the Supreme Court noted in the *Chrysler* [105] case that agencies could use their discretion in withholding or disclosing exempt documents. An agency could disclose exempt confidential business statistics, unless a statutory provision provided for its confidentiality. The development of that principle is discussed in chapter XVII.

The personal privacy exemption to the Freedom of Information Act balances the public's right to know certain information and the individual's right to privacy. If the public dissemination would be a clearly unwarranted invasion of privacy—more than just *some* intrusion—then the agency should withhold the information.[106] Because the Privacy Act is operative for some agency files, there is a set of information for which an agency must exercise its withholding discretion.[107]

The personal privacy exemption applies to personnel, medical, and "similar" files. Several labor-related cases have examined this exemption in some detail.[108] In general, intimate details or

---

[103] National Parks & Conservation Ass'n v. Morton, 498 F.2d 765 (D.C. Cir. 1974).

[104] The trade secret category is distinguishable from the commercial confidentiality category in 5 U.S.C. § 552(b)(4).

[105] Chrysler Corp. v. Brown, 441 U.S. 281 (1979).

[106] 5 U.S.C. § 552(b)(6) (1976).

[107] 5 U.S.C. § 552a (1976). For a discussion of its impacts on discretionary withholding, *see* Saloschin, Newkirk, & Gavin, *A Short Guide to the Freedom of Information Act*, in OFFICE OF INFORMATION LAW & POLICY, U.S. DEPARTMENT OF JUSTICE, FREEDOM OF INFORMATION CASE LIST i, 22-23 (1979).

[108] *See* Committee on Masonic Homes v. NLRB, 556 F.2d 214 (3d Cir. 1977).

personally embarrassing information is covered; the mere signing of a union authorization card is not covered.[109] When misconduct of a government agency's employees is asserted, there is a more difficult line-drawing exercise, with many problems in balancing the extent to which a clear invasion of the employee's privacy is counterbalanced by a public interest "warranting" dissemination.

CONCLUSION

Investigative files of labor enforcement agencies are difficult but not impossible to obtain under the Freedom of Information Act. By the time the information is available, it may not be useful to the litigating party. The curious episode of judicial legislating, which "corrected a flaw" in the Freedom of Information Act—a flaw that may in retrospect have been intended by Congress—makes this subject one of the most interesting, and least logically consistent, of all the subjects in this text.

---

[109] *See* chapter XIV *infra*; 2 J. O'REILLY, FEDERAL INFORMATION DISCLOSURE §§ 16.01-.14 (1977 & Supp. 1979).

The Freedom of Information Act and Representation Questions

One of the most controversial ways in which the National Labor Relations Board (NLRB) has been affected by the disclosure mandate of the Freedom of Information Act is the use of the Act to probe the validity of union claims to representation of workers. This is a different set of problems from the investigative files question discussed previously. Generally, a claim of **representation of a certain number of workers is manifested by** the union's presentation to the NLRB of the employee union authorization cards signed by current employees. The access by employers (and other unions as well) to those cards has been the focus of a group of disputed Freedom of Information Act cases.

AUTHORIZATION CARDS AS AGENCY RECORDS

The Freedom of Information Act applies to records of a government agency such as the NLRB, but not to private persons' records.[1] In the 1980 Supreme Court decisions in the *Kissinger* [2] and *Forsham* [3] cases, the Court drew a distinction between governmental records retained by agencies and the records that, although in private hands, might at some future time be available to the government when (and if) delivery of the documents is demanded. This distinction is significant in the labor relations

---

[1] A "record" of an "agency" is accessible. 5 U.S.C. § 552(a)(3) (1976). The term "agency" does not include nongovernmental institutions or entities. *See* 5 U.S.C. § 551 (1976).

[2] Kissinger v. Reporters' Comm. for Freedom of the Press, 100 S.Ct. 960 (1980).

[3] Forsham v. Harris, 100 S.Ct. 978 (1980).

area. If the Board representative views private documents such as authorization cards and leaves them in the hands of the union claiming to represent the workers, then the Board could not be forced by a Freedom of Information Act lawsuit to acquire and then disclose them. If, however, the Board had received and kept or copied and filed copies of the cards, a government "record" would exist, which might be accessible under the Freedom of Information Act.[4]

The record at issue in the union cards cases has been an individual employee's signed authorization card, in which the employee demonstrates a desire to affiliate with a particular union. The persons who may be interested in the contents of the cards are of two kinds. Employers are interested in the identities of which workers signed and in the accuracy of the union's claims to a certain percentage of workers represented. Rival unions will be interested in the accuracy of the number of cards to assure that their desire for designation as bargaining representative has not been thwarted by the card-holding union, which claims to hold a larger allegiance among the workers.[5] Moreover, rival unions will want to know which employees have signed cards in order to further their own organizing attempts.

EMPLOYER REQUESTS FOR AUTHORIZATION CARDS

Most of the litigation on the representation issue has focused on employer requests for disclosure of the actual cards. The leading case resulted from a dispute involving nursing home workers. *Committee on Masonic Homes v. NLRB* [6] was a dispute about the representation cards claimed to be held by an organizing union at a previously nonunion nursing facility. The employer's counsel won a preliminary injunction enjoining NLRB

---

[4] Although there is a plausible argument that the government merely had temporary possession of union property (the cards), the court will ignore the property rights issue when there is a possibility that a copy has been retained by the agency and proceed as if the documents were agency "records." Committee on Masonic Homes v. NLRB, 556 F.2d 214, 218 n.4 (3d Cir. 1977).

[5] *See, e.g.*, American Airlines, Inc. v. National Mediation Bd., 588 F.2d 863 (2d Cir. 1978).

[6] 556 F.2d 214 (3d Cir. 1977).

action on the representation petition until the disputed documents were produced.[7] The Third Circuit reversed.

The National Labor Relations Board's defense of withholding, upheld in *Masonic Homes*, centered on the representation process itself. The employer is not permitted to challenge the sufficiency of the union's showing of employee interest in that union. The Board may find it insufficient and refuse to order an election, but the employer cannot bring such a challenge.[8] It is impossible for the employer to learn which of the employees supported the union (at least in theory); although, if the union claimed a majority and demanded immediate recognition, a doubtful employer might have agreed with the union to have some neutral third party examine the cards to obtain acceptance of the union's claim without further litigation.[9] Because of this usual provision of a blanket of confidentiality for the records, the Board acted consistently when it claimed a Freedom of Information Act exemption on the information; however, the type of claim made and its acceptance by the courts were highly controversial.

In a 1972 case, a district court had allowed withholding of an entire representation case file on the basis of the internal memoranda exemption from disclosure.[10] In the 1976-77 *Masonic Homes* case, the NLRB asserted privacy rights of the workers as a supplement to its general claim of law enforcement exemption [11] and internal memoranda exemption [12] status as grounds for withholding the documents. When the courts considered the law enforcement status of the cards, they rejected the Board's position because there was no proceeding, and especially no

---

[7] Committee on Masonic Homes v. NLRB, 414 F. Supp. 426 (E.D. Pa. 1976), *vacated*, 556 F.2d 214 (3d Cir. 1977). Plaintiff's counsel gives an interesting perspective on the NLRB reaction to such disclosure cases, along with an active argument against the Third Circuit decision. Sobel, *An Example of Judicial Legislation: The Third Circuit's Expansion of Exemption 6 of the Freedom of Information Act to Include Union Authorization Cards,* 23 VILL. L. REV. 751 (1978).

[8] Linden Lumber Div. v. NLRB, 419 U.S. 301, 309 (1974).

[9] NLRB v. Gissel Packing Co., 395 U.S. 575 (1969); *see* Committee on Masonic Homes v. NLRB, 556 F.2d 214, 218 n.3 (3d Cir. 1977).

[10] Distillery, Rectifying, Wine and Allied Workers v. Miller, 68 Lab. Cas. ¶ 12,750 (W.D. Ky. 1972).

[11] 5 U.S.C. § 552(b)(7) (1976).

[12] *Id.* § 552(b)(5).

pending proceeding, involved in the election case.[13] The courts also rejected the claim of the internal memoranda exemption from disclosure, since the cards entered the Board's files from an outside source, the union. The outsider-generated documents could not become internal memoranda by operation of the Freedom of Information Act, the trial court held, for then all of the NLRB's documents "that might at some indefinite future date be relevant in an unfair labor practice charge would be exempt under the FOIA." [14] This narrow view of the law enforcement exemption preceded the Supreme Court's *Robbins Tire* decision,[15] but a post-*Robbins* case on similar election issues in the Fifth Circuit reached the same conclusion.[16]

The employer in *Masonic Homes* therefore had to attack the Board's position on personal privacy exemption status if it was to prevail. First, the files had to be shown by the NLRB to have some personal privacy connection.[17] Union cards state the intention to seek representation by a union at the workplace—hardly an intimate detail of the personal life of the employee. Union cards are signed in front of other employees, and the union may choose to deliver them to the employer as one tactic to provoke acquiescence in the union's representation of the employees.

It was significant as a sidelight on this important precedential decision that the union fighting for organization of the nursing home unit did not even assert the personal privacy claim on appeal, apparently seeing it as the weakest of its arguments in the losing arguments before the trial court.[18] The union preferred not to assert individual privacy issues. An amicus party, the National Union of Hospital and Health Care Employees, therefore introduced the issue before the Third Circuit.

The second element of the personal privacy exemption was the status of the files as "personnel" or "similar" files. Because

---

[13] 414 F. Supp. 426, 432 (E.D. Pa. 1976), *vacated*, 556 F.2d 214, 218 (3d Cir. 1977).

[14] 414 F. Supp. at 431, *vacated*, 556 F.2d at 214.

[15] 437 U.S. 214 (1978).

[16] Pacific Molasses Co. v. NLRB, 577 F.2d 1172 (5th Cir. 1978).

[17] This is a prerequisite to the use of exemption 6. 5 U.S.C. § 552(b)(6) (1976). A significant number of cases under that exemption have found various types of privacy invasions. 556 F.2d at 220; *see* 2 J. O'REILLY, FEDERAL INFORMATION DISCLOSURE § 16.05 (1977 & Supp. 1979).

[18] Sobel, *supra* note 7.

the cards showed something of an employee's classification and status, they satisfied a bare-bones test of "similarity" to personnel records in the eyes of the appellate court.[19]

The third element of the exemption was whether the files would cause *some* invasion of privacy. Privacy usually does not cover such a public declaration of interest in joining a group effort toward unionization.[20] The Third Circuit evaded the doubts as to privacy in this situation by finding a Freedom of Information Act analogue to the right of secret ballot election.[21] The National Labor Relations Act fosters policies in which each worker is entitled to a private choice of the union as his or her representative. The court also found the degree of invasion of privacy to be serious because of the fear of chilling the ardor of both union representation solicitors,[22] who gather the cards, and of the employees who sign them.[23]

The fourth and most critical issue in this privacy exemption case was whether the invasion of privacy was "clearly unwarranted," after balancing the public interest in having the information disclosed and the private interest in maintaining some privacy for personal choices.[24] The *public* nature of this test of

---

[19] 556 F.2d at 219 (*citing* United States Dep't of the Air Force v. Rose, 425 U.S. 352 (1976)).

[20] The court in *Masonic Homes* held that the union decision could be covered (556 F.2d at 221), but in the overwhelming case law trend, *Masonic Homes* is an aberration. Most cases, like *Rose*, look for something private or embarrassing about a person. *See generally* 2 J. O'REILLY, FEDERAL INFORMATION DISCLOSURE § 16.05 (1977 & Supp. 1979); Saloschin, Newkirk, & Gavin, *A Short Guide to the Freedom of Information Act*, in OFFICE OF INFORMATION LAW & POLICY, U.S. DEPARTMENT OF JUSTICE, FREEDOM OF INFORMATION ACT CASE LIST i, 11 (1979).

[21] *Committee on Masonic Homes* holds that dissemination would force the persons to "acknowledge in public their support of the union, in order to be given the right to vote in secret for the union." 556 F.2d at 221.

[22] The chilling effect upon persons who have no economic ties to the employer (e.g., a union representative employed by a union) is extremely unlikely; indeed, the organizational process often involves nonemployee organizers paid by the union simply because those organizers are unlikely to be coerced by an employer. The dissent adopts this view in NLRB v. Robbins Tire & Rubber Co., 437 U.S. 214 (1978).

[23] 556 F.2d at 221.

[24] 5 U.S.C. § 552(b)(6) (1976); *see, e.g.,* United States Dep't of the Air Force v. Rose, 425 U.S. 352 (1976).

benefits excluded the manufacturer in the Third Circuit's analysis: "We are not interested in the employer's benefit, though. Rather we must consider the public benefit that would result from the disclosure, to an employer or to anyone, of union authorization cards submitted to support an election petition." [25] The court could not perceive any public benefit to disclosure of the union cards. When the four reasons were added together, disclosure was denied because the employer had not overcome the "clearly unwarranted" standard and not disproved the court's assumption of a privacy connection to the cards. It was indeed odd that both the government defendant and the union intervenor defendant would drop an issue from the appeal and that then the appellate court would rest its whole opinion on that same issue as argued by an amicus party.[26]

Perhaps the Third Circuit was motivated by a desire to remain well away from the numerous judicial problems that would result from its intervention in an election case. The more deeply the courts enter the discovery phase of NLRB elections, the more likely that the courts would be dragged into what had heretofore been the NLRB's own (and rather mundane) problems. Alternatively, perhaps the court sincerely believed that the chilling effect on employees of disclosure of their signed cards would harm their unionization rights. The chilling effect argument seems to be a visceral reaction by the court, with no argument on the privacy point by the union that had attempted to organize the nursing home and no mention of the statutory protections against coercion that the Board could employ if the employer tried to misuse the verification process. Subsequent use of *Masonic Homes* in the Sixth Circuit *Madeira* decision suggests that it is a persuasive precedent on the Board's side in future representation proceedings.[27] It was followed by the Fifth Circuit in 1978 on similar facts in the *Pacific Molasses* decision.[28]

---

[25] 556 F.2d at 220.

[26] The outside amicus, a hospital employee union, recognized the weakness of the law enforcement exemption defense, although that set of defenses was the sole reliance of both the NLRB counsel and that of the Grain Millers, the union involved in collection of the cards, which were the subject of the litigation.

[27] Madeira Nursing Center, Inc. v. NLRB, 103 L.R.R.M. 2707 (6th Cir. 1980).

[28] Pacific Molasses Co. v. NLRB, 577 F.2d 1172 (5th Cir. 1978).

COMPETING UNION REQUESTS FOR
REPRESENTATION DATA

When two unions compete for the same employees, information on the number of authorization cards obtained by one union can be important to the competitive status of the other union. The Second Circuit held in *American Airlines, Inc. v. National Mediation Board* [29] that a union's own business of representing workers is part of commerce, that union activities are commercial, and that therefore the cards indicating how the union conducted its activities in certain facilities could be considered commercial confidential data of the union.

The decision in *American Airlines* was influenced by the nature of the dispute and the probable effect of disclosure. The nature of the dispute was a labor organization battle among unions. The Second Circuit frankly conceded its desire to stay out of "the very delicate area of labor relations," which had mired the same court in controversy over enforcement records in the *Title Guarantee* case.[30] The court also found that the union had a reasonable expectation of confidentiality, based upon the Mediation Board's confidentiality rules.[31] Although the reliance on a government promise was not binding on the legal status of the data as exempt, the court accorded it great weight. Interunion competitive injury from disclosure would fall upon the union that has the cards in hand, according to the Second Circuit.[32] So the Board had a legitimate interest in aiding the union to keep them secret.

In general, then, union authorization cards are not disclosable upon request. The cards are not available either from the NLRB or other agencies. Representation elections are thus not likely to be affected by the Freedom of Information Act in any significant way.

---

[29] 588 F.2d 863 (2d Cir. 1978).

[30] *Id.*

[31] *Id. See* the history of the mediation exemption status, 588 F.2d 869 n.14. The National Mediation Board, pursuant to the Railway Labor Act, handles representation cases in the railway and air transport industries.

[32] *Id.*

CHAPTER XV

Employer Suits to Enjoin Government Disclosure of Work Force Statistical Data

"Reverse-disclosure" suits are sometimes brought by employers against government agencies to protect the confidential status of employment statistics after the statistics enter government files. These lawsuits have developed out of a concern that competing firms could gain competitive advantage by access to private firms' submissions to federal civil rights agencies. Each of the major employers whose operations are subject to federal equal employment monitoring is vulnerable to the potential for this competitive dissemination of private data.

Because of space limitations, this discussion focuses only on the current case law and interpretations. A more detailed and historical view is available in other sources.[1]

GOVERNMENT COLLECTION OF EMPLOYER STATISTICAL DATA

The government agencies that monitor equal employment opportunity and have powers to gather private sector information are primarily the Equal Employment Opportunity Commission (EEOC), established by Title VII of the Civil Rights Act of 1964,[2] and the Labor Department's Office of Federal Contract Compliance Programs (OFCCP), established by executive order.[3] Their four types of employer-generated personnel statistics are

---

[1] *See* Saloschin, Newkirk, & Gavin, *A Short Guide to the Freedom of Information Act,* in OFFICE OF INFORMATION LAW & POLICY, U.S. DEPARTMENT OF JUSTICE, FREEDOM OF INFORMATION CASE LIST i, 24 (1979) ; and 1 J. O'REILLY, FEDERAL INFORMATION DISCLOSURE ch. 10 (Supp. 1979).

[2] Pub. L. No. 88-352, § 705, 78 Stat. 241 (codified at 42 U.S.C. § 2000e-4 (1976)).

[3] Exec. Order No. 11,375, 3 C.F.R. 320 (1967) ; Exec. Order No. 11,246, 3 C.F.R. 167 (1965).

(1) EEOC investigative files relating to the employer; (2) the form (EEO-1), which gives a racial group breakdown of broad categories of workers employed, e.g., Hispanic professional and managerial workers; (3) government contractor-prepared Work Force Analysis listings, detailing the facility's assignments, pay, etc., for the OFCCP; and (4) the Affirmative Action Plan, which contains the Analysis documents as well as narrative discussions, plans for hiring, etc.[4]

The set of documents that the EEOC collects, the first two types above, by authority of Title VII of the Civil Rights Act are given a special confidential status by that legislation.[5] The agency that collects such information as the EEO-1 forms is the agency charged with maintenance of their confidentiality. Section 709(e) of the Civil Rights Act made it unlawful for the Commission "to make public in any manner whatsoever" employer data that it obtained during its investigations prior to initiating litigation.[6] The intent of section 709(e) was to enhance the EEOC's investigations as part of its settlement package; sensitive data would not be disclosed except in the case of litigation. Because the EEOC and the courts could not control the information once it was released, the Congress gave the information a solid basis for confidentiality and forbade disclosure outside of the government. In that manner, voluntary cooperation would be fostered.[7]

---

[4] *See* 41 C.F.R. §§ 60-1.1 to -741.54 (1979) (OFCCP rules); *id.* § 60-40.2 (AAP disclosure); *id.* § 60-40.4 (EEO-1).

[5] 42 U.S.C. §§ 2000e-5(b), -8(e) (1976). *See generally* Connolly & Fox, *Employer Rights and Access to Documents under the Freedom of Information Act*, 46 Ford. L. Rev. 203, 237 (1977).

[6] 42 U.S.C. § 2000e-8(e) (1976).

[7] "[R]ealizing the lack of any effective mechanism for restricting the use of information once it leaves the hands of the EEOC, [employers might] refuse to comply voluntarily with investigative demands by the EEOC under § 709(e), thereby forcing the Commission to use subpoena power and suit in the district court in place of amicable negotiations. By doing so, employers would at least have the opportunity to persuade a court to impose effective restrictions on the scope of distribution. . . . [This would impede] the operation of the voluntary investigatory proceeding established by § 709(e) . . . in a fashion plainly not intended by Congress when it enacted the restriction on 'making public' data gathered by the Commission." With that comment, the Court of Appeals for the District of Columbia held the EEOC to a strict nondisclosure of business firms' submissions. Sears, Roebuck & Co. v. EEOC, 581 F.2d 941, 947 (D.C. Cir. 1978).

Section 709(e) was matched in the area of settlement negotiations by section 706(b).[8] Under this section, matters discussed in settlement negotiations absolutely could not be revealed by the EEOC without the employer's consent. As with the other section, the purpose of section 706(b) was to foster a candid exploration of possible avenues of settlement with less, or no, litigation.[9]

THE AVOIDANCE OF TITLE VII RESTRICTIONS

The EEOC, desiring to promote private litigation despite these two statutory barriers to information transfer, used two novel devices. First, it acted with several of the contract-monitoring agencies, whose authority came from executive orders rather than from Title VII, to establish a "Joint Reporting Committee." The EEO-1 forms filed by the affected employers all went to the "Committee," an entity created for the purpose of evading the confidentiality barriers.[10] Disclosure of the EEO-1s took place on a rather routine basis thereafter. The persons filing EEO-1 forms were refused relief by most of the courts, which credited the EEOC's claim that the Committee, and not its creator, was the custodian who was making the disclosure of the EEO-1 forms.[11] The second approach of the EEOC was to read "public" disclosure so that disclosure to a charging party was permissible.[12] The charging party who wished to file his or her own suit could do so with the EEOC's investigative documents.

The second approach was rejected by the most liberal of the courts (on civil rights disclosure issues), the District of Columbia Circuit. Although the EEOC had been successful in its first test case involving one charging party and a sparse in-

---

[8] 42 U.S.C. §§ 2000e-5(c), -8(e) (1976).

[9] EEOC v. St. Francis Community Hosp., 70 F.R.D. 592, 593 (D. S.C. 1976).

[10] The Joint Reporting Committee, Jeffersonville, Ind., is identified as the recipient for EEO-1 Forms on the forms themselves. The JRC has no independent existence.

[11] This approach to disclosure exalts form over substance but was credited as a valid argument in Sears, Roebuck & Co. v. GSA, 384 F. Supp. 996 (D. D.C.), *stay dissolved*, 509 F.2d 527 (D.C. Cir. 1974).

[12] This approach was firmly rejected by the District of Columbia Circuit as contrary to the letter and spirit of the statutes. Sears, Roebuck & Co. v. EEOC, 581 F.2d 941 (D.C. Cir. 1978).

vestigative file,[13] the District of Columbia Circuit threw out the
EEOC's disclosure rationale in *Sears, Roebuck & Co. v. EEOC*
in 1978.[14] The appellate court held that the absolute prohibitions of the statute, read in line with the intent to encourage
frank and confidential settlement discussions, made it impossible
for the EEOC to release the investigative file compiled under
Title VII to a charging party.[15]

When the particular statutory directive is considered in conjunction with one of the Freedom of Information Act's exemption provisions, the terms of Title VII are very protective.
When requested, the EEOC cannot give out the information
voluntarily. When a Freedom of Information Act suit is brought,
the prohibitive provisions of sections 706 and 709 fit within the
(b)(3) exemption so that disclosure need not be made of that
information.[16]

THE AFFIRMATIVE ACTION PLAN CONTROVERSY

In the middle of the 1970s, it became slowly and painfully
apparent to industry that a whole necessary corollary rule had
been omitted when the general rule of public access to information was codified in the Freedom of Information Act. The corollary was that confidential business data might intentionally not
be protected by a particular agency in a particular case. When
that information was the subject of a disagreement, the firm
that gave the data to the agency should have been able to assure
their legal protection. Otherwise, the Freedom of Information Act
would leave the owner of valuable rights powerless to protect
them.

After several years of litigation and extensive salvos on all
sides in the literature, the Supreme Court held that the omission indeed was present; that the Freedom of Information Act,

---

[13] H. Kessler & Co. v. EEOC, 472 F.2d 1147 (5th Cir.), *cert. denied,* 412
U.S. 939 (1973). *Kessler* was cited in *Sears* as not inconsistent with the
Sears result.

[14] 581 F.2d 941 (D.C. Cir. 1978).

[15] *Id.*

[16] Disclosure need not be made of specifically exempted materials; 5 U.S.C.
§ 552(b)(3) permits the agency to assert that a separate statute exempts
materials from the general disclosure requirements of the Freedom of Information Act. But note that the exemption may be available against certain
parties who have special access rights under Title VII. Charlotte-Mecklenburg
Hosp. Authority v. Perry, 571 F.2d 195 (4th Cir. 1978).

for whatever reason, failed to provide a basis for protection of confidential business data; and that protection of confidential information would have to find other legal bases than the Freedom of Information Act. In *Chrysler Corp. v. Brown,*[17] the Supreme Court had one of the best factual arguments for a legislative remedy to the Freedom of Information Act's omission. A manufacturer whose manning and staffing plans revealed extremely sensitive data related to labor costs, profit margins, and ultimately to price position in the competitive market entrusted those plans to a federal agency. The agency proposed to disclose the plans to any Freedom of Information Act requester. The agency refused to accept the firm's request for an advance determination that the Work Force Analyses would be kept in confidence.[18] The firm responded with a showing of routes of harm from the exposure, linkage between the employee data and profitability, and linkages between the worker assignment changes in several sequential years' plans and the economically efficient point at which certain operations could be mechanized.[19] For the firm, this was sensitive data acquired through costly trial and error. For the government agency, the arguments were insufficient to overcome a general desire to disclose the employment statistics.

The primary rationale against such disclosures is economic. Particularly where raw material costs are market-value commodity costs and where machinery costs and plant costs are well estimable, the degree of manpower and rates paid per group of workers become sensitive.[20] The Work Force Analysis is the blueprint for reaching into that information.[21] With it, profit-

---

17 441 U.S. 281 (1979).

18 Chrysler Corp. v. Schlesinger, 412 F. Supp. 171 (D. Del. 1976), *vacated,* 565 F.2d 1172 (3d Cir. 1977), *vacated sub nom.* Chrysler Corp v. Brown, 441 U.S. 281 (1979).

19 The trial court in *Chrysler Corp.* discusses many of the confidentiality issues involved in the factory statistics. The evidentiary record was sealed and remains sealed, so the actual statistical data—the *res* of the lawsuit—have never been exposed.

20 *See* Westinghouse Elec. Corp. v. Schlesinger, 542 F.2d 1190 (4th Cir. 1976), *cert. denied,* 431 U.S. 924 (1977).

21 The Work Force Analysis (WFA) document reaches into the departments and job assignments of the plant. The jobs may describe machines, e.g., "folder machine operator." Lack of reference to machines in the descriptions reveals an absence of machines. The detail of the analysis results from frequent bureaucratic rejection of finished WFA documents as insufficiently detailed to permit headquarters bureaucrats to review patterns of hiring

ability and, thereby, probable pricing and margins information can be obtained and used by a competing firm. The primary rationale for disclosure is social. When the pursuit of the societal goal of equal opportunity is entrusted to an agency of the federal government, which in turn is subject to public information access laws, the public should be able to monitor the government agency's effectiveness by monitoring its results.[22] The tougher question is, When should the public be excluded from some of the evidence to be used in making decisions at the agency level about the sufficiency of private firms' compliance?

BACKGROUND OF THE CHRYSLER DECISION

Most employers of a significant interstate character are in one way or another government contractors. The government contract authority of the Labor Department includes supervisory authority to monitor equal employment opportunity practices of the private sector employers, backed by the penalty of debarment from future federal contracts.[23] The regulations that implement the monitoring program require the collection of extensive data, preparation from the data of a plant-by-plant Work Force Analysis, and submission of the documents in the format of an Affirmative Action Plan.[24]

Prior to the *Chrysler* decision, the Labor Department's governing regulations had asserted authority for the Department to decide whether to release information that appeared in private firms' submissions of Affirmative Action Plans (AAPs).[25] Chrys-

---

and promotion in the workplace. Bureaucrats' powers to threaten debarment from future contracts are the means used to extract very sensitive, detailed data.

[22] And an argument was made by civil rights advocacy groups to the Fourth Circuit that this oversight requires detailed private sector information. The Fourth Circuit rejected the argument and ruled that the confidential business information deserved protection. Westinghouse Elec. Corp. v. Schlesinger, 542 F.2d 1190 (4th Cir. 1976), cert. denied, 431 U.S. 924 (1977). Daniel Clement, counsel for the losing advocacy groups, later coauthored the government's official policy on business confidentiality claims. *See* 1 OFFICE OF INFORMATION LAW & POLICY, U.S. DEPARTMENT OF JUSTICE, FOIA UPDATE (Winter 1979).

[23] 41 C.F.R. §§ 60-1.1 to -741.54 (1979); Exec. Order No. 11,246, 3 C.F.R. 167 (1965).

[24] 41 C.F.R. §§ 60-1.1 to -741.54 (1979).

[25] 41 C.F.R. §§ 60-40.2, .3, .4 (1979).

ler, a defense contractor, was informed of the government's intention to release the detailed statistics for two of its plants. It chose to challenge the release of its statistical data on the grounds that competitively sensitive confidential materials contained in the AAP would injure the commercial position of Chrysler if made available to the public, including Chrysler's competitors. At the trial court, Chrysler showed that the information would provide several benefits to competing firms, including labor cost data not generally known in the auto industry and vital information on the appropriate scheduling of automation planning in the firm's automotive plants. By comparing the 1975-78 annual statistics for a department that had heavy labor costs, for example, the competitor could find that the mechanization of a labor-intensive chore occurred in 1978, when Chrysler's work force showed a sharp decline in the laboring group and a redesignation of the remaining labor group as "technicians." Estimating the 1975-78 rates of output from that operation from publicly available sources, the competing plant operator could predict (at none of Chrysler's trial and error costs) that mechanization would be most profitable when the labor cost and units produced reached the point achieved at that Chrysler plant in 1978.[26]

Chrysler won an injunction against government disclosure in the trial court. On appeal, the Third Circuit reversed.[27] Regardless of the employer's meritorious arguments about use of the information, the appellate court held that the Freedom of Information Act did not contemplate lawsuits by persons other than aggrieved requesters of information. The appellate court did not accept Chrysler's argument that it could seek injunctive relief under the Freedom of Information Act by implication of a "reverse-FOIA" right.[28]

In the Supreme Court, *Chrysler Corp. v. Brown*[29] produced an odd result. The Court held that the Freedom of Information

---

[26] This system of divining confidential data from the AAP and WFA documents is amply described in Chrysler Corp. v. Schlesinger, 412 F. Supp. 171 (D. Del. 1976), *vacated,* 565 F.2d 1172 (3d Cir. 1977), *vacated sub nom.* Chrysler Corp. v. Brown, 441 U.S. 281 (1979).

[27] The court of appeals vacated and remanded for additional factual evidence in the trial court's record.

[28] 412 F. Supp. 171 (D. Del. 1976), *vacated,* 565 F.2d 1172 (3d Cir. 1977), *vacated* 441 U.S. 281 (1979).

[29] 441 U.S. 281 (1979).

Act did not permit reverse-disclosure suits by aggrieved submitters, as the government had contended, and that the exemptions from required disclosure were options that an agency could choose to invoke or not invoke as it desired.[30] The Court went further, however, to note that Administrative Procedure Act lawsuits to enjoin disclosure *were* permitted.[31] If a statute covered the type of documents in dispute, the statute could be invoked in the APA action to assert that disclosure was contrary to law. One of the widest statutes available was the criminal trade secrets statute,[32] which covered confidential private statistical data. That statute would protect a firm's private submission against an agency's desire to make disclosure only if the agency release was not "authorized by law." [33] Finally, to complete the analysis, the Court looked at the Labor Department rules to see if they were "authorized by law" and thereby were usable as a justification for dissemination of the private information. The Court ruled that the Labor Department rules were not legally valid and could not be used as a premise for disclosure.[34]

In *Chrysler*, the Supreme Court decision remanded the case to the lower courts, where it was remanded in turn to the Labor Department for reconsideration and another trip through the courts if any party to the outcome is dissatisfied.[35]

SIGNIFICANCE OF CHRYSLER

For employers, the *Chrysler* case means that judicial relief against disclosure depends predominantly on statutory grounds

---

[30] *Id.* at 294.

[31] *Id.* at 317-18. Because there are substantive limitations on an agency's discretion to disclose confidential business data (in such statutes as 18 U.S.C. § 1905), the agency is subject to full review under the Administrative Procedure Act. Whether the review should be *de novo* or limited to the (often sparse) record remains to be decided.

[32] 18 U.S.C. § 1905 (1976).

[33] Confidential statistical data are protected by the section, under its plain meaning, if the disclosure is not "authorized by law." *Id. See* 441 U.S. at 295-319.

[34] *Id.* at 316.

[35] Chrysler Corp. v. Brown, 611 F.2d 439 (3d Cir. 1979). The matter should be decided on the merits by the Labor Department in late 1980 and then will return to the federal courts. If the Department has a change of mind and protects the information, further proceedings would be dropped unless for policy reasons an intervenor or the parties wish to keep the case alive.

for nondisclosure. For example, if the criminal trade secret statute applies, it may be "dispositive" of the issues.[36] If another statute applies and covers the information, then likewise it may result in a defeat for the agency and a court order enjoining release.[37] Even absent a statutory basis, however, an Administrative Procedure Act challenge could be mounted against the agency's intended disclosure. If the agency fails to document *why* it is choosing to disclose—why, for example, some public benefit arises that outweighs the firm's competitive injury—then the absence of a reason for disclosure can make the agency decision seem arbitrary.[38]

For government agencies, the rush to release private information has been significantly slowed. There is a complex analytical process before agency attorneys can approve the dissemination of the confidential business information.[39] The agency needs some form of an administrative record if it expects to be sued. Conversely, if it withholds, it has a lesser likelihood of being sued, and it will have the persons most expert on the commercial value of the data on the agency's side carrying most of the weight of the defense.[40]

For the unions, disclosure is a mixed blessing indeed.[41] If a union already representing workers files a lawsuit to obtain staffing amounts, wage rates, etc., through litigation, using the Freedom of Information Act, its members may rebel. They could

---

[36] If 18 U.S.C. § 1905 applies to certain information, it cannot be disclosed, and that fact is "dispositive" of an Administrative Procedure Act challenge to the agency's proposed disclosure actions. 441 U.S. at 317.

[37] For example, if commercial information were offered in a settlement negotiation with the EEOC, another statute would absolutely bar EEOC disclosure, and the reverse-disclosure suit by the affected firm would succeed. 42 U.S.C. § 2000e-5(b) (1976).

[38] For an extensive discussion of the post-*Chrysler* burden on the government, *see* 1 J. O'REILLY, FEDERAL INFORMATION DISCLOSURE § 10.15 (1977 & Supp. 1979); Office of Information Law & Policy, U.S. Department of Justice, Statement Concerning the Supreme Court's Decision in Chrysler v. Brown (June 15, 1979).

[39] The government's current official position as this text goes to press is stated in detail in 1 OFFICE OF INFORMATION LAW & POLICY, *supra* note 22.

[40] The information owner will intervene and/or assist the preparation of the government's case because the owner is the real party in interest. Some agencies go so far as to demand cooperation, insisting on some form of advance assurances. *E.g.*, 21 C.F.R. §§ 20.1-.119 (1979) (FDA); 40 C.F.R. § 2.203 (1979) (EPA).

[41] *See* chapters II-VII *infra*.

have told the union the same thing; they could have obtained the same types of information in a useful but more general form, as discussed in the earlier chapters of this text.[42] For those unions that do not now represent employees in a firm, the information might be useful in a representation campaign. When the courts view the union in an organizational posture, seeking access to confidential business information of a firm, the courts are likely to accord the union the same skeptical treatment that they would give to direct competitors. Unions already have won their own reverse-disclosure suits with the argument that their organizing is a commercial activity done for profit and is thereby protected against the Freedom of Information Act access of competing unions.[43] It is doubtful that courts would ever welcome with open arms a union's lawsuit seeking to force disclosure of documents from a firm that it does not represent.

For individual workers, disclosure of their plant's sensitive data could hurt by assisting competing firms. For example, a unionized upstate New York electronic components plant supplying the Air Force competes with several Sun Belt competitors. Knowledge of precise manning levels and wage information by the union representing the New York workers is easily obtainable and requires little or no formality, but a competitor's acquisition of the same knowledge under the Freedom of Information Act from the Department of Labor, although it may require administrative effort and possibly a wait of several months, assists the competitor to undercut prices of the New York plant. The competitor's pricing is tied to the known profit margins obtainable from this "missing link" of labor cost data and is so designed as to undercut the competing firm with lower Sun Belt labor costs for a period of time sufficient to make the New York firm leave that market as noneconomic or insufficiently profitable. So the workers do not gain from the

---

[42] The union makes a difficult antagonist in a reverse-disclosure case because some amount of the contested information is likely to come into the union's possession through sympathetic employees researching the information for the union against the employer. The union is more likely to file an unfair labor practice charge to obtain the information than it would be to sue the employer for the data, except where unfair labor practice proceedings would take significantly longer than an FOI Act litigation might take. Sometimes, depending on the strength of the employer's resistance, the FOI route may be faster.

[43] American Airlines, Inc. v. National Mediation Bd., 588 F.2d 863 (2d Cir. 1978).

general public "right of access"; they gain information but lose employment. Disclosure by law to one is disclosure to all.[44] For firms that are not government contractors, the effects are not likely to be great. Equal Employment Opportunity Commission files on the labor forces of those firms will be protected under specific statutes already, especially Title VII's confidentiality sections discussed above.[45] If a prohibition against disclosure existed, then the agency's Freedom of Information Act discretion would be limited and disclosure would be denied.[46]

FUTURE DEVELOPMENTS

It is anticipated that the period 1980-82 will be a difficult time for confidential business data submitted to federal agencies. Court decisions so becloud the future protection of confidential data as to make worthless a government agency's promise of confidentiality. The *Chrysler* case will be back before the courts,[47] and other decisions may be important for the labor statistics confidentiality matter as well.

Legislation offered by Senator Dole in 1980 portends a new awareness of the need for protection of confidential statistical data.[48] Under the proposed revision of the Freedom of Information Act, much more of the sensitive business information would become confidential and exempted from the Freedom of Information Act. Employers would also benefit from procedural changes to provide advance notice and an administrative opportunity to object to disclosure.

---

[44] The agency cannot declare the information nonexempt for one firm and fail thereafter to disclose it for all. *See* 1 J. O'REILLY, FEDERAL INFORMATION DISCLOSURE § 9.07 (1977 & Supp. 1979).

[45] 42 U.S.C. §§ 2000e-5(b), -8(e) (1976).

[46] Chrysler Corp. v. Brown, 441 U.S. 281 (1979).

[47] Chrysler Corp. v. Brown, 611 F.2d 439 (3d Cir. 1979).

[48] S. 2397, 96th Cong., 2d Sess. (1980).

PART FIVE

*Frontiers of Disclosure:
The NLRB as a Source of
Safety and Equality Data*

CHAPTER XVI

Frontiers of Disclosure: Workplace Chemical Exposure and Identity Information

"Labor's right to know" has a ringing clarity of tone and an inherent sound of righteousness, which belies the complexity of the issues. This chapter addresses the complexities of balancing workers' own abilities to protect themselves through detailed knowledge of potential risks and the employer's legitimate expectation of confidentiality, where that confidentiality serves some defined competitive purpose or accords some advantage. The simple but attractive Coors beer can illustrates the quandary. In the *Borden* [1] case, discussed below, only that employer knew the one secret ingredient that made its can-coloring paint produce just the right shade and tone for cans of Coors beer. Workers had a desire to know, which some would call a right to know, the identities of the workplace chemical ingredients, while Borden had a desire, and others will say a right, to keep the identity of the secret ingredient hidden from the curious eyes of competing paint makers. Whose interests should predominate? Where can lines be drawn? The answer is a societal dilemma worthy of the best minds of our age.

ASPECTS OF WORKPLACE EXPOSURE

There are several distinct aspects to the matter of workplace exposures. *Ingredient, exposure,* and *effects* issues must be considered. First, *ingredients* present in the workplace are usually there for a profit-making purpose. For example, three separate chemical dyes mixed into a tankful of chemicals may be critical to the successful completion of a secret manufacturing process. The presence of each of the three may be masked by a code, with the code kept in the custody of a trusted manager. Or

---

[1] Borden Chemical, No. 32-CA-551 (NLRB, filed Apr. 25, 1979).

the dyes may bear a trade name if they are themselves mixtures, which prevents the dye user from mixing its own batch of the same materials, unless the user is analytically capable of discovering the composition of the proprietary mixture. The chemicals' identities may also be made known to the workers in some situations, depending on circumstances of the particular factory, process, and the workers' manufacturing functions.

Exposure information is the measurement of the extent to which workers in the plant are inhaling, absorbing, or otherwise coming into contact with a certain detectable substance. The exposure is monitored by a scientific testing apparatus appropriate for the nature of the particular chemical and the route of human contact being examined. The workers' exposure at a particular stage of production may be subject to controls by federal standards applicable to a type of operation and established by the Occupational Safety and Health Administration (OSHA).[2] Or they may be subject to recommended Threshold Limit Values (TLVs) of the American Conference of Government Industrial Hygienists (ACGIH), the quasi-official body responsible for setting air exposure measurement calculations. Usually, exposure monitoring data show only the amount of the substance and do not attempt to define which levels are or are not safe. This is a matter for health effects information.

Information on *health effects* correlates the known information about the workers with the known information about the substances to which they have been exposed. A chemical used at a concentration which allows 10 parts per million (ppm) to escape into the workplace air breathed by workers may produce wheezing and shortness of breath because of a reaction in the lungs and nasal passages. The health effects studied in the plant (e.g., a number of wheezing complaints reported and the number alleviated by removal of the worker from exposure to the chemical) will be written into a report that attempts to discover connections between the exposure, the chemical, and the observed effects.

THE LEGAL ISSUE OF CHEMICAL SECRECY

A "trade secret" is a piece of information, oral or written, which a person or firm possesses and uses in business pursuits,

---

[2] 29 U.S.C. § 655 (1976). For a description of standards, *see* J. O'REILLY, FEDERAL REGULATION OF THE CHEMICAL INDUSTRY § 9.09 (1980).

which others in the same field do not know or possess, and which gives the possessor some lasting advantage over competitors through its use.[3] The knowledge that phtalocyanine green at 4 percent with sodium chloride in a mixture of cotton and rayon will produce a certain fashionable color might be a trade secret for a textile dye firm that had independently discovered it. The same information could be independently discovered and kept secret by others as well, but their secrecy about the information would isolate its use so that the "secret" nature of the discovery would not be lost unless it is later disclosed through publication or commonplace public knowledge.[4]

For federal agency-maintained records, the concept of trade secrecy is important. A trade secret cannot be disclosed by a federal agency unless the agency has been delegated by Congress some substantive authority to adopt rules mandating the disclosure of those secrets.[5] Some statutes have tried to force the disclosure of information that could be a trade secret, usually with compensation,[6] but the majority of statutes are fully protective of information once it fits into the "trade secret" category.[7] Section 15 of the Occupational Safety and Health (OSH) Act requires that information containing trade secrets must be kept secret by the representatives of the Secretary of Labor, although the agency may disclose it to other federal officials in the course of their activities.[8] Section 1905 of the Criminal Code makes unauthorized disclosure of a trade secret by officials a criminal violation.[9]

---

[3] 4 RESTATEMENT OF TORTS § 757, Comment b (1938). The leading case on legal status of chemical trade secrets is Kewanee Oil Co. v. Bicron Corp., 416 U.S. 470 (1974).

[4] *See* R. MILGRIM, TRADE SECRETS ch. 2 (1967 & Supp. 1978).

[5] Chrysler Corp. v. Brown, 441 U.S. 281 (1979). *See* 5 U.S.C. § 552(b)(4) (1976); 18 U.S.C. § 1905 (1976).

[6] *See, e.g.,* Federal Environment Pesticide Control Act of 1972, § 3(c)(1)(D), 7 U.S.C. § 136a(c)(1)(D) (1976).

[7] For example, the trade secrets of an inspected firm are protected under the Occupational Safety and Health Act of 1970, § 15, 29 U.S.C. § 664 (1976); under the Food, Drug, and Cosmetic Act, § 301(j), 21 U.S.C. § 331(j) (1976); and under the Consumer Product Safety Act, § 6, 15 U.S.C. § 2055 (1976). Disclosure would also violate 18 U.S.C. § 1905 (1976).

[8] 29 U.S.C. § 664 (1976).

[9] 18 U.S.C. § 1905 (1976). *See* Chrysler Corp. v. Brown, 441 U.S. 281 (1979); Westinghouse Elec. Corp. v. Schlesinger, 542 F.2d 1190 (4th Cir. 1976), *cert. denied,* 431 U.S. 924 (1977).

A definition of *when* information is a trade secret remains quite controversial in the health and safety area. For example, the presence of statutory authority to disclose information from "health studies" under the Toxic Substances Control Act,[10] administered by the Environmental Protection Agency (EPA), is hard to reconcile with the mandatory confidentiality of confidential statistical data under OSH Act, whereby a study might be shared between agencies.[11] Usually, the statute under authority of which the information was collected will govern the ability of the agencies to disseminate the information to the public.[12] The problem of defining trade secrets is made more difficult when the agencies develop their own standards in different cases. Sometimes within the same agency, different administrative law judges may take different views on interpretation of the trade secret category.[13] In a particular case, to develop an understanding of the present legal limits of the "trade secret" category, the reader may wish to research the matter further. Textbooks, periodicals, and the like may be helpful, although for a particular substance, lack of any mention is considered a good sign of trade secret status.[14]

CONTROVERSIES OVER EXPOSURE DATA

The monitoring of worker exposure to potentially harmful substances in the workplace is a duty shared by the enforcement staff of the Occupational Safety and Health Administration (OSHA) and the scientific and laboratory organization of the National Institute for Occupational Safety and Health (NIOSH). The Occupational Safety and Health Act has a spe-

---

[10] 15 U.S.C. § 2613(b) (1976).

[11] 29 U.S.C. § 664 (1976).

[12] This approach is included in a number of joint agency agreements to speed the processing of the Freedom of Information Act requests to the appropriate agency. *See* the proposed Memorandum of Understanding between the Equal Employment Opportunity Commission and the Office of Federal Contract Compliance Programs in 45 Fed. Reg. 27,071 (1980).

[13] *See, e.g.,* Secretary of Labor v. Olin Corp., OSH Review Comm. Dkt. 77-4369 (1978), which applied a protective order in OSH Act proceedings over union objections.

[14] Absence of public knowledge of the substance or of its use will enhance the assertion that the information had not been part of the technology already known by others in the industry. If there were such widespread knowledge, the trade secret category cannot apply.

cific provision requiring that certain exposure data be disclosed to workers:

> The Secretary . . . shall issue regulations requiring employers to maintain accurate records of employee exposures to potentially toxic materials or harmful physical agents which are required to be monitored or measured under · section 6. Such regulations shall provide employees or their representatives with an opportunity . . . to have access to the records thereof. Such regulations shall also make appropriate provision for each employee or former employee to have access to such records as will indicate his own exposure to toxic materials or harmful physical agents.[15]

The method of monitoring will vary depending upon the chemical, type of system of production, and other factors. Worker access to information about the hazardous chemical exposures is not a right of access to all product information or all effects information. The statutory right relates to exposure data alone.[16]

There are several confidentiality problems with public dissemination of the exposure data. First, exposure monitoring is looking for a specific chemical or chemicals, the presence of which in the workplace may reveal a secret ingredient in a trade-named or -coded mixture.[17] If public data name a chemical not normally found, they give a clue to the other firms in the same field about the competitor's advantage. Second, the exposure data for periods of time (hourly samples for a week) show the competitive observer that the production schedule sets a certain time of day for the use of the chemical, e.g., an intermediate or byproduct of a certain heat-melting process. Following the charts of timing, a competing firm would be able to discern the manufacturer's cycle of production, the faster and slower times of the year or season (depending upon extent of data available), and even some details of the process by which the mixture is made. Variable results of the data over time allow a skilled competitor to reconstruct processes in some

---

[15] 29 U.S.C. § 657(c) (3) (1976).

[16] The statutory right covers "exposures to potentially toxic materials or harmful physical agents which are required to be monitored" only, not all chemicals. *Id.*

[17] For example, monitoring for an exotic material in a plant's air will disclose the presence of the material in the mixture although the material is at a level undetectable in the mixture by chemical analysis techniques.

cases.[18] Moreover, knowledge of the competitive firm's weakness in its control of emissions of a chemical may be an admission about a process weakness or about age or obsolescence of its machinery or buildings. Finally, applications themselves are an advance look into technological accomplishments of competitive firms in process control.

If the employer has a statutory duty to give the exposure data to the worker, should the same data be given to the government? The Act is not clear.[19] OSHA's controversial exposure records rule of 1980 decreed that such data must be retained and must be disclosed to the designated representative whom the employee authorizes to see those exposure data.[20] The rule has not yet been ruled upon in the courts,[21] but manufacturers have objected that the law does not give authority for access to detailed exposure data by OSHA, NIOSH, or to persons other than the actual exposed employees.[22]

As a policy matter, unions argue that their collective ability to analyze the workplace data with experts is far superior in its protective results to any attempt at self-help by individual workers. A special industrial hygiene expert from the international union may have expertise that would be unavailable to some employers as well as to employees; the expert will benefit the workers' own abilities to interpret the data in a useful manner.[23] The issue will be settled in the courts, perhaps by 1982.

---

[18] To be legally effective, trade secrets should not be obvious, commonly held knowledge in the industry. But a skilled competitive firm with enough money may be able to "reverse-engineer" a product. For anything other than the simplest discoveries, trade secret status can be applied. Case law support is discussed at length in R. MILGRIM, TRADE SECRETS § 7.07[1][a] (1967 & Supp. 1979).

[19] 29 U.S.C. § 657(c)(3) requires disclosure to workers, but 29 U.S.C. § 657(c)(1) limits OSHA and NIOSH inspectors to records that are required to be kept by a valid regulation. See the exposure records rule, 43 Fed. Reg. 31,371 (1978).

[20] Access to Medical and Exposure Records, 45 Fed. Reg. 35,212 (1980).

[21] The AFL-CIO filed a defensive notice of petition for review to force the rule's review in the "friendly" District of Columbia Circuit if it is reviewed as an OSHA "standard." See 29 U.S.C. § 655(f) (1976).

[22] *Access to Employee Medical and Exposure Records: Hearings Before U.S. Occupational Safety and Health Administration*, Docket No. H-112 (Mar. 1979) (brief for Chemical Manufacturers Association).

[23] For example, the union in Borden Chemical, No. 32-CA-551 (NLRB, filed Apr. 25, 1979), hired a consultant from Berkeley to assist in worker

CONTROVERSIES OVER INGREDIENT DATA

The widespread use of proprietary mixtures and secret ingredients in the workplace reflects the commercial sensitivity of ingredient information. The marketplace of product development suggests that some research is best compensated for by patents (e.g., photocopying techniques of Xerox Corporation), while other research into very complex formulations is better handled with traditional trade secret safeguards, e.g., the formula for Coca-Cola.[24] That commercial advantage *is* attached to chemical composition information is a marketplace fact; even those most ardently in favor of dissemination of constituent composition concede that commercial secrets do serve a societal purpose of enhancing the innovation cycle. Where controversies develop, they relate to the proper degrees of balance to be accorded the secrecy interest when those interests clash with some other desired goal. What appears to be a vocal minority would broadcast the data to maximize public awareness.

The legal protection of ingredient and formula data springs from the marketplace and societal situation of confidentiality. Under the leading interpretation, that of the *Restatement of Torts*, formula information is trade secret information if it is not known to the competitor firms in the same line of work, is not published or publicly available, is maintained as confidential data by some protective measures of the owner, and serves to provide a commercial advantage over competitors who do not know or use that secret information in their work.[25]

---

safety issues related to the nearby Borden facility at Fremont, California. The expertise of the union-selected academic researchers has increased because more sophisticated detection and analysis are required for chronic effects of certain chemicals. Such expertise was cited by OSHA in support of wider disclosure of exposure data. 45 Fed. Reg. 35,218-22 (1980).

[24] The serious problems of time, cost, and uncertainty of long-term enforcement ability make the patent system less attractive for a class of secret information than the informal trade secret system. The class of materials that are likely to be held as trade secrets are those that are difficult to detect through examination of the constituents of the finished product. That "reverse-engineering" process, using gas chromatography and mass spectroscopy, is not always successful in detecting trace materials, which can make an important difference in a mixture at low levels. Trade secrets and their relationship to patents are best discussed in R. MILGRIM, TRADE SECRETS ch. 2 (1967 & Supp. 1979).

[25] 4 RESTATEMENT OF TORTS § 757, Comment b (1938).

Many state laws prohibit the disclosure of formula data.[26] When the Supreme Court was asked to consider the interrelationship of ingredient trade secrets and the patent system, it ruled in 1974 that state protection of trade secrets was fully consistent with the federal patent system.[27] The desire to keep the innovative development system moving ahead, as reflected in state laws to protect trade secrets, was consistent with the parallel federal system of issuing patents for chemical compositions.

The environmental legislation of the 1970s and the health-related chemical regulation statutes of the same period often included statutory requirements for the disclosure of information that would assist a protected class of people in monitoring the government's enforcement of the new statutes.[28] For example, the Occupational Safety and Health Act required certain information to be made available to the workers who were protected by OSHA standards; if the standards required monitoring, the workers were entitled to review the monitoring data.[29] Each of the 1970s statutes, however, contained a protective provision for "trade secrets." By common as well as legal usage, the actual ingredients in a mixture were then (and are today) generally classed as "trade secrets."[30] When the identity of ingredients became relevant to some desired goal of protection, then the trade secret protective provisions clashed with some desires to place

---

[26] *See, e.g.*, N.Y. PUB. OFF. LAW § 87(2)(d) (McKinney Supp. 1979-80); OHIO REV. CODE ANN. § 1333.51 (Page 1979); W. VA. CODE § 29B-1-4(1) (1980).

[27] Kewanee Oil Co. v. Bicron Corp., 416 U.S. 470 (1974).

[28] Health and safety studies must be made public under the Toxic Substances Control Act. 15 U.S.C. § 2613(b) (1976). Emissions data must be available to the public under the Clean Air Act Amendments of 1970, § 12(a), 42 U.S.C. § 7607(a)(1) (1976), and the Federal Water Pollution Control Act Amendments of 1972, § 308, 33 U.S.C. § 1318 (1976 & Supp. II 1978).

[29] *Compare* 29 U.S.C. § 664 (1976) *with* 45 Fed. Reg. 35,212 (1980). The latter greatly increases OSHA's power.

[30] *See, e.g.*, the Toxic Substances Control Act's protection for formulation secrets in 15 U.S.C. § 2613(b) (1976). Mixture ingredients are frequently classified as trade secrets to preserve the research investment made by the mixture seller in the development of a more effective product. Full disclosure, or "cookbook labeling," is seen by mixture sellers as a direct disincentive to innovate because resources invested in the development could not be recouped from sales of the proprietary mixture. Ultimately, universal knowledge of contents would reduce net investment in nonpatentable (as most are not) mixture development projects.

full ingredient information in the public record. A balancing process ensued, with uncertain long-term results.

One of the most difficult areas for balancing private trade secret rights and public access rights has been in the workplace. The chemical identity of components of a mixture provides a special advantage to the owner of the mixture. When government surveys were taken of 4,636 workplaces in a 1972-74 sampling, 70 percent of the mixtures observed there were of unknown chemical components.[31] Proprietary mixtures traditionally do not reveal their composition. NIOSH criticized proprietary products sold by a chemical manufacturer whose product is known in the workplace only under its trade name.[32] The statutory provisions related to health and safety data disclosure, most notably section 14(b) of the 1976 Toxic Substances Control (TSC) Act,[33] required disclosure of effects of chemicals, although the law specifically protected ingredients and ingredient percentages.[34] Those disclosures under the TSC Act of chemical effects reach into workplace information and supplement the disclosures available under the Occupational Safety and Health Act;[35] however, the interaction of the two laws is still being determined. (Joint TSC Act-OSH Act rules to require certain labeling of chemical mixtures are discussed later in this chapter.) Whatever the statutes and regulations may require procedurally, the concept of trade secret protection still applies to confidential

---

31 Of mixtures discovered in the survey, 70 percent were trade-named mixtures whose chemical composition was not precisely known by the users; of those that contained OSHA-regulated products such as benzene, 32.5 percent were designated as trade secrets. NATIONAL INSTITUTE FOR OCCUPATIONAL SAFETY & HEALTH, THE RIGHT TO KNOW (1977).

32 *Id.* The report was prepared for and submitted to the Senate Committee on Human Resources.

33 15 U.S.C. § 2613(b) (1976). This section only applies to "health and safety studies." 15 U.S.C. § 2602(6) (1976).

34 15 U.S.C. §§ 2613(a), (b) (last sentence) (1976).

35 A set of joint chemical-labeling rules from the Environmental Protection Agency and the Occupational Safety and Health Administration under the TSC Act and the OSH Act is expected to be issued in summer 1980. After passage of the TSC Act, when NIOSH was asked to report to the Senate on the disclosure of ingredient identities, it stated: "Steps are being taken to promote voluntary disclosure. It may be possible for EPA to require that labeling of industrial chemicals include product composition. New legislation may be required if EPA is forced to go through the hearing process for each chemical constituent contained in trade name products." NATIONAL INSTITUTE FOR OCCUPATIONAL SAFETY & HEALTH, *supra* note 31, at 33.

ingredient data for purposes of state law protection, civil litigation, and most labor relations uses of chemical ingredient data.

APPROACHES TO RESOLVE DISPUTES ABOUT WORKPLACE EXPOSURE AND INGREDIENT DATA

Two extreme ways to resolve the disclosure problems for exposure data and ingredient data would be to disclose everything to everyone or nothing to no one. If all information on the chemical mixture were made publicly available on request of any person—worker, union, consumer, competitor, etc.—then the issue would be resolved. There might be a precipitous decline in innovation in the chemical specialty field, fewer new opportunities for development, weakened investment, and more imports from nations with secure systems of development incentives, but there would be no more disclosure problem. No one has seriously advocated that step.

The total prohibition of *any* disclosure of information, on the other end of the spectrum, would essentially be a rejection of some societal choices that have already been made, e.g., informing workers of known hazards in specific categories of chemicals which are subject to occupational safety standards. For social policy reasons rather than economic ones, the no-disclosure option seems unlikely to return to the American scene.

The most likely of the current options for information sharing is the system of *effects disclosure*. An employer or supplier provides warning information that is sufficiently detailed to permit the person handling a product to protect himself or herself from its consequences. Effects information is not the same as composition information, for a warning against skin contact, coupled with first-aid directions for alkalinity effects on the skin, need not contain the formulation of the alkaline material except in the case in which its peculiar characteristics require a particular emergency medical response.[36] The Material Safety Data Sheets program, which has the support of the Occupational Safety and Health Administration, is a means of communicating risk information to workers, and it serves to pass along special handling requirements for the customers whose receipt of the chemical

---

[36] Note, however, that chemical identity in general terms is required in caution labeling for nonindustrial, household products under the Federal Hazardous Substances Act, 15 U.S.C. § 1261(p)(1)(B), and that identity may be required by warning label regulations under 40 C.F.R. pt. 765 in summer 1980.

for processing may involve some dangers.[37] Effects data often include both a cautionary statement, a descriptive term for the hazard ("Corrosive," "Eye Irritant," etc.), and a brief statement of the first-aid treatment needed for the product's anticipated human effects.[38]

A variation of effects data is the disclosure of effects coupled with generic identity of the chemical or a trade name suggesting its principal component. The identity disclosure in that instance would usually help the understanding of the potential danger of the class of chemicals, without compromising its specific compositional secrets.[39] There are some ingredients so sensitive that code identity is the only appropriate disclosure, with effects labeling or attached sheets serving as a communications medium for the product's anticipated risks.[40] The less accessible the container

[37] Material Safety Data Sheets are developed by the manufacturer and sent to customers and others handling the chemical to advise them of precautions needed in handling the chemical substance. But some are critical of the sheets because they are sometimes out of date or have not been circulated by the recipient employers within the plant to actual users of the chemical in the workplace. Rodia, *States should adopt and enforce their own labeling requirements*, OCCUPATIONAL HEALTH & SAFETY, Mar./Apr. 1978, at 24. The sheets, OSHA Form 20, give only a generic identity name, along with appropriate caution and handling information.

[38] *Compare* OSHA's warning label requirements *with* the consumer label requirements in 16 C.F.R. §§ 1500.1-.272 (1980), which are imposed under the authority of the Federal Hazardous Substances Act. It is expected that OSHA and the EPA (Toxic Substances Control Act) regulations requiring labels will be issued at roughly the same time—fall 1980.

[39] For example, an organic peroxide's label with appropriate caution statements would be a description of a family of chemicals having similar hazards. The great problem in the identity categories issue is not whether similar chemicals can be grouped by class for acute hazards but whether their chronic hazard potentials can be equated among chemicals for which chronic toxic effects are found for one or two members of a ten-member chemical "family." Structure-activity relationships among comparably structured chemicals is a relatively new area of inquiry. At present, the predominant caution standard for industrial chemical labeling avoids the use of labeling based only upon structural analogues. AMERICAN NATIONAL STANDARDS INSTITUTE, PRECAUTIONARY LABELING OF HAZARDOUS INDUSTRIAL CHEMICALS § 3 (1976) (Standard Z-129.1).

[40] For an example of sensitivity, *see* Borden Chemical, No. 32-CA-551 (NLRB, filed Apr. 25, 1979); *Borden will appeal in worker-information case*, CHEMICAL WEEK, May 30, 1979, at 21. A single chemical substance, which took years to develop, is crucial to coloring of the famous Coors beer can; "the inclusion of a single raw material by Borden in its formula is the sole reason for its ability to produce a far superior 'Coors buff' ink." Brief on exceptions of Borden Chemical at 23, Borden Chemical, No. 32-CA-551.

and the larger its bulk, however, the less likely it is that disclosures will be of any immediate value to those exposed in a transportation or factory situation. The users may in those cases have a need to see documents relating to the shipment that supplement the bare warnings accompanying the containers.[41]

A different option for dealing with exposure information is government-operated review of the information and limitation of the chemical's specific uses or its levels of use. The exposure protection that these reviews would provide lies in their advance determination that the worker should never face the risks of certain exposures. As a surrogate of the individual worker, government agency technical experts make the decisions (through regulations) to put a limit on exposure. Then, by virtue of the general prohibitions or restrictions, the worker is *assured* that the exposure will not present a significant harm. Presumably, when scientific detection skills increase, the quality of the information passed on and the quality of the protective requirements will also increase, but this might be a large presumption, given budget priorities and other agency problems.

The theory of assurance implicit in government prescreening and government limitation standards falls flat if the government does not do its job or if workers mistrust the government's objectivity or competence. Recently, relationships on workplace information issues have been stormy between labor and the government; workers can challenge both the government's policy attitudes and, on occasion, its technical competence. When Occupational Safety and Health Administration officials were concerned with the details of an acceptable chemical labeling rule in 1979,[42] their work was hastened by intense political pressures from the AFL-CIO and by an unsuccessful lawsuit by a consumer-labor alliance.[43]

---

[41] For a useful discussion of current voluntary standards, *see* Jones, *ANSI Standard: Simple, Direct, Flexible,* OCCUPATIONAL HEALTH & SAFETY, Mar./Apr. 1978, at 29. The OSHA proposal will probably include a requirement for the posting of ingredient information in the workplace. Compare the present OSHA rules in 29 C.F.R. § 1915.57, 1916.1-.111, 1917.1-.84 (1979).

[42] A proposed standard on chemical identity labeling was expected in 1979, but its issuance has been postponed into mid-1980.

[43] Public Citizen Health Research Group v. Marshall, 485 F. Supp. 845 (D. D.C. 1980). The alliance of labor and consumer advocacy interest groups

The final option short of complete disclosure is a mandated regulation governing dissemination of chemical information under a legislative delegation of rulemaking authority. *If* the Toxic Substances Control Act or the Occupational Safety and Health Act expressly permit a requirement for disclosure of certain in• formation, then rules requiring that disclosure will probably withstand judicial challenges. The "if" is an expression of serious doubts. Dissemination of all information to a limited class of people—in effect, forced releases of the trade secret without general disclosure—is possible in some TSC Act proceedings, but only with protective orders to maintain the secrecy of the information.[44] Dissemination of *some* information to all people by placards and lists and signs is possible if one accepts the government's view of its legal authority in the workplace.[45] Dissemination of *some* information to some workers on a *need-to-know* basis is the predominant system in private sector use today.[46]

---

lost a suit, perhaps brought for publicity rather than legal merit, which argued that OSHA must issue regulations on chemical labeling. The court dismissed the suit and obliquely suggested in its dismissal that it is not entirely clear that OSHA has even a permissive authority for such labeling under 29 U.S.C. § 655(b)(7). It held that there is no obligation for the issuance of such rules whether or not the permissive discretionary authority exists.

[44] 15 U.S.C. § 2613(a)(4) (1976).

[45] There is no clear authority in Toxic Substances Control Act, § 6, 15 U.S.C. § 2605 (1976), for the issuance of a general standard requiring labeling. Indeed, the very specific-chemical approach required for justifications under this section suggests that the EPA could never blanket the entire chemical industry with a presumptive "unsafe if not labeled" rule. Absent a change in the statute, such a rule is unlikely to succeed, and there are significant doubts of the same type about the applicability of Occupational Safety and Health Act of 1970, § 6(b)(7), 29 U.S.C. § 655(b)(7) (1976), to all chemicals other than merely those for which a specific rule has been issued by OSHA. Congress has been aware of the labeling issue and has enacted some legislation requiring category or chemical-type labeling. *See, e.g.,* Federal Hazardous Substances Act, 15 U.S.C. §§ 1261-75 (1976 & Supp. II 1978). But neither the TSC Act nor the OSH Act adopted such an approach, and Congress never required that such a rule be imposed on all chemicals. *See* Public Citizen Health Research Group v. Marshall, 485 F. Supp. 845 (D. D.C. 1980), for a rejection of the contrary view adopted by an advocacy group.

[46] For example, worker training sessions are widely used, while listing and posting of precise components is virtually unknown. In a few states, disclosure of components has been advocated or required by state legislation encouraged by unions. *See, e.g.,* ME. REV. STAT. tit. 26, § 1701 (Supp. 1979); proposed legislation for chemical identity workplace disclosure in 1980 legislatures: New York Assembly Bill 7103 (1980); Connecticut Senate Bill 8 (1980); California Assembly Bill 1199 (1979-80).

THE NLRB AND THE DISCLOSURE OF INGREDIENT
INFORMATION TO WORKERS

The NLRB's ability to force the sharing of information between employers and employees [47] is one of the critical near-
future issues facing companies that have invested in development
of chemical products. Unpatented products need both to retain
commercial value and to avoid ready duplication by competing
firms from a disclosed list of ingredients, so *some* confidentiality
will have to be preserved. On the other hand, if the union is to
represent its members fully on issues of safety, which increas-
ingly involve toxicity and chronic hazard effects, the union may
have legitimate needs for detailed contents information. This
field of union-employer conflict is interrelated with the OSHA
medical records [48] and chemical ingredient labeling rules,[49] but
its mainspring is the NLRB's authority to determine the information to be shared under the mandatory duty to bargain in
good faith.

In 1977, the Oil, Chemical and Atomic Workers' Union
(OCAW) issued a directive to its local unions to begin writing
formal requests, using a standard OCAW form letter, for employers' special chemical identity and safety data for chemicals
in use in the workplace.[50] The explicit reason for the request
was the detection of sterility of chemical workers at a unionized
California plant; the sterility was attributed to the exposure of
the workers to certain manufactured pesticides.[51] It may be that
the implicit reasons were a general concern with chronic health
hazards then becoming publicized in the chemical industry—
about which that union had been most active during passage of
the Toxic Substances Control Act in late 1976—and union dis-
trust of the effectiveness of governmental agencies as monitors
of the workers' safety in chemical manufacturing plants. Once
the union obtained the information, it could employ specialists

---

[47] *See* chapters II-IV *supra.*

[48] *See* chapter X *supra.*

[49] OSHA's proposed rule of 1980 is discussed later in this chapter.

[50] Oil, Chemical & Atomic Workers Union ALERT, A-110, from A. F.
Grospiron to All Local Union Presidents, Subject "The Right to Know" (Oct.
11, 1977) [hereinafter cited as Grospiron letter].

[51] DBCP, a pesticide, was alleged to have rendered workers of Occidental
Chemical sterile through exposure to the chemical in the workplace.

to determine the risks to workers and bypass reliance upon the manufacturer's plant hygiene programs, the chemical suppliers' written assurances of safety, or the government's program of workplace safety monitoring.

The 1977 letter of the OCAW union was a milestone. The union's carefully drafted standard form letter anticipated and met many employer objections, e.g., that of forbidding access to medical records by nonmedical people. It also set the stage for later confrontations before the NLRB by phrasing the demands in a manner calculated to push the refusals of access to the information into NLRB hearings.[52] The skill and sophistication of the request letter's drafting would suggest that the union had a comparable level of quality in its ability to interpret the data received, but its interpretive task would begin only *after* the union had won its requested access to the documents.

Three years later, in January 1980, the full National Labor Relations Board heard three consolidated cases that arose out of employers' negative responses to the OCAW letter.[53] In the three cases, chemical identity was the primary issue. The Board's Administrative Law Judges had issued opinions generally favorable to the union viewpoint. Of the three cases, the *Colgate*[54] and *Minnesota Mining & Manufacturing Company*[55] cases involved blanket refusals to surrender the generic identity of chemicals. One case, *Borden Chemical,* also involved the specific chemical identity of special one-of-a-kind ingredients, the unique presence of which offered some special advantage for Borden in getting its products into marketplace acceptability.[56]

The position of the Board's General Counsel in each of the cases began with the same general presumption favoring union

---

[52] Grospiron letter, *supra* note 50. "This local union requests the company to submit the following information in order that it may properly carry out its representation responsibilities under the collective bargaining agreement." And the form letter stated that it is a "recitation of the information which the union believes it is entitled to under well-established NLRB precedents." The president's letter directed that no changes or omissions be made from the international's standard form letter to local employers when those letters were sent out by local union presidents.

[53] *Unions Not Entitled to Chemical Lists, Worker Records, Corporations Maintain,* CHEMICAL REG. REP. (BNA) 1644 (Jan. 25, 1980).

[54] Colgate-Palmolive Co., No. 17-CA-8331 (NLRB, filed Mar. 27, 1979).

[55] Minnesota Mining & Mfg. Co., Nos. 18-CA-5710, 18-CA-5711 (NLRB, filed Mar. 13, 1979).

[56] Borden Chemical, No. 32-CA-551 (NLRB, filed Apr. 25, 1979).

access to documents of potential or actual relevance to bargaining, and in each case, the Board asserted quite properly that health issues were bargaining subjects on which the union had a right to obtain information needed to protect worker interests.[57] The General Counsel argued, over vigorous employer objections, that the identity information was needed for the union to understand the adequacy of protection of the workers.[58] Waxing eloquent, an NLRB attorney said it would be the "hallmark of the dereliction of duty" for a union not to "address questions of safety" by demanding chemical-specific information.[59] The same advocate warned that confidential identities concealed potential mutagens, carcinogens, and sterilizers, "which strike at the very heart of the civil right of procreation." [60]

The General Counsel had two subsidiary arguments, one of particularity of the employer claim and one of remedy. The employer should be required to detail the items that are confidential and those that are not, segregating the very confidential information and justifying it.[61] This burden would be comparable to the litigation burden borne by agencies such as the NLRB in a Freedom of Information Act case or the burden borne by one opposing discovery in a trade secret dispute in federal civil litigation.[62]

---

[57] Briefs of NLRB General Counsel, Colgate-Palmolive Co., No. 17-CA-8331; Minnesota Mining & Mfg. Co., Nos. 18-CA-5710, 18-CA-5711; Borden Chemical, No. 32-CA-551. Before the Board, arguments included the presumptive relevance of the information as related to a "condition" of employment. General Counsel also argued that the union could not perform its duty of representation without the requested information. CHEMICAL REG. REP., *supra* note 53, at 1645.

[58] Brief of NLRB General Counsel, Borden Chemical, No. 32-CA-551.

[59] "[I]t is difficult to imagine how the effect of a worker's environment on his health could be considered anything less than the most important ingredient in 'conditions of employment'. . . . It would be the hallmark of the dereliction of duty for a union as the exclusive representative of employees to neglect to address itself to safety in the working environment, especially in [the chemical] . . . industry . . . where the hazards are not merely potential but real and present dangers." Brief to the ALJ of NLRB General Counsel, Minnesota Mining & Mfg. Co., Nos. 18-CA-5710, 18-CA-5711.

[60] *Id.*

[61] Brief of NLRB General Counsel in Answer to Respondent's Exceptions, Borden Chemical, No. 32-CA-551.

[62] *See* 5 U.S.C. § 552(b) (last sentence), which requires such segregation. Identification of which items constitute trade secrets would be required when one is asserting a privilege against discovery under the Federal Rules of Civil Procedure. Each of these is in a markedly different context than the

The General Counsel further argued that the employer had failed to exhaust an important remedy when it failed to negotiate with the union on a means for protecting the secrets once they were disclosed.[63] Some consent agreement might protect the employer's interest, according to this reasoning. Employers who object totally to the threatened release—and virtually all appear to do so—would have responded that the decision favoring the union weakens any posture by the employer that the information cannot be disclosed, so there is little on which to reach a compromise.[64] Also, there seems little remedy for the employer when such a contract to retain secrecy is breached by the union, making the union's contractual promise an illusory hope.[65] Nonetheless, the General Counsel urged negotiation of terms of a settlement instead of blanket refusal of access.

The employers raised a variety of defenses. When its case went up on appeal to the full Board, Borden Chemical, whose briefs and arguments were the best of the three, used a variety of defenses to attack the simple conclusions of the Board's Administrative Law Judge. Borden first raised the commonplace defenses of lack of demonstrated relevance and waiver of the demand,[66] but its trade secret defense was remarkable.

---

collective bargaining situation, so the substantiation burden may be inappropriate. Borden's brief to the Board asserted that no Board or court precedent could be found that requires a respondent to go beyond the existence of the legal "trade secret" into a showing of actual or impending damage. It can be postulated that such a showing may be no longer required in FOI Act cases. *See* 1 J. O'REILLY, FEDERAL INFORMATION DISCLOSURE § 10.12 (1977 & Supp. 1979).

[63] Brief of NLRB General Counsel in Support of ALJ's Decision and Opposition to Respondent's Exceptions, Borden Chemical No. 32-CA-551.

[64] Having won an order for disclosure, the union has little incentive to grant the employer an assurance of confidential treatment, especially where the union represents other competing plants in the same industry.

[65] The remedies for trade secret misappropriation are (a) criminal prosecution, which is politically unlikely where a disclosure occurs without *scienter* because of color of right from the discloser's union office; (b) injunctive relief against the recipient and the discloser, which will be difficult once general distribution of the list to many union groups has occurred; (c) damages, which is an unlikely remedy both because of the burdens of proof and the identity of the defendant as a long-term bargaining adversary of the plaintiff/employer; or (d) a request for the NLRB to issue a complaint, which when finally decided in three or more years will preclude the union from any *future* trade secret disclosures.

[66] *See* chapters III-IV *supra.*

The Coors beer can, an attractive buff-colored container familiar to millions of management and workers alike, obtains its buff color from a proprietary dye formulated by Borden Chemical. In the factory from which the charge of unfair practices arose, Borden manufactures that buff coloring mixture from a number of known ingredients and one secret ingredient not known to its dye-manufacturing competitors. If Borden disclosed the list of its ingredients used by that plant to an international union representing Borden and other competing dye plants,[67] the strong possibility exists that a leak of the information would destroy Borden's unique advantage, which Borden had spent years trying to develop. The competitor, gaining access to the list from whatever source, could compare its list to Borden's, determine the special ingredient, and duplicate the Borden color, with little experimentation and perhaps some chemical engineering adjustments to its process. Borden thus feared that the union would become, like some government agencies, a conduit for passage of trade secrets to competitive firms.[68]

Borden made a case in rebuttal of the union's safety argument. Because the union raised the issue of safety as a "condition" of employment, Borden's witnesses demonstrated the nature of its extensive industrial hygiene program. The firm then asserted, with general scientific consensus on its side, that ingredient names alone are of relatively little value without the levels of exposure at which workers are in contact with the material. For example, use of sodium chloride (salt) at high concentrations can be harmful, while use of a highly toxic intermediate in a tightly controlled, closed system need not be harmful. Because its hygienists and physicians monitored and controlled exposures, Borden argued, the effects of the chemicals were adequately controlled, and the union had ample opportunity to police that control system without ingredient disclosure.[69]

---

[67] It was conceded in *Borden* that the union, the OCAW, was also the bargaining representative for Borden's primary competitors. Brief for Respondent, Borden Chemical, No. 32-CA-551.

[68] The Board's Administrative Law Judge expressed doubt that any such transfers would take place. The union would worsen its relationships with management if this occurred, and the management would be less willing to supply information voluntarily in the future. The ALJ applied a "clear and present danger" test to measure the "temptations [toward] prejudicial disclosures." Borden Chemical, No. 32-CA-551.

[69] Brief for Respondent, Borden Chemical, No. 32-CA-551. But the union had engaged its own counterexpert to measure the same effects. Borden

THE FUTURE AFTER BORDEN

The future after decision in the *Borden Chemical* case and its appeals will be very interesting. OSHA promulgated sweeping, controversial rules on access to exposure records in 1980. NLRB decisions will ultimately determine access to ingredient information. With both sets of regulations, unions will (if they invest the considerable funds needed) eventually have a safety monitoring system that precisely duplicates and double-checks the employer's existing system. This would accommodate the Board's desires for full communication of chronic hazard information as a relevant "condition" [70] of employment. Discrepancies in findings would be a subject of bargaining.[71]

But the reader should stop and ponder what has been achieved and at what cost. Assuming that the state of scientific knowledge from experimentation will grow, assuming that human effects data will continue to be extrapolated from animal data as they have been for decades, and finally, assuming a greater governmental role in workplace safety through Toxic Substances Control Act [72] and OSHA requirements,[73] of what benefit is it for society to enforce the NLRB's creation of a redundant monitoring system for workplace exposure conditions? Will union members want to pay to double-check employer findings on a single set of discoverable data? If the employer's cost overhead already includes X dollars for exposure monitoring to obtain Y findings (and Y findings are readily inspected by both workers [74] and

---

Chemical, No. 32-CA-551, at 12. Borden countered the claim of independent experts with an offer for the union's expert to consult directly with the corporate staff hygienist most knowledgeable about Borden's conditions. *Id.*

[70] Conditions of employment are a mandatory subject of bargaining as to which the presumption of relevance may apply. *See* chapter III *supra.*

[71] For example, the method of sampling may differ so that results vary; however, employer findings and monitoring results are overseen by OSHA and NIOSH inspection authority as a means of verifying those results. 29 U.S.C. § 657 (1976).

[72] 15 U.S.C. §§ 2601-29 (1976). Reporting of workplace hazard allegations is required under 15 U.S.C. §§ 2603, 2608(c), 2608(e) (1976).

[73] 29 U.S.C. §§ 655-57 (1976); *see, e.g.,* OSHA's new carcinogens control policy in 45 Fed. Reg. 5002 (1980) (to be codified at 29 C.F.R. §§ 1990.101-.152).

[74] Worker review of exposure records is required by OSHA regulations. 45 Fed. Reg. 35,271 (1980) (to be codified at 29 C.F.R. § 1910.20(e)).

governmental inspectors),[75] is there a net benefit to forcing the disclosure of ingredients and of exposure data so that unions can independently duplicate Y findings? Unions may be suspicious of the quality of work done, but it will not be long before the overhead costs to the union of spending X dollars to duplicate the employer's results will pinch the union's members for more dues.[76] The workers' income taxes are already paying for government oversight of the employer's set of information.

The discussion above suggests that information transfer, as in the *Borden Chemical* situation, is not without significant cost-benefit questions. For Borden, costs in terms of lost trade secret advantage would be significant. Unenforceability of a union-employer contractual secrecy agreement is not the same problem here as would be, for example, an unenforceable no-strike clause. Instead, the breach of an agreement to keep a costly trade secret strictly confidential leaves the employer with virtually no remedy for the lost research investment. For the union, the cost of not getting the trade secret would be reliance on the employer and the government for the safety data.[77] The cost to the union of gaining access to the secret and then having the secret leak out would be minimal, for the union (as in *Borden Chemical*) suffers no net loss of membership as work shifts from one employer to another among a set of organized plants.[78] The union's loss would occur if the shifting went to nonunion facilities in the United States or abroad. For the union, there is no net benefit

---

[75] OSHA inspection authority is provided in 29 U.S.C. § 657 (1976). *See* OCCUPATIONAL SAFETY & HEALTH ADMIN., U.S. DEPARTMENT OF LABOR, FIELD OPERATIONS MANUAL ¶¶ 4331.4-1.6 (1974), *reprinted in* 1 EMPL. SAFETY & HEALTH GUIDE (CCH) ¶ 4251.

[76] The cost of medical experts to duplicate the company's medical experts is not inconsiderable. In *Borden Chemical*, the union had retained an outside consultant for study of plant chemicals, Dr. James Dolgren of the University of California at Berkeley. Borden Chemical, No. 32-CA-551 at 18.

[77] Although there may be cases in which an employer's nondisclosure of known information creates a harmful situation, for the most part the risk-situation reporting provision of the Toxic Substances Control Act, § 8(e), 15 U.S.C. § 2607(e), and the worker notification responsibilities of the Occupational Safety and Health Act alleviate the concern that employers would "bury" known adverse health effects information. For the contrary view, *see* Weiner, *Toxic Substances and the Workplace*, in TOXIC SUBSTANCES: DECISIONS & VALUES (National Science Foundation/Technical Information Project, 1979).

[78] The OCAW represented Borden's competitors as well as the Borden facility. The Board's Administrative Law Judge considered only the displacement as to the Borden unit alone.

to negotiation of a confidentiality pledge since the same set of information may be obtained under mandatory orders from the Board, depending on the outcome of *Borden Chemical*.[79]

THE IMPACT OF DETROIT EDISON

The Supreme Court's refusal to order disclosure to the union of certain testing data in *Detroit Edison* [80] was a major issue for argument in the *Borden Chemical* [81] case before the Board. *Detroit Edison* built in part upon the 1960 Board decision in *American Cyanamid Company*.[82] The *Cyanamid* decision involved worker evaluation papers that incidentally disclosed secret manufacturing processes and techniques used at the employer's plant. The Board there found no violation of sections 8(a)(5) or 8(a)(1) in the refusal of disclosure, because the information was highly confidential and the union adamantly insisted on the full set of secret information. *Detroit Edison* was a descendant of *Cyanamid*, but with testing validity at stake rather than chemical trade secrets.

In refusing to uphold the orders below, which would have delivered the actual tests to the union for its independent examination,[83] the Court noted in *Detroit Edison* that the NLRB appeared to believe that "union interests in arguably relevant information must always predominate over all other interests, however legitimate." The Court declined to accept that position.[84] It was significant that the Court took notice of the threat to continued secrecy that the union's possession of the employer's testing information would pose. The threat was twofold: if disclosure were inadvert by leaks or mistaken delivery, there would be no remedy; and if the value of the test were destroyed

---

[79] If *Borden Chemical* is upheld by the Board and courts, the union will have a vague and undefined obligation to "discuss" protective clauses but not an incentive or duty to protect the information as a necessary precondition to disclosure. Once disclosed to nonemployee representatives of the international union, without a secrecy agreement, trade secrecy would be breached. 4 RESTATEMENT OF TORTS § 757, Comment b(1938).

[80] *See* Detroit Edison Co. v. NLRB, 440 U.S. 301 (1979).

[81] Borden Chemical, No. 32-CA-551.

[82] American Cyanamid Co., 129 N.L.R.B. 683, 684 (1960). *See also* NLRB v. Truitt Mfg. Co., 351 U.S. 149, 153 (1956).

[83] Detroit Edison Co. v. NLRB, 440 U.S. 301 (1979).

[84] *Id.*

by voluntary passage of the information from the union to some third party, the most one could expect is a cease and desist order, and the least one might obtain is a nonreviewable NLRB General Counsel refusal to issue a complaint.

The analogies to *Borden Chemical*,[85] *Colgate*,[86] and *Minnesota Mining & Manufacturing Company* [87] reflect a greater cost of disclosure than that seen in *Detroit Edison*. The employer there could have hired a single psychologist or team of qualified test-preparation people and issued a new test. The chemical firms might have spent a great deal more time and money on chemical ingredient "recipes," which could be disseminated to competitors, without a real remedy available.

A final decision on the three cases is expected in late 1980.

OTHER FEDERAL DISCLOSURE SYSTEMS

In 1980, the Occupational Safety and Health Administration adopted a new and controversial final rule which requires the employer to provide easy and prompt access to exposure records to all employees, and to unions or other designated representatives.[88] Unions receive special consideration as "presumptive" representatives who need not state a reason or obtain worker consent to have access to all exposure information possessed by the employer (if the rule is ultimately upheld in the courts in its May 1980 final form).[89] Exposure data as a category are defined very broadly, so that a great deal of historical data becomes available for disclosure.[90] The breadth of disclosure is limited by three factors. First, medical records require individual workers' written consent, and certain exposure monitoring of personal medical conditions (e.g., sperm counts) is defined to be "medical" rather than "exposure" records.[91]

---

[85] Borden Chemical, No. 32-CA-551.

[86] Colgate-Palmolive Co., No. 17-CA-8331.

[87] Minnesota Mining & Mfg. Co., Nos. 18-CA-5710, 18-CA-5711.

[88] 45 Fed. Reg. 35,211 (1980) (to codified in 29 C.F.R. § 1910.20).

[89] *Id.* 35,279 (to be codified in 29 C.F.R. § 1910.20 (e) (2) (i)).

[90] *Id.* 35,277-78 (to be codified in 29 C.F.R. § 1910.20 (c) (5)).

[91] *Id.* 35,278 (to be codified in 29 C.F.R. § 1910.20 (c) (6) (i)).

The second limitation on exposure records allows manufactures to delete a very limited class of confidential process secrets and percentages of mixture ingredients when the exposure files are opened to unions or to workers.[92] Finally, the employer can obtain written confidentiality agreements from those to whom secrets are required to be disclosed. In an illegal overreaching of authority by OSHA—though merely in a preamble, so of doubtful legal value—the agency purported to limit opportunities for contractual agreements so that no contract could provide for damage or bonding clauses. This aspect of the standard's preamble is so divergent from the statutory authority that its continuing effect (other than as a union argument to avoid trade secret contracts) is doubtful.[93]

Every employer concerned with trade secret issues should read the medical and exposure records preamble carefully. If the rules are upheld on appeal, the preamble will be regarded as an interpretation of the agency's intent in the far-reaching generic rule.[94]

Also in 1980, OSHA is expected to propose a new regulation on labeling that would, for the first time, mandate a chemical identity disclosure program in the workplace for OSHA-regulated firms. The principal justification for the program is the belief that insufficient opportunity has been given to workers for self-protection. If workers knew the chemical identities of the workplace chemicals, they (or their unions) ostensibly would be better able to avoid chronic hazard situations, such as the inhalation of a toxic gas emitted by a proprietary solvent mixture.[95] The principal contrary argument is that effects, not chemical-specific identities, are the key to protective measures and that dissemination of warnings on chemicals' effects, together with sharing of particular identities with the physicians treating in-

---

[92] *Id.* 35,279-80 (to be codified in 29 C.F.R. § 1910.20(f)).

[93] *Id.* 35,275.

[94] The first petition for review was filed by the AFL-CIO on May 21, 1980, before the rule appeared in the Federal Register, so that the review would have to be held in the "friendly" District of Columbia Circuit.

[95] Address by Dr. Bailus Walker, Director, Health Standards Programs, Occupational Safety and Health Administration, at the City University of New York Labeling Conference (May 5, 1980).

dividual workers, would be a preferred course of response to workplace chemical exposure problems.[96]

The mechanics of how to label remain open to question. Drafts of the early OSHA rule would have required labels on all vessels, pipes, or other workplace "containers." Later drafts would allow placarding of vessels with the common or trade name of the material, with changes made by inserting new cards or placards into permanent holders. Then specific identities would be shown on a work-area list of chemicals to which the worker could refer for specific identity information.[97] An identity would be sufficient for many chemicals; for those which had some toxic effect or other hazard, such as flammability, warning labels would be required. These labels would be coordinated with the Environmental Protection Agency's Toxic Substances Control Act chemical label warnings, which are also under active development in 1980.[98] OSHA and the EPA each took account of the two existing warning label systems in federal agency rules, the Federal Hazardous Substances Act labels required by Consumer Product Safety Commission regulations,[99] and the Materials Transportation Bureau labels for transportation of hazardous materials, adopted under rules of the Department of Transportation.[100]

The OSHA labeling rule and the EPA rule have been purposely coordinated to maximize the consistency of labeling practices between the two agencies.[101] When political pressure from unions, the AFL-CIO, and legislative allies mounted on OSHA in 1978-79, the agency set several deadlines for action but revised the deadlines as it became apparent that practical obstacles, such as insufficient "hazardous chemical" definitions and the impossibility of labeling in some workplace situations, remained to be

---

[96] Address by Roger Batchelor, for Chemical Manufacturers Association, at the City University of New York Labeling Conference (May 6, 1980).

[97] Address by Dr. Flo Ryer, Occupational Safety and Health Administration Labeling Work Group, at the City University of New York Labeling Conference (May 5, 1980).

[98] The proposed regulation to be codified in 40 C.F.R. pt. 765 should be issued in late 1980. Address by Irwin Auerbach, Environmental Protection Agency, at the City University of New York Labeling Conference (May 5, 1980) [hereinafter cited as Auerbach Address].

[99] See 15 U.S.C. § 1261 (1976) ; 16 C.F.R. pt. 1500 (1980).

[100] *See* Hazardous Materials Transportation Act, §§ 102-12, 115, 49 U.S.C. §§ 1801-12 (1976 & Supp. II 1978).

[101] Auerbach Address, *supra* note 98.

solved.[102] So a Nader group, the Health Research Group, sued OSHA to impose a mandatory obligation for the labeling of workplace chemicals. The suit was dismissed, and the court agreed with the Labor Department that the Occupational Safety and Health Act had *not* required that such chemicals be labeled. The court suggested obliquely that the discretion to impose labels might be chemical-specific rather than a matter for general imposition upon all chemicals, but the court avoided any direct pronouncement on that subject.[103]

The legal question that remains, regarding an employer's duty to place chemical substance identity onto labels, is whether the two relevant laws (the TSC Act and the OSH Act) can be stretched to reach the broad coverage necessary to support mandatory labels. The Occupational Safety and Health Act might well permit a section 6 standard to be accompanied by a specific labeling rule.[104] Section 6, however, is not generic to all chemicals or hazards; it does not permit labels to be required on a blanket assertion that "without this label the chemical, of whatever type, is a hazard." Rather, its context suggests a rule-by-rule development.[105] Likewise, particularized findings are necessary for TSC Act labeling rules. Although the TSC Act permits categories of chemicals to be subjected to a single regulation,[106] the categorical power does not permit a blanket categorization that "items without this warning label are generically in violation of the law." It is likely that the chemical and related industries will challenge any mandatory ingredient labeling and possible that they may challenge any mandatory scheme for hazard labeling.[107]

---

[102] Probably the most difficult issue is the case of those chemicals which show one effect in laboratory animals and none or a lesser effect in actual observation in the workplace. For mixtures of 30 percent flammable chemical and 70 percent water, for instance, the absence of a real risk of flammability of the mixture must be considered.

[103] Public Citizen Health Research Group v. Marshall, 485 F. Supp. 845 (D. D.C. 1980).

[104] 29 U.S.C. § 655(b) (7) (1976).

[105] The section speaks of standards adopted under Occupational Safety and Health Act of 1970, § 6, 29 U.S.C. § 655 (1976), which is chemical-by-chemical specific in its approach.

[106] 15 U.S.C. § 2625(c) (1976).

[107] Hazard labeling is more likely to be accepted by most firms because of the prevailing acceptance of American National Standards Institute stand-

Future federal legislation for the labeling of identities or for warnings is a possibility, if the rules are successfully challenged in the courts after promulgation in 1980-81. The same debates regarding need, confidentiality problems, and related issues would then move from the bureaucracy, to the courts, to Congress, and ultimately back to the bureaucracy for a legislatively directed resolution of this complex problem.

STATE REQUIREMENTS

If no federal solution emerges, states may do their own regulating, and the multiplicity of solutions may motivate federal action to preempt the worst of the state rules. Workplace chemical disclosure has been an active subject of legislation. Maine was the first state to require what was essentially OSHA's first draft rule, for disclosure of chemical identities, but Maine allowed trade names or actual identities to be used on containers while reserving identities, Chemical Abstracts Service numbers, and Material Safety Data Sheets for retention elsewhere in the workplace.[108] The retained data would be open to employees, former employees, union representatives, employees' physicians, and state agents. Exposure records for individuals would be open to employees, former employees, union representatives, and officials of Maine's OSHA group.[109]

A less costly solution for the states would be mandatory disclosure to a central state agency. Michigan's statute of this type is a comprehensive information-gathering authority.[110] Virginia adopted such a statute shortly after the infamous Kepone incident at a Virginia manufacturing plant.[111] From the filings with the state, the opportunity arises for state scientists to plan the appropriate protective regulations for appropriate types of industries (e.g., metal finishing), and the state can backtrack from

---

ards of labeling for hazardous chemical substances. No present requirement exists for chemical identity disclosures, and indeed, most legal systems operate to protect those identities from disclosure rather than vice versa.

[108] ME. REV. STAT. ANN. tit. 26, §§ 1701-6 (Supp. 1979).

[109] *Id.* §§ 1703, 1705.

[110] MICH. COMP. LAWS ANN. §§ 286.81-.194 (1979); *see* pending amendment, Michigan Senate Bill 700 (1980).

[111] VA. CODE §§ 32.428-.438 (Cum. Supp. 1978).

incidents of occupational illnesses to the chemical substances that may be related to those illnesses.

Proposed legislation for various types of chemical disclosure in the workplace are in various stages of legislative development in California,[112] Connecticut,[113] and New York.[114] Because other states will probably consider similar laws with the assistance of the national offices of unions such as the Oil, Chemical and Atomic Workers, there may eventually be a change in industry's position on labeling of chemicals. Nationwide rules that preempt inconsistent state requirements may well be preferred to a multiple set of conflicting label regulations.

EMERGENCY HAZARD DISCLOSURE RULES

Employers may be subject to emergency disclosure situations in which government agencies must be advised in a manner which permits both government action and some disclosure to workers and the public of information about the workplace, its processes, or chemicals used there. For example, section 8(e) of the Toxic Substances Control Act may require a manufacturer of dyes to inform the Environmental Protection Agency upon revelations that strongly suggest that a dye used in the workplace causes acute kidney failure upon exposure through inhalation for longer than five minutes.[115] Experiments demonstrating human effects or discovery of a new academic finding based upon epidemiological studies not yet known to the EPA could be the type of data that trigger a section 8(e) report. The employer's report will be readily available to the employees and the public since this type of safety data is required to be available under section 14(b) of the TSC Act.[116] The status of the dye as a secret ingredient is not a defense to the duty to report, and once the matter is reported, even with confidentiality claims, the union and other dye manufacturers can be expected to learn of the hazard situation. Under those circumstances, it is perhaps preferable for the employer to share with the union the new

---

[112] California Assembly Bill 1199 (1979-80).

[113] Connecticut Senate Bill 8 (1980).

[114] New York Assembly Bill 7103 (1980).

[115] 15 U.S.C. § 2607(e) (1976).

[116] *Id.* § 2613(b).

knowledge that led to the hazard report so that the first notice received by the workers is not garbled or misleading when EPA sources release the information.

Comparable hazard-reporting obligations exist for the water pollution spill regulations of the EPA,[117] for product hazards to which manufacturing workers may be exposed in making a consumer product,[118] and for certain pesticides.[119] The bitter debate over chemical composition disclosure for chemical factories, discussed earlier in relation to *Borden Chemical*, began with a pesticide effects incident that would probably have been required to be reported to the EPA and would thereafter have been public.[120] In that instance, however, Occidental Chemical's workers and union knew of the physiological adverse effect (worker sterility) before the employer did.

TRAINING OBLIGATIONS AS A SOURCE OF DISCLOSURES

Occupational Safety and Health Administration training requirements are general and specific obligations. If there is a particular OSHA standard in place for a particular industry, workers in that industry may have rights to be trained in the processes and in the use of certain proprietary chemical mixtures. This may or may not present a conflict with confidentiality practices of the employer.[121] Disclosure of medical and ex-

---

[117] 33 U.S.C. § 1321 (1976).

[118] 15 U.S.C. § 2064(b) (1976).

[119] 7 U.S.C. § 136a-136y (1976).

[120] Sterility among workers making an agricultural pesticide was found by the workers themselves. The incident precipitated a letter-writing program by Oil, Chemical and Atomic Workers locals to determine the identities of chemicals used in OCAW-represented facilities. That in turn led to the confrontations in *Borden, Colgate,* and *Minnesota Mining & Mfg.* discussed above, all of which were pending before the NLRB for decision in 1980.

[121] The training may divulge in written form details of the manufacturing process that were not previously apparent to the workers; the loss of the written materials or their handling by the union presents some of the irremediable disclosure problems discussed by the Supreme Court in Detroit Edison Co. v. NLRB, 440 U.S. 301 (1979). The training process involves some risk of loss of the training material, while lack of training risks civil penalties and situations hazardous to workers.

posure records to the employee may be required; in the coke-oven emissions standard, workers are given a special right to their medical files.[122] And, finally, workers are often able to obtain information about workplace exposures through OSHA records, some of which can be obtained by use of the Labor Department's Freedom of Information Act procedures[123] and some of which are available under subpoenas when litigation is brought by individuals or unions against employers and when subpoenaed government information would be relevant and not privileged.[124]

---

[122] 29 C.F.R. § 1910.1029(m)(3) (1979).

[123] 29 C.F.R. §§ 70.1-.77 (1979).

[124] 29 C.F.R. §§ 1906.1-.7 (1979).

CHAPTER XVII

Frontiers of Disclosure: Affirmative Action in Employment

The period of 1978-80 was a time of rapid, revolutionary developments concerning the legal status of general public access to employment records of private employers. The earlier chapters of this text have discussed the National Labor Relations Act and many types of disclosure issues. The required transfer of certain employer information to collective bargaining adversaries has important ramifications beyond the employer-employee realm. This chapter attempts to integrate the legal authorities of the federal equal employment agencies with the NLRB's scope of authority. The likely trend of decisions for the 1980s appears to be toward more disclosure, more resistance, and more litigation.

THE FEDERAL IMPACT ON EMPLOYMENT STATISTICS

Before the 1970s, employer information about the racial, ethnic, or sexual composition of the work force was almost universally kept confidential, unavailable except to the extent that it might be relevant in a litigated discrimination suit.[1] In such suits, the plaintiff's discovery motions would seek the employer-defendant's personnel records, the defense would resist, and a protective order would be imposed.[2] The very wide reach of

---

[1] Of course, the union could reconstruct the visual data (except perhaps applicant data) from an internal discussion among union members within the plant unit, e.g., number of black machinists or women linemen.

[2] Protective orders in discrimination suits will follow Rule 26 of the Federal Rules of Civil Procedure. *See* 4 MOORE'S FEDERAL PRACTICE ¶ 26.60 (2d ed. 1979).

the federal antidiscrimination powers, manifest in legislation in the 1960s[3] and administrative regulations during the 1970s,[4] expanded the authority of the Labor Department and of the contract-issuing federal agencies to require the preparation and submission of detailed employment reports. Under authority of an executive order,[5] agencies required that a new set of paperwork be prepared: Form EEO-1, listing a statistical race and sex categorization of workers; Affirmative Action Plans, describing regulated firms' antidiscrimination programs;[6] and Work Force Analyses, describing the composition of the employee group. The new paperwork was to serve a contract-auditing purpose, allowing the government to oversee hiring practices of private persons so that corporate violators of antidiscrimination laws would be barred from future government contracts.[7] The proof of a violation must be constructed from statistical evidence; the evidence cannot be created sufficiently from outside of the firm; so the government utilizes employer-retained statistical reports and information to monitor the employer's conduct. If the government acquires the employer's documents in the course of an antidiscrimination investigation, then the Freedom of Information Act applies to their subsequent dissemination.[8] If the records remain in the custody of the employer, then the information generally remains confidential and is only seen by

---

[3] Title VII of the Civil Rights Act, §§ 701-16, 42 U.S.C. §§ 2000e to 2000e-15 (1976).

[4] 41 C.F.R. §§ 60-1.1 to -741.54 (1979).

[5] Exec. Order No. 11,246, 3 C.F.R. 167 (1965); Exec. Order No. 11,375, 3 C.F.R. 320 (1967).

[6] 41 C.F.R. § 60-40.1 to -40.8 (1979).

[7] The basis for the regulations is discussed in Chrysler Corp. v. Brown, 441 U.S. 281 (1979). Debarment from future contracts is the penalty established by the Executive Orders.

[8] That Act applies to disclosures of agency records generally. 5 U.S.C. § 552(a)(3) (1976). Prior to *Chrysler*, the administering agency, the Department of Labor, had regulations (invalidated in *Chrysler*) authorizing and encouraging disclosure of the AAP data. 41 C.F.R. §§ 60-40.2 to -40.4 (1979). The AAP disclosures reflected a policy decision by the Labor Department to make as much AAP information as possible available to the public, notwithstanding any effect that this action could have upon contractors' cooperation with the AAP system. Brief Amicus Curiae of Dep't of Labor at 8-9, Westinghouse Elec. Corp., 239 N.L.R.B. No. 19 (Oct. 31, 1978), *appeal docketed*, No. 78-2067 (D.C. Cir. Nov. 1, 1978).

the employer's staff and by any visiting representative of the government.[9]

Until very recently, the unions representing employees at the companies that held government contracts did not bother with demanding access to copies of governmental equal employment statistics. Since the data were compiled to meet government requirements and had no value other than as evidence in suits brought against the employer by aggrieved persons or government agencies, the unions had no incentive to demand access to the documents.[10] The growing number of suits, however, alleging that unions had in some ways fostered discrimination—by failing to represent fairly the interests of minority and female workers [11]—gradually began to motivate unions to protect themselves against potential liability.[12] This self-interested concern took the form of a new interest in employers' hiring patterns. Direct government pressure against the International Union of Electrical Workers (IUE)[13] was predominantly responsible for the events that precipitated the landmark NLRB case in *Westing-*

---

[9] Information not within a federal agency's custody or control is outside the "agency record" class and therefore is outside of the FOI Act. *See* Forsham v. Harris, 100 S.Ct. 978 (1980); Kissinger v. Reporters' Comm. for Freedom of the Press, 100 S.Ct. 960 (1980).

[10] And the lack of precedents in the NLRB field on the subject of this information prior to 1973 suggests that few if any contract disputes involved this affirmative action data. Recognition of the duty of fair representation is discussed in Emporium Capwell Co. v. Western Addition Community Organization, 420 U.S. 50, 64 (1975); Vaca v. Sipes, 386 U.S. 171 (1967).

[11] Emporium Capwell Co. v. Western Addition Community Organization, 420 U.S. 50 (1975); Vaca v. Sipes, 386 U.S. 171 (1967).

[12] Under this duty, unions faced "millions of dollars of back pay liability for local unions and the International" if their practices were found to be in violation of members' rights. Letter from IUE President Jennings to District Presidents (Oct. 11, 1973), *quoted in* International Union of Elec., Radio & Mach. Workers v. NLRB, No. 79-1682, app., at E37-38 (D.C. Cir., filed July 2, 1979).

[13] A Commissioner's Charge initiated by the Equal Employment Opportunity Commission was filed against the IUE on August 30, 1973, and against General Motors and several other unions, asserting violations of employee/union member civil rights. Likewise, the IUE insisted on information from Westinghouse through its locals, reminding them of the large amount of money penalties which the union might face. Brief of Westinghouse Electric Corp., International Union of Elec., Radio & Mach. Workers v. NLRB, No. 78-2067 (D.C. Cir., filed Nov. 1, 1978) (Westinghouse was an intervenor in this case). The union locals then pressed Westinghouse to obtain this information.

house in 1978.[14] The extent to which unions were sincerely committed to the civil rights aspect of the process varied; in at least one case, a union's representative said that its demand for records access could be dropped if the employer promised by contract to pay any damages the union might suffer in the event of a lawsuit for any of the alleged hiring discrimination.[15] In others, sincere commitment existed.

As discussed earlier in this text, however, unions have not been active users of the Freedom of Information Act.[16] The advocacy groups, who are frequent FOI Act users,[17] only gained the attention of the unions when they joined both employers and unions as defendants in their discrimination charges. Unions are the most active users of the unfair labor practice process, however, and it is understandable that their pressures for disclosure from employers would be pursued through NLRB remedies.[18]

---

[14] Westinghouse Elec. Corp., 239 N.L.R.B. No. 19 (Oct. 31, 1978); *appeal docketed*, No. 78-2067 (D.C. Cir. Nov. 1, 1978).

[15] Bendix Corp., 242 N.L.R.B. No. 8 at 14 n.22 (May 8, 1979), *appeal docketed*, No. 79-1479 (D.C. Cir. June 19, 1979) (dissent by Murphy): "Such a comment is hardly consistent with a burning desire on the part of the Union to unearth and eliminate any possible employment discrimination by Respondent."

[16] Interviews with Elizabeth Medaglia, Deputy Solicitor, Federal Labor Relations Authority; David Vaughn, General Counsel, Federal Mediation and Conciliation Service; Constance duPre, Associate General Counsel, Equal Employment Opportunity Commission; Soffia Petters, Associate General Counsel, U.S. Department of Labor; Stan Weinbrecht, Associate General Counsel, National Labor Relations Board, in Washington, D.C. (Jan. 14/ Feb. 7, 1980). On occasion, unions will seek information not available by bargaining agreements, such as the chemical reporting forms filed by ninety-two employers in the chemical industry, requested from the Environmental Protection Agency in February 1980 by the Oil, Chemical and Atomic Workers' representative R. F. Goss. EPA Freedom of Information Act Log, RIN 594-80 (1980).

[17] For example, civil rights and minority advocacy groups, not the UAW which represented workers at both plants for which disclosure was requested, were the principal requesters in the *Chrysler* case. Chrysler Corp. v. Brown, 441 U.S. 281 (1979).

[18] In several briefs filed with the District of Columbia Circuit, unions frequently referenced the availability of unfair labor practice remedies as a justification for their access to these detailed statistical data. International Union of Elec., Radio & Mach. Workers v. NLRB, Nos. 78-2067, 78-2262, 79-1654, 79-1682, 79-1864, 79-1892 (D.C. Cir., filed from Nov. 1, 1978, to Aug. 13, 1979). As to their use of the NLRB procedures, see McDOWELL & HUHN, NLRB REMEDIES FOR UNFAIR LABOR PRACTICES (Labor Relations & Public Policy Series No. 12, 1976).

THE NLRB DECISIONS

A series of NLRB-decided cases between 1978 and 1980 have caused a major change in the legal status of employment information. The Board decided in 1978 in a pair of companion cases, *Westinghouse* [19] and *East Dayton Tool,* [20] that unions had a right to receive employer-held copies of the papers prepared and/or submitted by employers for government equal employment monitoring. Although the dissemination of the previously confidential papers could have been prohibited by an employer's court action if government officials had attempted to release the documents,[21] the Board's decision forced the employer to forego confidential handling and to pass the information along to the unions whose members worked at the plant sites.[22] (The labor law consequences of this trend of Board opinions has been discussed earlier; [23] this discussion focuses on the federal law consequences of the dissemination in other contexts.)

Some private statistics about employee composition, assignment, hiring, and training have legitimate private value that would be lost through public disclosure. For example, in the rubber tire industry,[24] employers are concerned that competitors should not be able to learn their exact labor costs for tires produced at certain plants. Knowledge of that missing element—labor cost—in an industry whose raw materials, shipping costs, and capital investment figures are well known can provide foreign or domestic tire firms with a "missing link" in the calculation of profit margins. Once a tire manufacturer's true costs per unit

---

[19] Westinghouse Elec. Corp., 239 N.L.R.B. No. 19 (Oct. 31, 1978), *appeal docketed,* No. 78-2067 (D.C. Cir. Nov. 1, 1978).

[20] East Dayton Tool & Die Co., 239 N.L.R.B. No. 20 (Oct. 31, 1978), *appeal docketed,* No. 78-2395 (D.C. Cir. Dec. 12, 1978).

[21] Such a case would have arisen under the reverse-disclosure Administrative Procedure Act suits permitted by Chrysler Corp. v. Brown, 441 U.S. 281 (1979). *See generally* 1 J. O'REILLY, FEDERAL INFORMATION DISCLOSURE §§ 10.01-.17 (1977 & Supp. 1979).

[22] The unions, of course, argued that their rights were not diminished by the access of the public, or lack thereof, which the FOI Act provides. Briefs of International Union of Elec., Radio & Mach. Workers at 35 n.15, International Union of Elec., Radio & Mach. Workers v. NLRB, No. 78-2067 (D.C. Cir., filed Nov. 1, 1978), make this argument against limitation of union rights.

[23] *See* chapters II-V *supra.*

[24] *See* Connolly & Fox, *Employer Rights and Access to Documents Under the Freedom of Information Act,* 46 FORD. L. REV. 203 (1977).

and profit margins are calculated, a competitor's planned erosion of the pricing in the market for that item may cripple the employer firm's ability to compete. Before these labor costs were known, there would be available only a broad guess of actual unit cost.[25] With the statistical missing link, a great deal of competitive strategic planning would be possible. In some cases, declines or increases in the work force would show up first in the government-required statistics.[26] The firm's planned expansion to a third shift to meet rising demand would show up in large training classes,[27] expanded hiring plans,[28] and projections for the growth of total, female, and minority categories of the work force.[29]

The sensitivity of this information has led to a number of bitterly contested lawsuits against government disclosure of this information. In the Equal Employment Opportunity Commission's enabling legislation, there is a special statutory barrier to disclosure.[30] For other agencies, which receive the same information through a disclosure device constructed to evade the disclosure barriers, the Joint Reporting Committee,[31] there is *some* discretionary power over the disclosure of the information. The extent of that discretion was partially resolved in 1979 in

---

[25] For most plants, competitive firms would have to count workers' cars, solicit a copy of the union's wage agreements from the union local, or in some other manner combine numbers of workers in total with job class rates. This gross averaging could be off by 20 percent from actual costs, and more if there is a multiproduct plant or larger group of workers. Confidential business information, however, is that which is difficult—not impossible—for others to learn. The standard for legal protection does not require burglar-proof storage or absolute assurance of no possible inadvertent leaks. If it did, the military ability to claim FOI Act exemptions would be virtually nonexistent. Purposeful disclosure to competitive firms does, however, forfeit protection. Hughes Aircraft Co. v. Schlesinger, 384 F. Supp. 292 (C.D. Cal. 1974); Union Oil Co. v. Andrus, No. 77-2077-LTL (C.D. Cal. 1978).

[26] As the projections appear from year to year or in midyear compliance review reports, the competitors will learn of the planned movement before it takes place or before its occurrence becomes public knowledge.

[27] Training status is a part of the utilization portion of the AAP.

[28] Plans for hiring and applicant flow are part of the AAP.

[29] Projections for work force growth are found in both the narrative and Work Force Analysis portions of the AAP.

[30] 42 U.S.C. § 2000e-8 (1976).

[31] The basis for the Joint Reporting Committee is 29 C.F.R. § 1602.7 (1979).

the Supreme Court's *Chrysler Corp. v. Brown*[32] decision. As *Chrysler* and related cases have developed, it has become a general rule that employment statistics having some commercial value *can* be protected from public disclosure if (1) they were secret, (2) their disclosure would cause some harm, (3) statutory prohibitions against dissemination by the government of private statistical data applied to that type of information, and finally (4) the disclosing agency lacked some statutory authority for the dissemination of the information.[33]

The National Labor Relations Board, with apparently more naiveté than intention, upset the balance of power in this legal controversy by blithely finding that the employment statistics could *not* be kept secret.[34] The Board's approach was a surprise to many non-labor lawyers, who had observed the careful construction by courts of rationales for or against dissemination of the business confidential statistical data.[35] The development of legal rationales restraining government disclosure would be worthless if the same statistics came to public attention from wide union dissemination.[36] A major principle of trade secret law,[37] implanted as well in the Freedom of Information Act commercial data exemption from disclosure,[38] is that secrecy is fragile, and as soon as any person not contractually bound to secrecy (e.g., an international union) obtains unrestricted possession of copies of the document, it will no longer be legally a "secret."[39]

---

[32] 441 U.S. 281 (1979).

[33] *Id.* at 317-18.

[34] This is the net effect of Work Force Analysis disclosures in Westinghouse Elec. Corp., 239 N.L.R.B. No. 19 (Oct. 31, 1978), *appeal docketed*, No. 78-2067 (D.C. Cir. Nov. 1, 1978).

[35] *See, e.g.*, Chrysler Corp. v. Brown, 441 U.S. 281 (1979); Westinghouse Elec. Corp. v. Schlesinger, 542 F.2d 1190 (4th Cir. 1976), *cert. denied*, 431 U.S. 924 (1977).

[36] Public dissemination destroys the "confidential" and "secret" prerequisites to exempt status. 5 U.S.C. § 552(b)(4) (1976). Without exempt status, they cannot be withheld. Chrysler Corp. v. Brown, 441 U.S. 281 (1979).

[37] 4 RESTATEMENT OF TORTS § 757, Comment b (1938).

[38] 5 U.S.C. § 552(b)(4) (1976). This subsection relies partially on 4 RESTATEMENT OF TORTS, *supra* note 37.

[39] 4 RESTATEMENT OF TORTS, *supra* note 37; *see* 1 J. O'REILLY, FEDERAL INFORMATION DISCLOSURE § 14.08 (1977 & Supp. 1979).

The NLRB decision in *Westinghouse*[40] in 1978 is currently on appeal to the District of Columbia Circuit, brought to that court on a procedural fluke[41] at the request of the unions that won the case. Until a final decision is reached—and until the Board determines to follow a particular court decision as controlling precedent—the *Westinghouse* and subsequent cases[42] are the controlling legal interpretations of the employer's duty to transmit the employment statistics to the unions. The numerous *amici curiae* in the proceeding underscore its precedential significance.[43]

It is significant that, as the Board majority viewed the issue in *Westinghouse,* all of the commercial secrecy defenses raised in the Freedom of Information Act case law on employment statistics were irrelevant.[44] Trade secret status had been the focus of the disputes between government and employer, but the Board regarded that issue as an insufficient defense to a charge of failure to supply information in collective bargaining.[45] Its only recognition was in the Board's refusal to order

---

[40] Westinghouse Elec. Corp., 239 N.L.R.B. No. 19 (Oct. 31, 1978), *appeal docketed,* No. 78-2067 (D.C. Cir. Nov. 1, 1978).

[41] International Union of Elec., Radio & Mach. Workers v. NLRB, 610 F.2d 956 (D.C. Cir. 1979).

[42] General Motors Corp., 243 N.L.R.B. No. 19 (June 29, 1979), *appeal docketed,* No. 79-1682 (D.C. Cir. July 2, 1979); White Farm Equipment Co., 242 N.L.R.B. No. 201 (June 22, 1979), *appeal docketed,* No. 79-1654 (D.C. Cir. June 26, 1979); Bendix Corp., 242 N.L.R.B. No. 170 (June 11, 1979), *appeal docketed,* Nos. 79-1609, 79-1795 (D.C. Cir. July 23, 1979); Kentile Floors, Inc., 242 N.L.R.B. No. 115 (June 4, 1979), *appeal docketed,* Nos. 79-1641, 79-2055 (D.C. Cir. n.d.); Bendix Corp., 242 N.L.R.B. No. 8 (May 8, 1979), *appeal docketed,* No. 79-1479 (D.C. Cir. June 19, 1979); East Dayton Tool & Die Co., 239 N.L.R.B. No. 20 (Oct. 31, 1978), *appeal docketed,* No. 78-2395 (D.C. Cir. Dec. 12, 1978). The District of Columbia Circuit has consolidated *Westinghouse, General Motors,* and *White Farm.* The remaining cases have been stayed on agreement of the parties.

[43] In *Westinghouse,* the Equal Employment Advisory Council filed for the employer, while the National Education Association, the AFL-CIO, and the United Auto Workers filed for the union. The U.S. Department of Labor filed for the union at the Board, but not at the District of Columbia Circuit.

[44] 239 N.L.R.B. No. 19 (Oct. 31, 1978), *appeal docketed,* No. 78-2067 (D.C. Cir. Nov. 1, 1978).

[45] For the Board, trade secret disclosures should be handled by negotiations to achieve protections. The employer cannot refuse the data on grounds that release to competitors would be competitively injurious, according to the Brief of the NLRB at 45 n.16, International Union of Elec., Radio & Mach. Workers v. NLRB, No. 78-2067 (D.C. Cir., filed Nov. 1, 1978).

disclosure of the entire Affirmative Action Plan (AAP) of the employer.[46] Instead, the Board regarded the commercial confidentiality issues as having been avoided when it ordered only the dissemination of the work force analysis documents and related statistics. Observers who are knowledgeable in the use and sensitivity of the data would regard the information that was ordered disclosed to be the most significant in the AAP. It would be of great help as a legal means of indirectly forcing the disclosure of information that could have received protection within trade secret and exempted categories in other contexts.[47]

It is significant that the dissent written by Member Murphy in *Westinghouse*[48] and in each of the successive disclosure cases[49] was not rebutted by the majority. Instead, the majority paid attention to the positions of its most liberal member, who consciously strove to make the Board information process an adjunct of the government's affirmative action programs.[50] That function for the Board remains unaccepted as a policy ideal by the remaining members of the majority and was bitterly criticized by Murphy as an effort to create a "mini-EEOC" within the labor-dispute resolution authority of the Board.[51]

---

[46] Westinghouse Elec. Corp., 239 N.L.R.B. No. 19 (Oct. 31, 1978). The Board believed that the same information for which Westinghouse had won appellate court protection in Westinghouse Elec. Corp. v. Schlesinger, 542 F.2d 1190 (4th Cir. 1976), cert. denied, 431 U.S. 924 (1977), contained no confidential information. 239 N.L.R.B. No. 19 at 28. So, the Board counsel argued that the effort to obtain a protective order as a condition of disclosure "was an unjustified interference with the union's representative functions." Brief of NLRB at 44, International Union of Elec., Radio & Mach. Workers v. NLRB, No. 78-2067 (D.C. Cir., filed Nov. 1, 1978).

[47] Note, however, that the courts, more familiar with trade secret disputes than the Board, have been extremely willing to protect employment statistical data against disclosure, while the Board has refused on grounds that it is not "confidential." *See* 1 J. O'REILLY, FEDERAL INFORMATION DISCLOSURE §§ 14.07, 10.11 (1977 & Supp. 1979). *See also* chapters II-V *supra*.

[48] 239 N.L.R.B. No. 19 at 28. (Oct. 31, 1978), *appeal docketed*, No. 78-2067 (D.C. Cir. Nov. 1, 1978).

[49] Bendix Corp., 242 N.L.R.B. No. 8 (May 8, 1979), *appeal docketed*, No. 79-1479 (D.C. Cir. June 19, 1979); Safeway Stores Inc., 240 N.L.R.B. No. 138 (1979); East Dayton Tool & Die Co., 239 N.L.R.B. No. 20 (Oct. 31, 1978), *appeal docketed*, No. 78-2395 (D.C. Cir. Dec. 12, 1978).

[50] Member Jenkins's views are seen in 242 N.L.R.B. No. 8 at 5 n.6 (May 8, 1979), *appeal docketed*, No. 79-1479 (D.C. Cir. June 19, 1979); 239 N.L.R.B. No. 19 at 16 n.36 (Oct. 31, 1978), *appeal docketed*, No. 78-2067 (D.C. Cir. Nov. 1, 1978).

[51] 239 N.L.R.B. No. 19 at 16 (Oct. 31, 1978), *appeal docketed*, No. 78-2067 (D.C. Cir. Nov. 1, 1978).

After *Westinghouse*,[52] and its companion case, *East Dayton Tool*,[53] were decided, the Board followed those cases with rapid development of related principles. Additional statistics on racial and ethnic makeup of the work force beyond the federal reports were found relevant in *General Motors*,[54] despite the fact that the volume of information required to be processed far exceeded that which was commonly assembled for government reports. Excessive paperwork was not a sufficient defense. The Board suggested as it had in earlier cases that costs be negotiated and shared if the employer claimed them to be excessive.[55] For GM, the cost would be 20,000 man-hours of work to prepare 300 charts for five plants with statistics covering twenty years.[56]

Charges and complaints regarding the existence of discrimination in the workplace were found to constitute a set of relevant information to which the union was entitled.[57] The names and identifying details of charging persons were, however, deleted because the unions failed to show relevance of such identities to the policing of the contract. Even with names deleted, there still exists the opportunity (by indirection) for the curious or hostile bystander to identify which of the workers was the complainant.[58]

Relevance of the allegations and charges of discrimination might be denied where a union had failed to show need for the copies of such charges, but the Board found in cases such as *Bendix* [59] and *General Motors* [60] that a union showing both the existence of an antidiscrimination clause and some instance of need to police the effectiveness of the contract would satisfy

---

52 239 N.L.R.B. No. 19 (Oct. 31, 1978), *appeal docketed*, No. 78-2067 (D.C. Cir. Nov. 1, 1978).

53 239 N.L.R.B. No. 20 (Oct. 31, 1978), *appeal docketed*, No. 78-2395 (D.C. Cir. Dec. 12, 1978).

54 243 N.L.R.B. No. 19 (June 29, 1979), *appeal docketed*, No. 79-1682 (D.C. Cir. July 2, 1979).

55 *Id.* at 2 (citing Food Employer Council Inc., 197 N.L.R.B. 651 (1972)).

56 Brief for General Motors at 16, International Union of Elec., Radio & Mach. Workers v. NLRB, No. 79-1682 (D.C. Cir., filed July 2, 1979).

57 243 N.L.R.B. No. 19 (June 29, 1979), *appeal docketed*, No. 79-1682 (D.C. Cir. July 2, 1979).

58 Brief for General Motors, *supra* note 56.

59 242 N.L.R.B. No. 170 (June 11, 1979), *appeal docketed*, Nos. 79-1609, 79-1795 (D.C. Cir. July 23, 1979).

60 243 N.L.R.B. No. 19 (June 29, 1979), *appeal docketed*, No. 79-1682 (D.C. Cir. July 2, 1979).

the requirement for a showing of relevance. In each of the cases in which the Board found that such need had been shown, the Board's opinion suggests an unstated desire to have a larger role as a watchdog against discrimination, perhaps exerting its authority into areas unsuccessfully reached by the EEOC and the OFCCP authorities. One can question the Board's means without questioning a common end—the elimination of discrimination—for there is truly no evidence that an organization with the structure, tradition, and hierarchy of the Board could do an effective job as a third partner in the EEOC-OFCCP tandem efforts against discrimination. Had the Board thought through its efforts and priorities, it perhaps would have done something to join the veteran civil rights agencies much earlier. Instead, EEOC pressure on a union, union pressure on employers, and employer resistance to the Board's views appear to have "backed" the Board into its present posture.[61]

Member Murphy, a strident minority before her departure from the Board in 1979, issued ringing dissents from the trend toward an NLRB affirmative action disclosure program,[62] but her comments failed to sway the Board, while Member Jenkins pushed from the opposite direction to steer the Board fully into EEO matters under the banner of disclosure of relevant information.[63]

Serious students of the conflict are encouraged to read the briefs of the several parties and *amici curiae* before the Court of Appeals for the District of Columbia Circuit. Exposure of the reports could lessen candid self-examination and frank reporting to the government,[64] employers argued, while the Board

---

[61] The history of the IUE's actions to get the information and of the Board's activities begins with an EEOC Commissioner's charge of discrimination against the union in 1973, at which point the union began insisting that local unions demand the information from employer plants. Dates and events are listed in Brief for General Motors, *supra* note 56. In addition to this particular circumstance, however, the government desires unions to participate in the AAP process. *See* the proposed role in 44 Fed. Reg. 77006, 77010, 77012 (1979) (to be codified in 41 C.F.R. §§ 60-1.9(c), 60-1.25(d)).

[62] *See, e.g.*, her dissent in General Motors Corp., 243 N.L.R.B. No. 19 at 8 (June 29, 1979), *appeal docketed*, No. 79-1682 (D.C. Cir. July 2, 1979).

[63] Bendix Corp., 242 N.L.R.B. No. 8 at 5 n.6 (May 8, 1979), *appeal docketed*, No. 79-1479 (D.C. Cir. June 19, 1979); Westinghouse Elec. Corp., 239 N.L.R.B. No. 19 at 16 (Oct. 31, 1978), *appeal docketed*, No. 78-2067 (D.C. Cir. Nov. 1, 1978).

[64] Brief of appeal for Westinghouse, International Union of Elec., Radio & Mach. Workers v. NLRB, No. 78-2067 (D.C. Cir., filed Nov. 1, 1978);

argued that it would not have that effect.[65] The Board articulated several grounds for disclosure:

1. Contracts with antidiscrimination clauses must be policed by unions, using whatever data the union finds relevant and necessary; and

2. The duty of fair representation is a continuing obligation of the union during the contract's term; therefore

3. Unions have a "continuing right to demand and receive whatever information concerning discrimination may be necessary to its good faith discharge of its duty of fair representation throughout the bargaining process." [66]

The employer arguments were a comprehensive assault on the theory presented by the Board and the unions. A final decision is expected in 1980, and Supreme Court review is possible.

THE "BACKDOORING" PHENOMENON

When the Freedom of Information Act was used as a means of gathering information about NLRB investigative proceedings, the Board vehemently objected that employers were trying to "backdoor" the discovery process (or lack thereof) in Board procedures.[67] It is ironic that the Board now backdoors the Freedom of Information Act. Although the Act exempts certain federal files containing private data from federal agency release obligations and the Administrative Procedure Act permits private data owners to object legally to the agency's exercise of FOI Act discretion to release their data,[68] neither statute operates in the private sector. When private sector data are no longer "confi-

brief of appeal for General Motors Corp., International Union of Elec., Radio & Mach. Workers v. NLRB, No. 79-1682 (D.C. Cir., filed July 2, 1979).

[65] Brief of NLRB, International Union of Elec., Radio & Mach. Workers v. NLRB, No. 78-2067 (D.C. Cir., filed Nov. 1, 1978) (citing the Department of Labor's *amicus* brief in support of disclosure filed during the Board proceedings).

[66] *Id.* at 32-33.

[67] Title Guarantee Co. v. NLRB, 534 F.2d 484 (2d Cir.), *cert. denied,* 429 U.S. 834 (1976); *see* Note, *Backdooring the NLRB: Use and Abuse of the Amended FOIA for Administrative Discovery,* 8 LOY. L. J. 145 (1976).

[68] If an exemption applies, such as the commercial confidentiality exemption codified in 5 U.S.C. § 552(b)(4), then review under the Administrative Procedure Act may be sought. 5 U.S.C. § 706 (1976). Chrysler Corp. v. Brown, 441 U.S. 281, 317 (1979).

dential," they cannot be withheld under the FOI Act's commercial confidentiality exemption.

Removing the private sector status of the data as "confidential" accomplishes by indirection what the Freedom of Information Act had not done, releasing the data to the public. This would, indeed, "backdoor" the FOI Act processes.

The Board's response to this problem is that unions will not disclose the information. Traditional trade secrecy principles suggest that international union officials who have no contractual obligations upon them to maintain secrecy of what they are permitted to see are treated as any member of the public would be. Thus, one "public" disclosure would occur, terminating trade secret status.[69] Sometimes a union has been willing to agree to nondisclosure, but the most that has been promised in the pending AAP cases before the District of Columbia Circuit is the IUE's "willingness to discuss disclosure of the Affirmative Action Plans on terms that might protect any valid interests of the Company."[70] For Westinghouse, this offer is perhaps an ironic or illusory promise, for Westinghouse had been one of the few national firms to win a conclusive court battle to establish the confidential legal status of its AAP information against a threatened government disclosure.[71]

The outcome of the pending District of Columbia Circuit cases may or may not alter the NLRB's position. Barring some legislative change or a definitive Supreme Court decision, the employment statistics cases may remain unresolved for several years.

CAN A UNION KEEP A "SECRET"?

Despite the willingness to discuss terms of disclosure proffered to the District of Columbia Circuit by the unions as a rationale

---

[69] 4 RESTATEMENT OF TORTS § 757, Comment b (1938). This would seem apparent even though the union official is an indirect beneficiary of the employer-employee contract.

[70] Brief of the IUE at 36, International Union of Elec., Radio & Mach. Workers v. NLRB, No. 78-2067 (D.C. Cir., filed Nov. 1, 1978).

[71] Westinghouse Elec. Corp. v. Schlesinger, 542 F.2d 1190 (4th Cir. 1976), *cert. denied*, 431 U.S. 924 (1977). Note, however, that many firms have failed to convince courts of their protectable data's need for injunctive relief, including Goodyear, Union Oil, Hughes Aircraft, Sea-Land Service, Burroughs, and Metropolitan Life Insurance. *See generally* 1 J. O'REILLY, FEDERAL INFORMATION DISCLOSURE § 10.11 (1977 & Supp. 1979).

for upholding the Board's *Westinghouse* order,[72] unions have generally resisted the granting of access with limitations upon their use of further disclosure of the AAPs.

In *Westinghouse,* if the appellate court finds that a union secrecy promise, once made, could be enforced, its decision would recognize a new right for employers. If the court finds that the Board does *not* have the power to force the submission to the union of this private but essentially government-mandated data, then the pre-1978 situation will prevail.[73] If the Board forces the information to be readily available to the unions but it does not insist on protective provisions, then it is likely that the information will leak out of the union so rapidly that employers will lessen the quality and quantity of their governmental reporting.[74] This would run contrary to efforts to improve legislatively the protection of confidential private data.[75]

The question of protective orders is one of tangled contract and labor law significance. There is virtually no state criminal code protection for the dissemination of this material by an employee representative.[76] Given the political climate in most states, no larceny of trade secret prosecutions will likely be brought against unions. On the other hand, a moral obligation not to disclose might be imposed and might be respected by many unions. The Supreme Court's *Detroit Edison*[77] case limited the dissemination of the confidential testing materials because it would have significantly damaged the testing process. In that case, the Court recognized the uselessness of a claim that the union could promise to keep a secret:

---

[72] Brief of the IUE, *supra* note 70, restated the IUE's "willingness to discuss" the issue of protection.

[73] Assuming that other circuits, and eventually the Board, will agree.

[74] No remedies would then exist since the unions would be able to refuse to accept what Board counsel has called an "unjustified interference with the union's representative functions," i.e., a protective order. Brief of the NLRB at 44, International Union of Elec., Radio & Mach. Workers v. NLRB, No. 78-2067 (D.C. Cir., filed Nov. 1, 1978).

[75] S. 2397, 96th Cong., 2d Sess. (1980), would restrict the ability of the NLRB to disclose the information from its own files and might inspire legislative action against the Board's forced transfer approach.

[76] Employee organizations are unlikely to be covered by such statutes as OHIO REV. CODE ANN. § 1333.51 (Page Supp. 1979).

[77] Detroit Edison Co. v. NLRB, 440 U.S. 301 (1979).

The restrictions barring the Union from taking any action that might cause the tests to fall into the hands of employees who have taken or are likely to take them are only as effective as the sanctions available to enforce them. In this instance, there is substantial doubt whether the Union would be subject to a contempt citation were it to ignore the restrictions. . . . Moreover, the Union clearly would not be accountable in either contempt or unfair labor practice proceedings for the most realistic vice inherent in the Board's remedy—the danger of inadvertent leaks.[78]

Because the Court found that the disclosure to the union was with "such scant protection to the Company's undisputed and important interests in test secrecy," it reversed the Board and held that a requirement for the company to turn over sensitive materials to the union was not properly imposed by the Board.[79] The same comment could be made about sensitive employment statistics. It is apparent in the disputed employment statistics cases that union disclosure of the information in whatever format to competitor firms would destroy the claim of the employer that the government cannot disseminate the employer's "secret" statistical data.[80]

If the union represents multiple facilities, including those of competing employers—as the union in the *Westinghouse* information disclosure case does—then the same erosion of secrecy may be found to occur as soon as the union obtains the information. The remedy available may be either delivery of documents under protective order solely to the local union or delivery of the information to a third party who is competent to assess the statistical data on the union's behalf. Such a person might be committed to protect that information against further dissemination without the employer's consent. Of course, these contractual remedies are not as useful as secrecy per se, but that secrecy may have to be compromised if the courts uphold the attitude of the present NLRB on the issue of employment statistics.

---

[78] *Id.* at 315-16.

[79] *Id.* at 316.

[80] Once public, the material cannot regain its confidential status and thus cannot reassume its FOI Act exempt status. 5 U.S.C. § 552(b) (4) (1976).

PART SIX

Concluding Remarks

CHAPTER XVIII

Concluding Remarks

The epigram that seems to best fit this text is "This and all other generalizations are false." To generalize about information rights and duties is to fall into confusion. Unions have much greater power to obtain employers' information than the average observer would expect. Unions currently have an excellent position from which to examine many sensitive aspects of the employer's affairs. Unions also have a great deal of opportunity to gain personal information about their members by a system of access for "designated representatives" under contract, state law, or federal regulations.

Employers have not, however, given the keys to all the files to their employees' bargaining representatives. A growing consciousness of file protection to preserve medical privacy and individual (personnel records) privacy is counteracting union pressures for greater access. Government agency access is becoming more attuned to individual rights than to some theory of government-advanced promotion of collective authority for the union. The presidential privacy initiatives discussed in the employment and medical records privacy chapters illustrate the movement toward individual rather than collective judgments about which records should be released to which recipients.

Neither have employers given away all their trade secrets. The chemical regulation statutes, for example, each permit or require the withholding of trade secret ingredient information by government agencies and permit the closed-door discussion of trade secret ingredients when the regulatory agencies are properly notified of a trade secrecy claim. Dissemination of secret information to a union might be required by NLRB order, but the Board permits trade secret issues to be resolved between the owner of the secret and the recipient union. There may be a confidential disclosure contract between recipients and owners, for example, providing that the union recognizes the state criminal penalties for unauthorized trade secret disclosure, that the union acknowledges that it may be sued for damages if the information is leaked, and that the purpose of the disclosure was exclusively for the compilation of epidemiological findings by a union's consulting scientific group, such as a university medical school.

The specific nature of the disclosure problems for employers in the 1980s will turn upon several factors which are outgrowths of 1970s developments. Though history loves to disprove such generalizations, the reader will note that, as the text has progressed, the author has suggested that basic foundations of disclosure are already set and firm, with the details yet to be filled in. There will not be another Privacy Act in the foreseeable future; there may not be another round of vigorous debates over disclosure in labels and disclosure of exposure records, as the 1977-80 period experienced. The generalization can be offered that cosmic issues have been settled—frequently against the employer's desire—in favor of disclosure, and the shorter-range issues of when and with what safeguards are well on the way to resolution. Disproving that hypothesis by developments in the law or in government policy is possible, but from present positions, it is unlikely.

Apart from that forecast of expanded disclosure, the reader will want to pay close attention to several 1980-82 developments:

1. the appeals of the OSHA exposure and medical records generic rulemaking, to be filed in late 1980 in various courts;

2. the NLRB decisions in *Borden Chemical* and the related chemical ingredient disclosure cases, and courts of appeals decisions in those cases;

3. the outcome of pending appeals and future certiorari petitions in the employment statistics cases such as *Westinghouse Electric*, discussed in chapter XVII; and

4. the development of state privacy-related statutes that inhibit or rigidly structure the passage of personal data about employees from employer files to third parties, including unions and other interested data recipients.

For other nations with different systems of data handling and systems for mandatory disclosure to unions, the American system may appear to have evolved haphazardly on several parallel fronts at roughly the same time. The impression of disorganization is a fair one. We as a society have not yet sorted out the balancing of privacy concepts, proprietary protections of business data, union access rights, government passage of business data from one competing firm to another, and all the myriad of "information law" issues which confront employers and employees. Only one thing is certain—that this text will have to be written over, before 1990, to keep pace with developments in this rapidly changing area of the law. Whether that rewriting is premised on a smoothly organized and well-functioning system of data sharing or on a retrospective assessment of reasons for the systems' failures will have to be decided later. And the future yields none of its secrets to anyone, preferring to keep its information as confidential (and impervious to laws, lawsuits, and regulations) as it has ever been.

Index of Cases

265

Racial Policies of American Industry Series

Order from: Kraus Reprint Co., Route 100, Millwood, New York 10546

STUDIES OF NEGRO EMPLOYMENT

Vol. I.   *Negro Employment in Basic Industry: A Study of Racial Policies in Six Industries (Automobile, Aerospace, Steel, Rubber Tires, Petroleum, and Chemicals)*, by Herbert R. Northrup, Richard L. Rowan, et al.   1970.   *

Vol. II.   *Negro Employment in Finance: A Study of Racial Policies in Banking and Insurance*, by Armand J. Thieblot, Jr., and Linda Pickthorne Fletcher.   1970.   *

Vol. III.   *Negro Employment in Public Utilities: A Study of Racial Policies in the Electric Power, Gas, and Telephone Industries*, by Bernard E. Anderson.   1970.   *

Vol. IV.   *Negro Employment in Southern Industry: A Study of Racial Policies in the Paper, Lumber, Tobacco, Coal Mining, and Textile Industries*, by Herbert R. Northrup, Richard L. Rowan, et al.   1971.   *

Vol. V.   *Negro Employment in Land and Air Transport: A Study of Racial Policies in the Railroad, Airline, Trucking, and Urban Transit Industries*, by Herbert R. Northrup, Howard W. Risher, Jr., Richard D. Leone, and Philip W. Jeffress.   1971. $13.50

Vol. VI.   *Negro Employment in Retail Trade: A Study of Racial Policies in the Department Store, Drugstore, and Supermarket Industries*, by Gordon F. Bloom, F. Marion Fletcher, and Charles R. Perry.   1972.   *

Vol. VII.   *Negro Employment in the Maritime Industries: A Study of Racial Policies in the Shipbuilding, Longshore, and Offshore Maritime Industries*, by Lester Rubin, William S. Swift, and Herbert R. Northrup.   1974.   *

Vol. VIII.   *Black and Other Minority Participation in the All-Volunteer Navy and Marine Corps*, by Herbert R. Northrup, Steven M. DiAntonio, John A. Brinker, and Dale F. Daniel.   1979.   *

Order from the Industrial Research Unit
The Wharton School, University of Pennsylvania
Philadelphia, Pennsylvania 19104

* Order these books from University Microfilms, Inc., Attn: Books Editorial Department, 300 North Zeeb Road, Ann Arbor, Michigan 48106.